The Case Against the Reckless Congress

Edited by Congresswoman
Marjorie Holt

GREEN HILL PUBLISHERS, INC.
Ottawa, Illinois 61350

NOTICE

The chapters in this volume, covering a wide range of current policy issues, were each written by a Member of Congress who has specialized in the problems under discussion. Although all the authors represented here share a common basic political philosophy there are, of course, individual differences on some points. I would like to stress, therefore, that *each chapter reflects the point of view of the individual author* and that viewpoint is not necessarily shared by all the authors of other chapters.

Marjorie S. Holt

Green Hill Publishers, Inc.
236 Forest Park Place
Ottawa, Illinois 61350

Library of Congress Catalogue Card Number: 76-1806
Manufactured in the United States of America.
ISBN: 0-916054-08-½

CONTENTS

INTRODUCTION A View of the Reckless Congress
                                        Marjorie S. Holt   3

THE ECONOMY 11

1. A Nation's Energy Policy:
   Let There Be Light   William L. Armstrong   13

2. The Bloated Budget   John H. Rousselot   25

3. Tax Reform: The Key to
   Jobs Creation   Jack F. Kemp   37

BIG BROTHER 49

4. Who's That Looking Over
   My Shoulder—and Why?:
   A Case for Regulatory
   Reform   William M. Ketchum   51

5. OSHA: The Businessman's
   Burden   Robin L. Beard   61

6. The Disarming of
   Citizens   William F. Goodling   69

7. Bureaucracy: Paternalism
   on the Potomac   Sam Steiger   79

8. Politics and the Civil
   Service: A New Spoils
   System   Edward J. Derwinski   89

SOCIAL SERVICES 93

9. Let's Not Wreck American
   Medicine   Philip M. Crane   95

10. Taming the Welfare
    Problem   Clair W. Burgener   107

11. Food Stamps: Good
    Intentions Distorted ...
    or Hidden Intentions
    Fulfilled?   William L. Dickinson   117

12. Social Security: Going
    the Way of New York
    City?   Barry M. Goldwater, Jr.   131

EDUCATION AND THE ENVIRONMENT   141

13. Feeding at the Trough:
    A Case Study of Federal
    Grants   Robert E. Bauman   143

14. An Environment for
    People   Thomas M. Hagedorn   155

15. Protect Citizens; Punish
    Criminals   Trent Lott   167

16. Federal Regimentation of
    Schools   Steven D. Symms   177

NATIONAL SECURITY   189

17. Our Foreign Policy: A
    Time for Re-evaluation   David C. Treen   191

18. In Defense of Freedom   Floyd D. Spence   203

TABLE I : Votes   212

TABLE II: Positive Proposals   234

REPUBLICAN STUDY COMMITTEE   247

ORDER FORMS   249

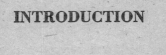

INTRODUCTION

BIOGRAPHY
of
The Honorable Marjorie S. Holt
Maryland

Marjorie S. Holt, a leader in the struggle to cut non-essential spending from the federal budget, is serving her second term in the United States House of Representatives.

She was elected to the Congress with a landslide victory in 1972, and won reelection by a similar large margin in 1974. She represents the Fourth Congressional District of Maryland, which includes all of Anne Arundel County and Southern Prince George's County.

Mrs. Holt, the first woman ever elected to Congress in a Maryland general election, has been a member of the House Armed Services Committee since her first days on Capitol Hill.

Her diligent work and perceptive mind have won recognition among her colleagues. At the start of her second term, she was elected chairwoman of the Republican Study Committee, the conservative caucus for research and coordination on legislative matters.

She also serves on the Budget Committee, and the Technology Assessment Board, which oversees the work of a research staff created to inform the Congress on technological advances in society.

Mrs. Holt and her husband, Duncan, an engineer, live in Severna Park in Anne Arundel County. They have a son, two daughters, and three grandchildren.

The Congresswoman has a strong interest and concern for education. She has been a fighter against the disruptive imposition of racial quotas on schools, and she has worked to protect local school districts from harassment by the Department of Health, Education and Welfare.

An attorney, Mrs. Holt is a graduate of the University of Florida Law School. Before winning her Congressional office, she was elected to two terms as Clerk of the Anne Arundel County Circuit Court.

Introduction

by
Congresswoman Marjorie S. Holt

Two hundred years ago a proud people in pursuit of individual liberty declared their independence from the government of Great Britain. Today we ask whether the noble American experiment in freedom is dissolving into a new tyranny, in which omnipotent government engulfs us all in a smothering embrace with ceaseless murmurs about what is good for us.

Seventy million taxpayers in the productive sector of the economy are compelled to support government payments of one sort or another to 80 million recipients. Some 44 percent of the federal budget is allocated for grants to individuals. The federal government in the 1976 fiscal year spent approximately $80 billion more than its revenues, borrowing and printing cheap money to cover the deficit. The value of the dollar has declined 25 percent in the past three years. Our national debt has exceeded $600 billion, and interest payments alone cost us more than $100 million a day. Our children and grandchildren will be paying for today's extravagance.

Spending by all levels of government in these United States consumes 37 percent of the gross national product, the total value of all goods and services produced each year. The worker is supporting government with 37 percent of the fruits of his labor. By taxation and inflation, government drains away so much of our savings that we lack the capital necessary for investment in expanding private industry and creating jobs.

More than 18,000 Internal Revenue agents operate across our landscape to enforce an incomprehensible tax code that only a curious cult of specialists can understand, and then only imperfectly. In Washington, bureaucrats confer importantly on the design of bathtubs and lawnmowers, typewriters ripple incessantly, papers are whisked from an "in" box to an "out" box and thence to the next "in" box, and the Federal Register establishes a new record by publishing 60,000 finely-printed pages of new rules and regulations in a single year.

How did we get into this mess? The answer is that

Congress has brought us here. For three decades Congress has consistently demonstrated incompetence to do anything except promise more and spend more, but the wildest surge in spending has come within the last five years. We experienced the consequences in 1974 with double-digit inflation, and in 1975 with the deep recession caused by consumer reaction against intolerable price increases.

In consideration of this experience, the 94th Congress must be ranked as the "worst" in memory. It has done nothing to slow the growth of government, and has actually proceeded to accelerate that growth. Remember the grand talk of "reform" when the new Congress with so many fresh faces assumed office in January of 1975? Let us see how they have reformed:

• They adopted a budget that is nearly $80 billion higher than revenues, causing inflation and high interest rates to continue.

• They indulged in the political trickery of offering a tax cut without a reduction in spending, thereby expanding the inflationary deficit.

• They attached themselves to cost-of-living pay raises for federal employees (see vote 1 in Table I), expanded their staffs, increased their travel allowances, and appropriated tax dollars to pay for newsletters to their constituents.

• Not content with expanding all the existing federal programs and bureaucracy, they voted to create a large new bureaucracy called the Agency for Consumer Advocacy, thus contributing to an increase in the consumer's greatest burden, the cost of government. (see vote 2 in Table I).

• Another vote for irresponsible and burdensome legislation was the vote in favor of the conference report on the Common Situs Picketing bill, which would have permitted a strike against a single subcontractor to close down an entire construction site. This would have caused further unemployment in the construction industry as well as higher costs to the consumer. It was prevented from becoming law by a Presidential veto. (see vote 3 in Table I).

• They saddled the energy industry with impossible, constricting controls—controls that can only increase the prices on the consumer.

Perhaps this last was the most serious failure of the 94th Congress. Playing the game of political expediency instead of considering the nation's future energy needs, the Congress maintained price controls on crude oil produced from American wells, and even insisted on a price rollback (see vote 6 in Table I). This, of course, has had the effect of encouraging high consumption of oil while removing both incentive and funds for exploration, development, and production of domestic resources. Have we learned nothing from the critical shortage of natural gas resulting from many years of price controls?

The worse effect of price controls is to make us more dependent on the high-priced oil of the foreign cartel, on which we currently rely for more than 40 percent of our petroleum needs. While Congress dithers with domestic price controls and devises schemes to allocate shortages, citizens become dangerously vulnerable to foreign producers and their price-fixing.

The actions taken by Congress on energy are certain to make our problems worse in the long run. What we need is to encourage large-scale private investment not only in oil development and production, but also in various alternative sources of energy. This investment will not occur as long as domestic oil prices are controlled at artificially low levels. Time and time again, the 94th Congress has cynically grasped for short-range political advantage at the expense of the nation's future.

• The program Congress chose to deal with New York City's financial crisis displays further irresponsibility, a refusal to seriously consider long-term policy effects. Few people will deny that the politicians managing the City's financial affairs are responsible for the crisis that occurred: they are the ones who decided to please everyone while trying to harm no one (an economic impossibility, of course—someone must pay.) The liberal policies of the City caused expenditures to increase three times as fast as tax revenues; high taxation encouraged the tax base to flee the city; extremely liberal program benefits caused poor and disadvantaged people to flock to New York; the city borrowed extravagantly to meet its daily operating expenses. Instead of requiring the City to assume responsibility for its own extravagance (including a massive, tuition-free university, for example), the Congress followed President Ford's recommendation that the federal government loan the city $2.3 billion, thus allowing the City to go further into debt at the expense of taxpayers throughout the country. (See vote 4 in Table I; a "yes" vote is in favor of lending up to $2.3 billion to New York City.) Apparently the Congress was persuaded to do so because they

5

felt the people of the City should not have to suffer for the financial mistakes of New York politicians. However, why should the rest of the nation pick up the burden? The residents of New York, not Omaha, received the benefit of the irresponsible spending. Not only did the Congress make the mistake of approving the initial bill, but a short while later the House rejected the opportunity to reduce the amount of the loan to $1.3 billion, which President Ford determined would be sufficient, instead of the $2.3 billion he initially suggested. (See vote 5 in Table I; a "yes" vote is in favor of reducing the loan to $1.3 billion.)

We may survive 1976 without economic calamity, but what about 1977 and beyond? The sad conclusion is that this Congress has demonstrated inability to think beyond the next election. While the Congress pours our wealth into a thousand domestic programs administered by a monstrous bureaucracy fiddling with statistics, charts, and reports weighing tons, it cuts the strength of our national defense to perilous weakness.

If the federal government has one unique and vital mission which neither the states nor localities can perform, it is national defense. In this curious age, however, many Members of Congress perceive federal priorities in sidewalks, housing, rat-control, health planning, public schools, storm water drainage and recreation, but national defense is considered a prime target for budget-cutting. While the Congress behaves in the manner of county councilmen, the Soviet Union pursues a military expansion unmatched in history to roll toward its persistent goal of world empire. The American military budget has remained relatively constant for several years, which means that it has sharply diminished because of inflation. Defense is a declining percentage of the federal budget, claiming only 24 percent in the 1976 fiscal year, when Congress cut the requested appropriations by $7.4 billion.

Analysis of relative Soviet-American military strength shows a sorry picture. We have fallen behind. The Soviet Union has approximately 500 more intercontinental ballistic missiles than we have, 100 more submarine-launched ballistic missiles, 350 more strategic bombers, 250 more combat ships (including a huge advantage in submarines), 30,000 more tanks, and more than twice as many military personnel. It is true that sheer numbers cannot be the only measure of strength. We continue to have a technological advantage and more sophisticated weapons systems, including the cruise mis-

6

sile. But what is clear is the trend: a massive Soviet drive to shift the world balance of power. And Congress shows no signs of willingness to compete, although our very survival is at stake.

American political leaders have been trusting souls who have interpreted "detente" to mean faith in peaceful Soviet intentions. This is a dangerous illusion. It could mean catastrophe for the United States. The enormous war machine of the Soviet Union has not been built for peace.

- "Detente" means a flow of Russian arms that enabled Communist North Vietnam to overrun all of Vietnam, Cambodia, and Laos and to threaten Thailand.

- "Detente" means that the Soviet Union arms Syria and Iraq and inspires them to aggression against American allies in the Mid-East.

- "Detente" means that the Soviet Union established major military bases in Libya and deploys a vast fleet toward the goal of making the Mediterranean a Soviet lake.

- "Detente" means that the Soviet Union arms the Portuguese communists to attempt takeover of a nation where the people overwhelmingly voted against communism in a free election.

- "Detente" means that Soviet arms and many thousands of stooge Cuban troops attempt to take over Angola and establish Soviet military power on the Atlantic coast of Africa.

The record of "detente" is a continuing story of aggressive acts by the Soviet Union on a worldwide scale, and it should not surprise us. Remember Poland, Hungary, and Czechoslovakia where Soviet tanks and armies crushed national independence and remain stationed to this very day? Nothing has changed.

Alexander Solzhenitsyn, the great Russian author who was exiled to freedom in 1974, has devoted his time to warning us of our peril. These are his words.

A concentration of world evil, of hatred for humanity is taking place, and it is fully determined to destroy our society.... Must you wait until it comes with a crowbar to break through your borders, until the young men of America have to fall defending the borders of their continent?

Do we really have to wait for the moment when the knife is at our throats? Couldn't it be possible, ahead of

7

time, soberly to assess the worldwide menace that threatens to swallow the whole world?

These are the words of a Russian who endured the hell of Siberian labor camps, an intellectual who has intimate knowledge of communist barbarity and intentions. He speaks on the subject with greater authority, both practical and moral, than any American.

Americans who have a realistic understanding of the predatory enemy that confronts us are not demanding a preemptory war against the Soviet Union. We are insisting only that the United States recognize the menace and maintain both the will and the strength to resist it.

The world struggle is both military and political, and we cannot ignore either. In the political sphere, our greatest weapon is food, the product of an abundant agriculture of a free people, and we should use it. It is intolerable that the Soviet Union runs a war economy, wholly committed to world conquest, while it relies on American grain to feed its masses and purchases American technology to build its war machine. An America that slides toward socialism at home and weakness abroad cannot remain free for long.

In domestic policy, the fundamental issue is whether Americans will be ruled by a paternal federal bureaucracy that offers benefits in return for submission to central planning and control of every significant aspect of their lives. Remember, social and economic planning by the central government is the surest road to tyranny, because a plan can be enforced only by the exercise of tyranny. The people are best served by policy set at the state and local levels. The cause of freedom is best served at a level where the individual voice can be heard.

Consider Thomas Jefferson's ideal:

A wise and frugal government, which shall restrain men from injuring one another, which shall leave them otherwise free to regulate their own pursuits of industry and improvement, and shall not take from the mouth of labor the bread it has earned. This is the sum of good government.

*　　　*　　　*

I consider the foundation of the Constitution to be laid on this ground: that 'all powers not delegated to the

8

United States by the Constitution, nor prohibited by it to the states, are reserved to the states or to the people.' To take a single step beyond the boundaries thus specially drawn around the powers of Congress, is to take possession of a boundless field of power no longer susceptible of any definition.

*   *   *

I am for reserving to the states the powers not yielded by them to the Union, and to the legislature of the Union its constitutional share in the division of powers; but I am not for transferring all the powers of the states to the general government, and all those of that government to the executive branch.

Compare those quotations from Jefferson at the dawn of the Republic with what has actually happened, especially within the past decade. How far we have drifted from the ideal of freedom and self-government! I believe the PEOPLE sense what is wrong. I believe they are ready for a rollback of big government that makes decisions for them in central offices of Washington. Congress is always lagging behind the people, and it may take some time for the political system to bring about the changes desired by the people. But we must awaken more quickly to the dangerous trend of military decline. The survival of America depends absolutely on our military strength and a foreign policy that bespeaks our resolute commitment to freedom.

This Congress has failed on both the domestic and foreign issues, pursuing a course of more government and less defense. In this year of celebrating the 200th anniversary of the American War for Independence, we must recommit ourselves to a strong, free America.

THE ECONOMY

BIOGRAPHY
of
The Honorable William L. Armstrong
Colorado

A second term Congressman from the Fifth District of Colorado, Bill Armstrong came to Congress after serving 10 years in the Colorado General Assembly, the last four as Majority Leader of the State Senate.

Born in Fremont Nebraska, on March 16, 1937, Representative Armstrong and his wife Ellen are the parents of two children. Mr. Armstrong is presently President of radio station KOSI in Aurora, Colorado, as well as President of the Colorado Publishing Company.

Congressman Armstrong presently serves on the House Appropriations Committee. His two terms are marked with responsible conservatism. He has proposed specific legislation to balance the federal budget and has fought against needless growth of the federal government. As Chairman of the House Republican Task Force on Energy, Mr. Armstrong has been a leader in the fight to restore free market principles to energy production.

A NATION'S ENERGY POLICY:
LET THERE BE LIGHT
by
Congressman William L. Armstrong

"They ought to call this the OPEC Relief Act of 1975; the only people who will be helped by what we're doing are the Middle East oil producers." Thus one GOP lawmaker summed up Congressional action on energy legislation during the 1975 session. Although too bitter in tone, his appraisal is essentially correct.

After months of wrangling, during which more than 90 different House and Senate committees claimed some jurisdiction over energy legislation, the first regular session of the 94th Congress adjourned in an atmosphere of confusion and frustration. Final action to bolster the nation's dwindling natural gas reserves was postponed. And the session's main energy bill, the so-called Energy Policy and Conservation Act (see vote 6 in Table I), will, in the opinion of many experts, cripple already faltering U.S. efforts to regain energy independence.

Although the energy act contains a hodge-podge of controls, restrictions, incentives, loan guarantees, subsidies, and other provisions, its crucial defect is the legislated reduction of the market price of domestic crude oil. The effect of the omnibus bill will be to lower domestic oil production and consequently to increase U.S. dependence on higher-priced foreign oil. A heavy loss of jobs for American workers will result.

Under the new law, the composite average price of domestic crude oil will initially be limited to not more than $7.66 per barrel, a sharp reduction from the $8.75 estimated actual selling price of the average barrel of U.S. crude at the end of 1975. By rolling back the market price to a level that affords little or no economic motivation to producers—a level that is actually below cost in some instances—the legislation establishes a powerful disincentive to production. So a further decline in domestic crude oil output is inevitable.

Although the 94th Congress may prefer to ignore the inescapable logic of this conclusion—that production is bound to decline when prices are held below a level that offers incentives to producers—it is demonstrated by the actual results of oil price controls during the preceding three years. From

1973 to 1975 price controls were only partially applied. But production incentives were sufficiently curtailed to cause a noticeable decline in domestic production, which had previously risen steadily. And despite a modest, probably temporary, slack in demand, U.S. reliance on foreign oil sources increased as a result: from 36 percent in 1973 to an estimated 46 percent during 1975, according to data supplied by the Federal Energy Administration.

Effects of Price Rollback

Debate continues regarding the exact consequences of the newly enacted oil price controls. But there can be little doubt that controls will severely affect both supply and demand. Data Resources, Inc., a respected private economic consulting firm, estimates U.S. oil consumption will be 500,000 barrels per day higher in 1976 and 477,000 higher in 1977 as a result of extra usage induced by controlled prices. But predicted domestic production will drop by 300,000 barrels daily in 1976 and 630,000 barrels in 1977. The result will be an increase in the nation's reliance on foreign oil sources of 800,000 to 900,000 barrels per day in 1976 and 1.3 to 1.4 million barrels per day by the end of 1977.

An even gloomier prediction, from the nonpartisan Congressional Research Service of the Library of Congress, estimates the U.S. will be forced to import 50 percent more oil within two years. The study estimates the U.S. may bring in 16 billion barrels of oil in the next five years with imports climbing from the current 6 million barrels per day to 9 million in 1977 and 10 million by 1980. CRS also warns that the proportion of U.S. oil imports produced by the Organization of Petroleum Exporting Countries (OPEC) will rise because other suppliers, such as Canada and Venezuela, are curtailing production to prolong the life of their oil fields. As America becomes more and more dependent on OPEC, the study continues, "Energy may well become the Achilles heel of U.S. foreign policy the same way as agricultural shortages are for the Soviet Union." Other implications of dependence on OPEC include serious military and strategic considerations, balance of payments problems, and the prospect of another OPEC oil embargo to enforce demands—for higher prices or any other political considerations. Under the circumstances, it's no wonder some of my colleagues think OPEC will be the chief beneficiary of this ill-advised legislation.

Price Reductions for Gasoline Users: Fact or Illusion?

One stated purpose of the price rollback is to ease the burden on American gasoline consumers. By cutting the price of domestic crude oil, backers of the legislation aim to force a retail gasoline price reduction of about one cent per gallon. In the absence of price controls, they say, the price per gallon could increase five to six cents.

But by now it seems obvious that approximately half of the nation's oil volume and perhaps two-thirds of the dollar value of the nation's oil usage will come from foreign nations whose prices are not subject to U.S. control. As the proportion of domestic crude oil in the average gallon of American gasoline declines and the percentages of OPEC oil goes up, the more likely result is an increase in retail gasoline prices —particularly if OPEC puts still higher prices into effect, as most observers expect. This is exactly what happened during the last three years when gasoline prices skyrocketed despite stringent federal controls on U.S. crude oil prices. The pattern is certain to repeat itself.

Lost Jobs

One additional side effect of this harmful legislation deserves further comment. As more and more of the nation's oil needs are supplied by overseas sources, the loss of American jobs will become painfully evident. Drilling activity has already diminished and will undoubtedly grow worse as domestic production continues to shrivel. Data Resources' analysis indicates the extent to which the legislation just adopted will discourage capital investment in the petroleum industry:

In particular, the uncertainty in the petroleum sector which has been viewed as a temporary problem will now become institutionalized because the Congressional bill does not expire in any specific period. (Although controls are scheduled to expire in 40 months, the authority to reimpose them does not. Given the difference between U.S. and world oil prices which is expected to exist in 40 months, most producers will probably anticipate that they will be continued). The continued level of uncertainty will reduce producers' willingness to invest in projects such as advanced secondary recovery programs, where the high cost requires prices at or above current levels prevailing in world markets. Investments in other programs will be reduced not only by the institutional-

15

ization of uncertainty, but also by the reduction in cash flow. This program will, at a minimum, reduce after-tax cash flow of the petroleum sector by $1.5 billion in 1976 *above and beyond* the $2 billion lost with the removal of percentage depletion.

This investment decline means the loss of a huge number of jobs that would have otherwise been created in the domestic petroleum industry. In effect, American jobs will be exported to OPEC nations.

Ending the Natural Gas Shortage

The outlook for legislation to end the nation's natural gas shortage is considerably more encouraging. It seems inexplicable that Congress, within a few weeks or months after imposing oil price controls, would recognize the futility of the same kinds of controls over natural gas and abolish them. Yet this may soon happen.

I have introduced legislation (H.R. 5550; see proposal A in Table II) permitting eventual deregulation of all "new" natural gas in interstate commerce. Prior to the end of the 1975 session, the Senate passed such legislation. The House failed, however, to act before adjourning. But a growing number of Members are beginning to realize that natural gas shortages, which have plagued areas of the nation and caused countless school and factory closings, are the direct result of federal price controls. How the nation came to be short of natural gas is a depressing but simple story.

Until eight years ago America enjoyed an abundant supply of this efficient and environmentally desirable fuel. Gas consumption rose dramatically, but production easily kept pace. Year after year more new gas was developed than was consumed; reserves steadily increased. But in 1968 the Supreme Court upheld the Federal Power Commission's complicated system of price regulation, which was imposed on all natural gas sold for transmission in interstate commerce.

The effect was dramatic. Incentive to produce new gas for interstate commerce vanished. The nation's total gas production leveled out after rising for years, and people soon were using more gas than was being produced. By 1973 new reserve additions were less than one-third of consumption and the nation's total natural gas reserves dropped from a 15-year supply in 1967 to a 10-year reserve (see Table I).

Meanwhile, an increasing proportion of production was

16

being diverted from the price-controlled interstate market to unregulated intrastate customers (see Table 2).

Shortages soon began to develop throughout the nation, except in gas-producing areas. In my own state of Colorado lack of natural gas to meet peak demand closed schools, shut down factories, and brought new home construction to a standstill.

General softening of the economy has subsequently eased demand for new natural gas permits for residential construction, but when demand increases again, economic recovery will be severely curtailed by lack of gas permits for residential construction, particularly in rapidly growing and metropolitan areas.

In Colorado Springs, for example, all interruptible customers have been cut off almost all winter. Virtually no new firm customers have been added for over two years. In Denver the waiting list for natural gas is ten months long; Public Service Company sees no improvement in sight. Some builders are switching to all-electric heat, a more expensive and less energy-efficient alternative.

By 1977 gas supplies to Colorado, including those now committed and contracted for, will not meet projected needs. The state's major gas supplier sees no prospect of new supplies. So-called firm customers, including homeowners, will be forced to cut back on usage.

It is obvious that industries located in states with supplies of natural gas have a significant competitive advantage over firms that must rely on other sources of energy. Consequently, firms are foregoing plans to expand in nonproducing areas and relocating plants in a handful of states where natural gas is produced.

The magnitude of this trend—and the extent to which this premium fuel is being diverted from home heating to use by industries that could use oil or coal with proper environmental safeguards—is revealed by the consumption statistics. Four gas-producing states already consume 34 percent of all natural gas used in the nation. Of this amount, 91 percent is used industrially. A large part of this consumption is used to generate electricity. Nationwide about 20 percent of all natural gas production is used to generate electricity. Four gas producing states account for 65 percent of that amount. In summary, electric production in just four states accounts for 15 percent of all natural gas consumption in the entire nation. Homeowners and industries elsewhere who are, in ef-

17

Table 1. Natural Gas Production and Reserves, 1950-75
(in trillions of cubic feet)

	Domestic consump- tion	Domestic produc- tion	Reserve addi- tions	Year-end reserves	Supply (in years) at current use	Supply (in years) at 1974 use
1950	5.9	6.3	12.0	184.6	31	8
1955	8.9	9.4	21.9	222.5	25	9
1960	13.0	12.8	13.8	262.2	20	11
1964	15.7	15.3	20.1	279.4	18	12
1966	18.0	17.5	19.2	286.4	16	12
1968	20.0	19.3	12.0	287.3	14	13
1970*	22.6	21.8	37.1*	290.7	13	13
1971	23.5	22.6	9.8	278.8	12	13
1972	23.5	22.5	9.6	266.1	11	13
1973	23.6	22.6	6.8	250.0	11	12
1974	22.1	21.6	8.7	237.1	10	11
1975	20.1	19.7	N/A	N/A	—	10

*Alaskan gas included for the first time in 1970.

18

Table 2. Percentage of New Natural Gas Reserves for
Interstate and Intrastate Use, 1964-74

Year	Intrastate	Interstate
1964	47%	53%
1966	26	74
1968	21	79
1969	27	73
1970	100	0
1971	70	21
1972	100	0
1973	83	17
1974*	90	10

*Estimate

fect, prohibited from bidding on natural gas are being forced to switch to higher-priced substitutes.

For example, in Colorado Springs, the city council spent $1 million for equipment to inject a propane-air mixture into natural gas lines at times of peak demand. This cost, and the use of higher-priced propane, became necessary simply because regular gas supplies were inadequate to maintain pressure in the gas lines on coldest days, when peak demand occurs.

Other Colorado communities have responded in other ways: Burlington maintains a large supply of fuel oil for emergency use if their interruptible supply of gas is cut off, leaving the power plant and city buildings, including the hospital, without service.

As more municipalities and other priority users are forced to depend on propane, oil, and coal the price of these substitutes is bid up in response to demand. Mobile homeowners who use propane for heating and farmers who use it extensively in crop drying were horrified when the price per gallon jumped from around 18 cents to over 60 cents within a few months. Although this price increase has moderated somewhat recently, propane is still twice as expensive as it was three years ago. An even worse supply-price crunch may develop in the future. The price of coal has been similarly affected.

Other Areas of the Nation

Although I have mentioned hardships and dislocations in my own state the shortage of natural gas is causing similar consequences elsewhere. Recently the Federal Power Commission turned down an oil company's request to supply domestic natural gas to New York State users at a cost of 52 cents per thousand cubic feet. Instead these users were forced to import liquefied natural gas from overseas at rates up to $1.86 per thousand cubic feet.

In New Jersey gas curtailment levels last winter (1974-75) averaged about 28 percent. If they rise to 30 percent this year, officials estimate that 120,000 workers could be laid off and working hours of another 40,000 employees would be reduced. In Ohio in 1970 a ten-day shutdown of natural gas caused 1,500 person-years of unemployment.

These are a few of many dislocations that have resulted from the federal government's destructive attempts to substitute administrative judgments and regulations for the efficient working of the free market. Even the Federal Power Commission, the agency that regulates the field price of gas, recently called for legislation to decontrol gas altogether. FPC studies and much other evidence indicate that decontrol is the only feasible way to assure the nation a dependable supply of gas.

Objections to Decontrol

The main objection to returning to free market pricing seems to be the fear of a drastic increase in home heating costs. Is this fear justified? Are much higher prices likely?

Only about 10-20 percent of the price paid for home heating is accounted for by the fuel cost. The balance represents distribution charges—the cost of the pipeline. So even if the field price of gas were to double or triple—a pessimistic estimate, I believe—the effect on most homeowners would be relatively modest, and certainly would be far less than the cost of converting to other fuels. And such increases would probably be phased over many years.

What are the alternatives? If regulation continues, the volume of gas carried in interstate pipelines will decline. The shrinking volume of gas will necessarily become more expensive as the cost of the pipeline—the major component of user cost—is amortized over fewer and fewer units of natural gas. In fact, some experts believe that price increases resulting from decontrolling the wellhead price will be less than price increases inherent in the present regulatory structure. As FPC Chairman John Nassikas pointed out, "Whatever the cost of deregulation may ultimately be, it will be far less than the costs associated with current and anticipated curtailments of gas deliveries, idle pipeline capacity, and high cost supplemental supplies."

A Free Market Alternative

Whether the 94th Congress will be able to overcome its aversion to free market economics long enough to deregulate natural gas remains to be seen. We hope so. But in view of recent experience, a more basic question should be raised: Why is Congress so quick to impose controls and so loathe to loosen them?

In talking with individual Members about such issues during the past three years, I have heard many explanations. Some are sincerely convinced controls are desirable or at least necessary under the circumstances. But a great many others are simply taking the easy way out. It is more politi-

21

cally advantageous and personally gratifying to tell constituents they have legislated to reduce oil prices than to explain why such controls will fail and will finally hurt the nation. So they rationalize and duck tough issues instead of meeting them head on. Based on my contact with Colorado voters, I believe these Members underestimate the intellect and willingness of their constituents to face economic reality. They do a grave disservice to the nation.

Another major reason for Congressional attitudes toward energy legislation is the current attitude toward the oil industry. Those who berate Big Oil are picking on an already unpopular victim. Anyone foolhardy enough to refute charges against the oil barons—or to defend them—is likely to be scorned. Many people still believe that oil companies gouge their customers, take unfair advantage of shortages, lie about their reserves, doctor their profit-and-loss statements and, in general, deserve summary punishment.

So the industry has become the focal point of our country's latent antibusiness populism and it is not surprising that Congress has enacted punitive legislation. Nor is it remarkable that the *Congressional Record* bulges with proposals to punish the industry. But the shrillness of many voices now being raised recalls Irving Kristol's perceptive description of the "temper and state of mind which too easily degenerates into political paranoia, with 'enemies of the people' constantly being discovered and exorcised and convulsively purged. The paranoia takes the form of an instinctive readiness to believe anything reprehensible, no matter how incredible, about the machinations of 'big business'." Clearly much of the incessant criticism of the industry verges on such paranoia. And while it is not my purpose here to defend the nation's oil companies, it does seem to me we'd better think seriously of the consequences of further weakening, or altogether destroying, the nation's oil industry with legislation already enacted or now pending. If that happens, who will produce the oil? Who will decide how much oil will come to market? How shall it be distributed? What will the price be?

Throughout most of our nation's history such decisions have been made in a free market economy in the natural interaction between buyers and sellers. This arrangement has led to the harnessing of untold energy resources for the benefit of consumers. It has fostered a standard of living and general prosperity without parallel. If, as critics contend, shortcomings and injustices are inherent in our traditional free

22

market system, what is the alternative? More government intervention? Perhaps a complete takeover of the industry by federal administrators, as some of my colleagues have hinted?

We have seen the results of government intervention: a decline in domestic production, increased reliance on OPEC, a larger federal bureaucracy, more federal spending, and higher gasoline prices. On the record, it would seem obvious to any but the most dogmatic federal interventionist that the market system has performed far better than government. Historically, unregulated private firms are generally more efficient and responsive to consumers than those firms which have been most closely regulated for the longest period of time—the nation's railroads, for example—and more viable by far than the Post Office, HEW, the food stamp program, the State Department, the District of Columbia, and other enterprises directly managed by the federal government.

It may be argued that immediate price decontrol will unjustly enrich oil producers. If this is true, Congress could enact windfall profits legislation—incorporating a plowback provision to encourage firms to reinvest in domestic production as proposed long ago by the President.

But the main thing is to eliminate price controls and other regulations that hamstring efforts to increase domestic oil production. Geologists assure us America has an almost infinite potential for energy production, from conventional sources of oil, from natural gas, and from offshore oil and gas, shale oil, coal, solar power, geothermal power, nuclear power, and power generated from wind, tides, ocean thermals, and many other possible sources. We are a nation brimming with energy potential that can and will be realized if Congress will abolish or loosen existing controls and forswear new controls.

This will happen when the nation's voters elect a Congress more understanding of free market principles and less addicted to bureaucratic controls. Let us hope that day is not far distant.

BIOGRAPHY
of
The Honorable John H. Rousselot
California

John H. Rousselot began his career as a Congressman in the 87th Congress.

Born on November 1, 1927, Mr. Rousselot attended schools in San Marino and South Pasadena and graduated from Principia College, Elsah, Illinois, in 1949 with a B. A. degree.

By 1954 he had established the John H. Rousselot & Associates public relations firm. He was the manager and owner of this firm until 1958 when he joined the Federal Housing Administration as its Director of Public Information (1958-1960). From 1967 to 1970, Mr. Rousselot was a management consultant.

His service as a representative to the U.S. Congress from California has been in two non-consecutive terms: from the 25th District (1961-1963) and from the 24th (later the 26th) by a special election in June of 1970.

Active in party politics, Mr. Rousselot has served as a delegate to a Republican National Convention, as President of the California Young Republicans and as a member of the Executive Committee of the Republican State Central Committee. He is also on the Executive Committee of the National Republican Congressional Committee.

In addition to his membership on the Committees on Banking, Currency and Housing and Post Office and Civil Service, Congressman Rousselot serves on the Joint Economic Committee. In 1975 Congressman Rousselot led the fight for a balanced budget in the House of Representatives.

THE BLOATED BUDGET
by
Congressman John H. Rousselot

Throwing huge amounts of dollars and bloated bureaucracies at problems has, for the past four or five decades, become the popular solution in Washington, D.C. to the economic and social ills of our country.

The Federal Budget is a huge book of thousands of pages. No one person is ever likely to read all of it; it is not as exciting as an investigation of the CIA; it does not have the publicity value of a series of hearings on pollution; it does not have the glamour of high-level conferences on foreign policy.

And yet, as we all know, nothing can be done effectively without an adequately planned budget. If the government runs short of money, then many politically popular programs will come to a grinding halt. No one will benefit, and millions of people may be hurt. Balancing the budget may not be an exciting job, but it is a necessary one.

Many bureaucratically created programs are not only expensive but they are also futile. When, under the prodding of various administrations and interest groups, huge, expensive bureaucracies are created by Congress, and ceaseless demands are made upon the government's budget by all areas of society, the very stability of our American way of life is threatened.

Congress, through the appropriations and budget process established in the Constitution, is assigned to control the purse-strings and provide restraint against this onrush of irresponsible demands. Unfortunately, until 1974 and the passage of the Congressional Budget Impoundment and Control Act, there was no understanding in Congress for how far out of hand the process was and of how indulgent the expenditures really were.

Is Deficit Spending Inevitable?

Every year, Congress struggles through a long list of issues: energy supplies, funding of Social Security, tax reform, unemployment, rising interest rates, and a host of others. However, it is apparent that a majority of problems have one underlying cause—*the inability of Congress to deal with excessive federal spending.* Few appropriations bills that have come before this Congress have received my support. *Every single one* has contributed substantially to the increase in our national debt. When the federal treasury is forced by over-spending on the part of a reckless Congress to go into the marketplace to borrow money to finance its deficits, it re-duces the amount of capital available to the private sector. Irresponsible federal spending limits the money available to the private market for investment in home mortgages, for in-dividual investments, for outlays for business growth and pro-ductive development and research, and for other operations that help to increase total output of goods and services and to create jobs.

Overspending by the federal government also clearly limits the availability of funds that could otherwise be used for lo-cal bond issues, public works projects, rapid transit systems, and other important community needs. To finance its deficits, the federal government is now absorbing over 50 percent of the available funds in the private money markets, and this creates an almost impossible task for mayors, county supervi-sors, and city councils to fund the programs they feel are needed at the local government level.

Some will argue that deficit spending is inevitable, or even desirable, and that there is no way to reverse the trend and bring the budget into balance. But we continually see proof that deficit spending is the wrong solution to the pressing economic problems of inflation, recession, and unemploy-ment. The plight of New York City is a good example, and attempts by the reckless spenders in Congress to implement New York's policies at the national level must be stopped.

One of the major reasons why many Congressmen advo-cate budget deficits is rooted in an outmoded economic the-ory. In the 1930s the English economist John Maynard Keynes theorized that a country would move out of the de-pression by spending more. Many economists believe Keynes would have a different view if he were alive today, because even he did not advocate deficit spending in every national budget. Nevertheless, many liberal Democrats still rely upon this 40-year-old theory. They reason that when the economy is not producing at full employment it is necessary to increase government spending to create demand and to increase pro-duction. Budget deficits incurred in recession years would be offset by budget surpluses in boom years.

This approach has tantalizing appeal, but it fails to con-sider a number of points. For instance, in the budget resolution in late 1975, the 1974 recession was a major consideration leading Congress to adopt high spending levels. However, that "stimulative" spending would normally not have an impact until mid- to late-1976. It is hard to see how this helps bring the economy out of recession, since the upturn in the economy had already begun in May of 1975. So the "stimulation" usually comes at least a year late. An upward cycle in the economy does not provide an absolute guarantee against recession, but the point remains that the long-time lag drastically reduces the value of Congressional action calculated to "fine tune" the economy. What it may do, in fact, is stimulate inflation and encourage another recession in the future—a process similar to the stimulation in 1971-72 that produced the 1974 recession. In short, fiscal action designed to bring about a certain effect in the short run may have exactly the opposite effect in the slightly longer run. The problem is compounded by a tendency to pursue one goal blindly—in this illustration, fiscal stimulation—and ignore other important effects of deficit spending.

This economic ignorance is compounded by attitude and ideology. One can point to facts and experience to inform free-spending Congressmen that their policies will be counterproductive, but facts are frequently ignored for ideological reasons. In the name of collectivist goals, they take advantage of the federal taxpayer to assure employment and prosperity for various elements of their constituency and to offer welfare to the group they call the disadvantaged.

We shall see that actions that seem in the short run to help disadvantaged groups may actually do them more harm than good. These actions perpetuate the dependence that binds them to big government. Furthermore, even when the deficiencies of this situation are demonstrated to the liberal Congressman, the motivation to help someone under the name of "emergency" legislation causes him to repeat his earlier mistake. A clear example is funding for public works projects. The budget resolution adopted in late 1975 included a $5 billion authorization for accelerated public works to create jobs for the unemployed. But the big spenders in the House were refusing to learn from their experience two years earlier with the Public Works Impact Program (PWIP), which had the same goal. Did PWIP help the unemployed? Not much. Of the entire cost of the program, only 7 percent went to wages.

Furthermore, 59 percent of the jobs went to skilled workers who were already employed but changed jobs. And roughly 56 percent of those receiving jobs were not residents of the area ostensibly receiving aid. All told, to hire one man for one month cost taxpayers $10,000.* Similar problems were seen in the Comprehensive Employment and Training Act, under which 90 percent of the "created" jobs would have existed anyway. Each job in the program paid $10,000 per year and the cost of actually creating one new job under that program was around $100,000 per year.** Recent policies continue to repeat earlier mistakes, indicating not only that ignorance is a problem, but also that it is compounded by refusal to learn from experience.

Another major factor contributing to foolish budget policy is the structure of the political system. It is designed so that the Congressman who is most successful (gets reelected) is the one who does the most favors for the largest number of special interest groups. Most national politics require handouts to various groups to gain their votes. The big-spending Congressman knows that the interest groups have a lot of voting power, and he responds to this incentive by catering to their needs. If we wish to see fiscal responsibility in the form of lower taxes, lower spending, and lower deficits, the disadvantaged *taxpayer* needs to be heard. This can come about through election of Members of Congress whose "special interests" consist in limiting the size and scope of government and removing the incentive to use taxpayers' funds as political payoffs.

---

* Economic Development Administration, Department of Commerce, *An Evaluation of the Public Works Impact Program*, January, 1975; cited in the "Minority Views" of Mssrs. Latta, Cedeberg, Schneebeli, Broyhill, Clawson, Hastings, Shriver and Conable, in House Report #94-145, "First Concurrent Resolution on the Budget—Fiscal Year 1976," prepared by the Committee on the Budget, April 14, 1975, p. 91.

** The Office of the Assistant Secretary for Planning and Evaluation of the Department of Health, Education and Welfare stated that the figures cited were based on the following studies: (1) George Johnson and James Tomola, *An Impact Evaluation of the Public Employment Program*, Technical Analysis Paper #17, Office of the Assistant Secretary for Policy Evaluation and Research, Department of Labor, April, 1974. (2) National Planning Association, *An Evaluation of the Economic Impact Project of the Public Employment Program*, May, 1974 (Department of Labor contract numbers 43-2-001-11 and 63-11-73-04; Report MEL 74-06). (3) Alan Fechter, *Public Employment Programs: An Evaluative Study*, Urban Institute.

How to Finance a Deficit

The preceding section gives us some idea why Congress is motivated to spend so much and why essentially all of the increased spending goes to "social programs," especially transfer payments. We must also consider the major reasons why the Democrat-controlled Congress' budget policy is wrong—in terms of the real effects of large budgets and large deficits.

The deficits for each year have consistently grown. The most recent Congressional authorization (December, 1975) was for a $74 billion deficit in fiscal year 1976, and the deficit for each of the past several years has typically been in the tens of billions of dollars. Unfortunately, this spending habit has encouraged the Congress to regard deficits as a way of getting more than you pay for, with the belief that it is a way of "stimulating" the economy. This policy has the long-run effect of contributing to inflation and economic instability.

The financing of even a small federal deficit causes two economic problems. First, deficit financing forces the Treasury to go to the private market to borrow. The debt is financed by selling government debt instruments (notes and bonds) to the public, requiring the Treasury to compete with private borrowers. Often they compete by offering a higher rate of interest. But the money paid is drawn away from private markets; that is, if the government had not borrowed it, the money would have been available to a private borrower, and could have been used to finance the expansion of the productive segment of the economy directly. Most firms rely heavily on borrowing in order to finance expansion—to increase productivity, hire more workers, and generally increase the wealth of society. But when the government enters the private markets and draws investment away from private borrowers, "crowding out" occurs: market interest rates go up, private investment is reduced, and the ability of the economy to expand is generally limited. Then after limiting the capacity of the economy to grow, the government turns around and spends the money it has borrowed from the private sector on public programs designed to stimulate demand. The combination of the increased government demand and limited ability of the private sector to respond by increasing production causes prices to rise.

The second alternative for financing a deficit is to sell government debt instruments to the Federal Reserve instead of to the public. The Federal Reserve does this by increasing the money supply. But now, since there are more dollars available to buy the same number of goods, and each dollar is worth less, prices will rise. This process is described as *inflation;* that is, a general loss of purchasing power resulting from a relative increase in the quantity of money compared to the quantity of goods.

It is clear that no matter how small the federal deficit is in a given year, it causes some combination of "crowding out" of private investment and inflation. The problems are especially serious with deficits as large as the $74 billion authorized for fiscal year 1976. Even with a smaller deficit in fiscal year 1975, total federal government borrowing absorbed 50.9 percent of the entire credit market. The result is a general reallocation of spending power from the private to the public sector, which stifles the ability of private industry to expand and create jobs. Other problems arise when deficits occur year after year and the national debt accumulates. Deficits have occured in 15 of the last 16 years and in 40 of the last 48 years.

Buy Now, Pay Later (Maybe)

The recent financial crisis in New York City illustrates what happens if debts are permitted to accumulate. The City reached the point where its credibility had diminished, where investors demanded a higher rate of interest to compensate for the risk, and where, finally, lenders refused to finance the City's spending because the total indebtedness was so high. The major difference between New York City and the federal government is that the latter can "create" money; this really means that it can dilute the value of everyone's money, reduce the value of the money it has to repay, and create a new source of demand for the bonds. But a gradual loss of confidence is inevitable and in order to compete with fiscally sound private businesses, the government will have to offer a continually higher rate of interest.

Interest payments on the federal debt are the third largest item in the budget—roughly $38 billion this year—following defense spending and human resources payments. As the debt grows larger (*$623 billion* is authorized for 1976) the interest payments grow along with it. As interest rates rise, the amount the government has to pay in interest rises more rapidly than the total debt itself. With big spenders in control of Congress, there is no end in sight. For these reasons, it is clear that the phrase "fiscal responsibility" is hollow and meaningless. The underlying premise of deficit spending is

30

that the Congress can buy now and make the taxpayers of the future pay later. A deficit is, by its nature, the equivalent of a credit card that can be used now in the name of current taxpayers; the bill, which will be due and payable in a number of years, will go to other taxpayers. But what is the outcome of this scheme? No liberal Congress will ever choose to pay the bill from preceding years. Each one will decide to borrow more from taxpayers farther in the future. Thus responsibility for one's own debts is avoided and the national debt and its interest payments continue to grow indefinitely.

The record of 1975 is not surprising: The Congress decided to authorize an increase in the "debt ceiling" (above which the Treasury cannot raise the public debt) three times during the year (in February, June, and November). At the beginning of 1975, the ceiling was $495 billion; the latest increase, in November, raised the limit to $595 billion (see vote 7 in Table I). A few days earlier, the Congress had refused a ceiling of $597 billion, and the liberals used the vote to go on record as supporting "fiscal responsibility" and control. However, their *real* sentiments on controlling their spending are shown by their decision to raise the ceiling to $595 billion, and by their acceptance of the budget resolution in December of 1975 (see vote 8 in Table I) which declared that for the quarter beginning July 1st, 1976, a debt limit of $641 billion is "appropriate." (In other words, the Congress is predicting that another 6 months of spending will make it necessary to raise the debt limit by another $46 billion.)

Ultimately, the dead weight of the federal debt reduces the viability of the nation's economy and the standard of living of the American people. Problems associated with large budgets and deficits are aggravated by inaccurate government accounting practices. Private businesses are required by law to use an accrual accounting method, which means that any debt (a promise of future payment) must be recorded when it is incurred, and any expense must be recorded when the transaction takes place, rather than when payment is made. In contrast, however, the government records only some of its liabilities, such as the bonds it sells. There are other debts (to be paid in future years) which the government incurs, but does *not* record. The result is that while the government reported a total national debt of $486 billion in 1974, its *real* liabilities totalled $1.141 trillion, and the difference between total liabilities and total assets (that is the total real deficit) was $812 billion. In that same year, the government reported

31

a (one-year) deficit of $3.5 billion, but actually, incurred a deficit of $95 billion (the amount by which expenses exceeded revenues). This sort of distortion is typical of government accounting, and deceives both the public and the Congress about the financial situation of the government. As a result, it is much easier for the Congress to legislate a large deficit each year, when the *recorded* deficit which the Congress recognizes is much smaller than the *real* deficit that occurs. The solution, of course, is to require the federal government to meet the same standards of honesty which it imposes on businessmen, namely, the accrual method of accounting. The Truth in Government Accounting Act, whose principal sponsor is Rep. Philip M. Crane, has been proposed for this purpose, and is included as proposal B in Table II.

However, in the absence of major reforms, the budget situation is not at all encouraging.

What Next?

We know what the future holds if liberals continue to control Congress: higher and higher deficits, accumulation of the national debt, higher interest payments, more inflation, and less investment and a stifling of the economy's ability to expand output, productivity, and wealth. If liberals continue to control policy, they will seize upon this massive economic failure as evidence that *more* government action is necessary—further illustrating their inability to learn from experience. These fiscal and monetary policies have restricted investment to such an extent that productivity has grown only 0.7 percent annually over the past decade. If the current trend continues, the big-spending Congress will take it as a failure of the economic system rather than a failure of their own policies, and our ability to correct past mistakes will diminish even more.

However, the trend *can* be reversed and past mistakes can be corrected. A change in who controls Congress is the first necessary step. There are more than enough potential spending cuts if the Congress is willing to make them—some are small, some large. The size of the current budget is no surprise when one considers the many examples of waste that occur throughout the federal government:

• In the military: Golf courses cost $13.9 million a year. The Pentagon spent $375,000 studying frisbees.

• The National Science Foundation has spent $135,000 to find out whether chimpanzees can talk, $25,000 to study primate teeth, $84,000 to find out why or how people fall in love, and $112,000 to study the climate of Africa during the last Ice Age.

• The Federal Aviation Administration spent $57,800 to conduct a study on the body measurements of airline stewardess trainees.

• Several agencies spent more than $1 million studying marihuana's effect on sexual arousal, hypnosis, facial expressions of Americans, the use of marihuana by the Zulus, and the use of qat by the people of North Yemen.

• Other agencies have spent $500,000 to determine why rats, monkeys, and humans clench their jaws—apparently because of anger—stopping smoking, loud noises, and the feeling that one has been cheated. Other studies accounted for $70,-000: the smell of perspiration of Australian aborigines; $71,-000: preparing a history of comic books; and $19,300: why children fall off tricycles.

Of course, cutting the budget both to balance and to reduce it will require many major cuts, not merely relatively trivial examples of waste. An organized system of budget reductions was proposed by several of my colleagues in a Special Order led by my able colleague, Congressman Bill Armstrong of Colorado, which I was pleased to take part in.

In addition, I introduced a substitute for the Second Budget Resolution of 1975 (H. Con. Res. 466), which was mentioned earlier in this chapter, (see vote 9 in Table I). My proposal would have balanced budget outlays with anticipated revenues, and would have held the increase in the public debt to $14.2 billion. While I prefer no increase in the debt ceiling, this minimum increase is necessary primarily to account for the expenditures of the federal off-budget agencies. I saw no reason why last year the U.S. government could not live within its means, namely within a $300 billion per year cash flow.

Reducing government spending over the long run requires an awareness on the part of Congress of the real economic consequences of its policies, combined with careful scrutiny of the various programs which either have been enacted or are likely to be created (given the current trend).

As long as there are a significant number of liberals in the Congress, long-run budget control will be impossible without adoption of a requirement that the budget be balanced (except in times of declared war or national emergency). The temptation to create new deficits, year after year, is too strong. A large number of bills have been introduced for this purpose, generally in the form of a Resolution in favor of a Constitutional Amendment which would prohibit the Congress from spending more than it will receive in revenues. Some other bills would institute additional controls to insure the fiscal integrity of the federal government. And even in the absence of a permanent requirement in the Constitution, the substitute I offered for the Second Budget Resolution would have balanced the fiscal year 1976 budget. (These various zero add-on deficit proposals are combined in proposal C in Table II.)

What should be kept in mind is that there is nothing magic about a large budget or a budget deficit. Liberal Democrats have spent years trying to convince us that deficit spending will make all of us better off, despite evidence to the contrary. They have spent years trying to deny that their programs caused or aggravated problems, though that was, in fact, what happened. A change in budget policy is essential to economic and social health; that change will be brought about only by replacing the liberal Democratic Congress with a Republican, free-market-oriented Congress that recognizes that responsible fiscal policy is essential to the long run health of our nation's economy.

BIOGRAPHY
of
The Honorable Jack Kemp
New York

Representative Jack Kemp, a third term Congressman from the 38th District of New York, came to Congress in his first bid at elected office in 1970.

Born in Los Angeles in 1935, Mr. Kemp received his B.A. from Occidental College and did graduate studies in education and political science while playing professional football.

During his 13 years as a quarterback in the American and National Football Leagues, Mr. Kemp led the Buffalo Bills to AFL championships in 1964 and 1965 and won the AFL's Most Valuable Player Award in 1965. He is a co-founder of the AFL Players Association, helped to negotiate the first comprehensive collective bargaining contract in professional football, and was Association president from 1965 until 1970.

Congressman Kemp served as a special assistant to Governor Reagan of California in 1967 and as a special assistant to the Chairman of the Republican National Committee, Rogers Morton, in 1969, concurrent with his football career.

Chosen as one of the 200 outstanding young leaders in America by TIME magazine in 1975, Mr. Kemp was re-elected to the 94th Congress with a 72% vote in a year of Democratic victories. His was the largest number of votes of any Republican candidate for Congress in 1974.

His efforts for the working men and women in his District and his ability to sell free enterprise principles have resulted in strong support throughout Western New York from blue collar workers.

As a member of the Committee on Appropriations, as an economic analyst, and as the principal author of the Jobs Creation Act, Congressman Kemp has had a long-time interest in the relationship between capital formation and job creation.

TAX REFORM: THE KEY TO JOBS CREATION
by
Congressman Jack Kemp

A nation's tax policy determines whether or not the costs of government are spread among people in proportion to the benefits they receive; it also affects the attitudes of the people and their relationship to the state. A nation's political and economic character cannot be independent of its tax policy.

When the purpose of taxation is to raise revenue, people remain responsible for their own economic welfare. When people are responsible for their own welfare, that very fact unites them in resisting any attempt by government to erect, in the words of the Declaration of Independence, a "multitude of new offices and send hither swarms of officers to harass our people and eat out their substance."

Today, taxes take about 40 percent of total personal income, as compared to 15 percent in 1930. Unless present trends are reversed, by 1985 the government will take 54 cents from every dollar of personal income.

By turning taxation from its original purpose of raising revenue and making it into a method for redistributing income, the Democrat majority in Congress has created constituencies known as special interest groups, each with its own lobby organization. The special interest lobby organizations all want as large a share as possible of the taxes that are collected from the taxpayers. Obviously, these special interest groups have a stake in higher taxation, because the taxes extracted from the taxpayers are used to benefit the interest groups that lobby for the redistributed monies. The huge growth in government bureaucracy since 1930 indicates that bureaucracy also benefits from redistribution.

By thus breaking what was once a unified resistance to higher taxes, the Democrat majority in Congress has removed a principal constraint that limited the size of government. When the purpose of taxation is to redistribute income rather than to raise revenue, the opportunity for more and more people to live on the public's purse causes more and more efforts and abilities to be directed away from productive work and into political action.

Harmful Effects of the Redistributive Tax Policy

The leaders of the Democrat Party have emphasized income redistribution as the basis of tax policy. This emphasis has been in effect long enough for us to reach conclusions.

The main economic effects of redistributive tax policy have been a reduction in the rate at which the economy's productivity increases and the appearance of unemployment and inflation simultaneously. Let us see why redistributive taxation has reduced productivity and caused both unemployment and inflation.

A redistributive tax is a tax designed to make people more equal as consumers than they are as producers. Therefore, it is a tax on productivity.

A tax on productivity not only encourages people to *produce* less, it encourages them to *save* less of the amount they produce. A person's taxes increase if he puts part of each paycheck into a savings account. He must pay income tax on the wage or salary he earns and also on the interest his savings account earns. People learn that they can minimize their tax bill *by spending more than they earn*, because *the interest cost associated with borrowing is tax deductible*.

In short, just as a tax on productivity reduces people's incentives to work and encourages them to spend more of their time in leisure and less in work, it reduces people's incentives to save and causes them to spend more of their income in consumption.

Savings are the source of capital—a term that is applied to machinery, equipment, buildings, and other productive resources—and capital is the source of productivity. The number of jobs and the level of real wages cannot grow unless productivity grows. But productivity cannot grow unless capital grows, and capital cannot grow unless savings and investment grow. A tax on productivity is a tax on capital that biases people away from savings and toward consumption. Obviously, that means less capital, therefore lower productivity, fewer new jobs, and a lower rate of growth in real wages. Fewer new jobs mean more unemployment.

Unemployment and a lower rate of growth in real wages are both consequences of and setbacks to the redistributive tax policy. This produced a dilemma because the liberal majority in the Congress was not willing to give up trying to redistribute income. Yet, to finance the redistributive schemes through legislating higher tax rates would cost the votes of many taxpayers.

The solution adopted by the liberal majority in the Congress was to spend more than the government receives in taxes—that is, to create a deficit, which is "covered" by the sale of bonds (borrowing). This "solution", however, either reduces productivity further or causes inflation, depending on who buys the bonds.

In order to sell the bonds to individuals or organizations in the private sector, including banks, the government must bid against other bond-sellers (borrowers), such as local governments and private firms. Bidding takes the form of offering a higher interest rate to the investor. If the government successfully sells its bonds, this indicates that the private investors have decided to lend their money to the government *instead* of, say, a private firm, which would use the money to build a new plant and hire more people.

Private investors can only use their money once—either to buy government bonds or to invest in the productive sector of the economy. Therefore, when the government successfully sells bonds, it draws money away from the private sector, and private investment is "crowded out" of the market. If government expenditures were investment-oriented, this "crowding out" might be less harmful. But government transfer payments are designed to encourage consumption, and thus do *not* replace the private investment that was "crowded out" by the government bonds.

If private investors for the bonds cannot be found, the bonds *must* be bought by the Federal Reserve. The only way the Federal Reserve can purchase them is by "creating" more money. This means that the number of dollars in the system increases, but the number of goods does not increase. As a result, each individual dollar is worth less than before. *This process is inflation*.

Inflation itself cuts into productivity by increasing taxes automatically. In a progressive tax system if a taxpayer's money income increases to keep pace with inflation, he or she moves into a higher tax-rate bracket even though his purchasing power has not increased. Thus *real* income (after taxes and after adjusting for inflation) actually goes down, leaving the taxpayer with less ability to save. In 1974 inflation (during that *one* year) caused personal income taxes to increase by almost as much as the tax rebate enacted in the Tax Reduction Act of 1975. In addition to the tax rebate for 1974, that Act provided for a tax reduction for 1975. However, despite the cuts, the total tax burden per household rose *12 percent* in fiscal year 1975; in the same period, total personal income rose at a slower rate than inflation, so real income declined. In short, the enacted tax cuts did not prevent a real tax increase, even though real income declined.

While comprehensive tax reforms are desirable, this specific problem—increased real taxation as a result of inflation—can be dealt with through a relatively simple reform, namely tax indexing, which is the purpose of the Cost-of-Living Adjustment Act and several similar bills (see proposal D in Table II). Under an indexed tax system, people cannot be pushed into higher tax brackets by inflation. It would no longer be possible for the Congress to increase taxes through inflation; nor could they claim credit for a tax "reduction"—like the Tax Reduction Act adopted in early 1975—which merely restored the effective tax rate which existed before the most recent year of inflation.

Inflation has a similar effect on businesses by exaggerating corporate profits (because of phantom "inventory profits" and understated depreciation costs); the result is overtaxation of business income—by roughly $10 billion in 1974 alone—leaving less funds for investment. Thus, though the Congress discovered a way to increase taxes—through inflation—without explicitly legislating the increase, the further effect has been to reduce productivity and increase the government's share of national income.

Because it increases the effective tax on productivity, inflation further cuts into savings and capital, aggravating inflation and unemployment. Inflation produces more money with which to demand goods but less capital with which to employ labor in the production of goods.

The Congress has been less successful in redistributing income from the more productive to the less productive than in redistributing resources *out of investment and into consumption*. The result of the redistributive tax policy has been to increase past consumption at the expense of present and future income and employment. The redistributive tax policy has produced a damaging capital shortage, the minimum estimate of which is $575 billion over the next ten years. A capital shortage of this magnitude means rising rates of unemployment and inflation.

Economic Freedom Is Endangered

There is still some hope that an informed electorate will realize that inflation, unemployment, high taxes, big government, and big bureaucracy are all components of the same explosive package. It is not too late for the electorate to take action to prevent further departures from a free society.

Advocates of big government will attempt to misrepresent the capital shortfall, *which they have caused*, as a failure of private enterprise. This failure, they will insist, requires the government to plan investment. As inflation, taxation, and government borrowing shrink the sources of investment capital, government loans may become the main source of business funds, as has happened in Britain.

If that point were reached the socialization of investment would be complete and the independence of private property would be destroyed. Perhaps underlying the drift toward socialization of investment is the belief among advocates of big government that control over investment would allow more control over the distribution of income, and thus over the lives of individuals.

This is the shape of the battle that must ultimately determine the future political character of the nation and the relationship of the people to the state. The advocates of big government have long been mobilizing to force the issue. They have made demagogic use of political offices to convince the people that it is easy for those with high incomes to avoid paying taxes and that investment incentives, which some liberal Democrats call "corporate tax loopholes for the benefit of fat cats," result in "revenue losses" that American workers must make up out of their pockets. Demagogues have fanned envy in their battle to redistribute and enlisted it as an ally.

Academic apologists for big government have invented the concept of "tax expenditures"—a term describing a potential source of tax revenue as an expenditure of tax revenues because it was not collected. (Under this concept, the personal exemption you declared on your income tax form last year represented an "expenditure" of federal funds!) Through this concept, the Democrats have fostered the misconception that income earned by businesses and individuals is the *property of the government*, and that any income that is not taxed represents a gift to the earner at the expense of the U.S. Treasury.

These same academic apologists have been spreading doctrines for three or four decades which undermine the confidence of individuals that they have control over their own lives. By arguing that a person's employment prospects are unrelated to his own efforts, that the responsibility for being employed lies not with the individual but with the government, reliance that people once placed on themselves is shifted to the government.

The political effect of this shift is ominous. When people lose self-confidence and self-reliance, they cannot expect their opinions to count politically. When all responsibility for looking after the people has been shifted to the government, the people will be ruled by government; American democracy will no longer exist. There can be no individual liberty without individual responsibility. The advocates of big government pose as progressives, but in fact they are reactionaries.

The Cause For Hope

And in that fact there is hope. The American people are not a reactionary and envious people. Born of a revolutionary and generous spirit, they have no craving to be stifled by the state. The growing libertarian movement has brought back into use our revolutionary slogan: "Don't Tread On Me!"

Some liberal Democrats themselves are beginning to face the fact that the liberal program of big government does not minister to the real discontent of the people. Senator Edmund Muskie, D-Maine, in a speech at the New York Liberal Party's annual dinner in October, 1975, acknowledged, "in the past decade, liberals have developed an ideology and state of mind that is narrow, unimaginative and often irrelevant."

"Why can't liberals talk about fiscal responsibility and productivity without feeling uncomfortable?" he asked. "When there is talk of cutting costs or just wondering why our Federal budget is now almost $400 billion," he noted, "you simply don't find liberals involved in the discussion." And he put his finger precisely on the problem when he said of his own Party, ". . . our emotional stake in government is so much that we regard common-sense criticism of government almost as a personal attack."

It remains to be seen how the Democrat Party will respond to such forthright talk by one of its leaders. If it responds by bringing itself back into the mainstream of American politics, Republicans will face increased political competition. But the battle drawn by that Party's ideological leaders may not have to be fought. A return of the Democrat Party to the mainstream of American politics will not shatter the commonality that has been the basis of the nation's political unity.

Thus far, many liberals in Congress have not shown a willingness to face economic reality, but political reality has forced them to compromise somewhat. Initially, the Congress passed the tax reduction extension, which provided short-run relief but ignored long-term consequences. After the President vetoed the bill, the responsible position was supported strongly enough to sustain the veto (see vote 10 in Table I, a "yes" vote is in favor of overriding the President's veto).

But there is no reason for Republicans to stand in abeyance while Democrats deliberate. We know our values and can reflect them in creative, progressive programs within the American political tradition. A program which reflects what is right in America will succeed with the people. The Jobs Creation Act (see proposal E in Table II), which restores the productivity of the economy, and the Fiscal Integrity Act (see proposal F in Table II) which restores a constraint on the size of government, are part of such a program.

An Alternative to Big Government, Inflation, and Unemployment

The program of the liberal Democrats places more emphasis on income redistribution than on employment, seeks income equality even at the cost of lower incomes, and makes people increasingly financially dependent on the government by putting disincentives on saving. Our alternative is the Jobs Creation Act.

The Jobs Creation Act addresses itself to unemployment. It would create millions of new jobs in the private sector and would remove the people's dependence on government for employment.

The Jobs Creation Act attacks the capital shortage. It would generate one quarter of a trillion dollars in new capital outlays over a three-year period, helping our economy catch up with the demands placed on it.

The Jobs Creation Act faces the need for fiscal responsibility and stable prices. It would generate $45 billion in new federal revenues over a three-year period to help offset the deficits caused by previous Congresses.

Economic Effects

A major economic study undertaken by the Washington consulting firm of Norman B. Ture concludes that in the first year after its enactment the tax reduction provision of the Jobs Creation Act would generate increases of $151.4 billion in the gross national product (GNP), $74.6 billion in capital outlays and $5.2 billion in federal revenues. The second year after enactment would see additional increases of $200.5 billion in GNP, $77.9 billion in capital outlays, and $14.6 billion in federal revenues. The third year would see further increases of $248.9 billion in GNP, $81.1 billion in capital outlays, and $25.2 billion in federal revenues. These are real increases, not increases resulting from higher prices.

How would these increases in real GNP affect employment and real wages? If all of the increased productivity goes into hiring new workers, there would be increases in employment of 8.7 percent in the first year, 10.6 percent in the second year, and 12.4 percent in the third year. These percentage figures translate into *7.2 million new jobs* in the first year of enactment, *9 million new jobs* in the second year, and *10.9 million new jobs* in the third year.

On the other hand, if all the increased productivity were to go into higher real wages for those already working there would be increases in real wages of 8.2 percent in the first year, 10.3 percent in the second year, and 12.1 percent in the third year. These percentage figures mean almost $2,000 additional real income for every employee in *each* of the three years.

Since some of the increased productivity would go into hiring new workers and some would go into paying higher real wages, it is obvious that the Act would generate millions of new jobs and substantial gains above the wage level that would otherwise occur. These millions of new jobs (and higher incomes) would be resting on healthy expansion of the economy and a stronger base of invested capital, rather than relying on annual government handouts at the expense of productive workers. They would be productive, tax-generating jobs rather than tax-consuming jobs. By generating full employment, the Act would eliminate the necessity of many unemployment-related government expenditures, further reducing the deficit in the government budget.

There is no other way to create millions of new real jobs, not jobs that are just another form of welfare (federal transfer payment) that benefits the recipient at the expense of others, but jobs that result from the creation of new income and new production.

Some people may find it startling that it is possible to have such large increases in income and employment. But that is because in the last four decades this country has not relied on the approach embodied in the Jobs Creation Act of fostering full employment and price stability through production.

In addition to these employment and income effects that

stem directly from reduced taxes on business (through reducing the corporate income tax rate, improving the investment tax credit and the asset depreciation range), the Act creates similar effects by providing individuals with incentives to save and invest through the following provisions (summarized briefly):

• Give tax credits to individuals for savings in such forms as savings accounts, life insurance investments, and stocks and bonds.

• Exclude from gross income the dividends paid to the taxpayer by corporations, and the first $1,000 of capital gains.

• Enlarge the dollar amount for individual retirement accounts.

Other sections of the Act help preserve family businesses and family farms from the tax collector.

The Jobs Creation Act is a program that benefits all sectors of the economy and all segments of the citizenry—labor, pensioners, small business, farmers, investors, professionals, and large corporations. It is a program not of fighting over how to share a small pie but of producing a bigger pie. It encourages work, not political lobbying. It is a program that lets people look to the future without the fear that they will be robbed by Washington of what they produce. The Jobs Creation Act is a program of stimulating production.

The Economics of Stimulating Production

Everyone knows that real jobs originate in industry's ability to produce and that only increased production can enlarge the tax base and increase tax revenues. Even the advocates of deficit spending claim their purpose is to increase production by stimulating consumption. They have in mind to increase production indirectly by directly increasing consumption. The idea is that as business finds the demand for products rising, it will invest more to be able to produce to meet demand.

But this indirect approach often fails. As we have seen, the government deficits will produce inflation or "crowd out" investment. The impact of the government deficit is contradictory: while stimulating consumption, it removes the investment capital that businesses need to increase production. Private savings that could have financed investment and new jobs go instead into government bonds or are lost to inflation, thus limiting the economy's ability to grow.

Tax reductions designed to increase consumption cannot simultaneously increase saving. People cannot save what they consume. And there will not be more consumable goods unless people have first saved and invested more to provide the increased production.

On the other hand, tax reductions designed to lessen the existing tax bias against saving—which results from failure to allow tax deductions for initial saving or return to saving—will directly encourage production. Reducing the tax bias against saving encourages people to save more because it reduces the amount of current consumption they must forego in order to increase their future income.

Tax reductions of this sort increase the value of the after-tax income from the investment, thereby lowering the pre-tax rate of return that must be anticipated if the investment is to be undertaken, thus increasing the range of profitable investments.

A Pro-Jobs Program

The alternative we offer to the tax policy of liberal Democrats is to stimulate production, not envy. We know that redistribution both divides and fails. Our tax policy is not a program to make some better off by making others worse off, but a program to make all better off through a more rapidly growing economy that is beneficial to all. Our tax policy is a program of helping our productive capacity catch up with the demands that are placed on it. Our tax policy is a program of full employment without inflation-fueling deficits. Our tax policy is a program to get government out of America's pockets and off of our citizens' backs.

The Fiscal Integrity Act: A Pro-Taxpayers Program

The Fiscal Integrity Act complements the Jobs Creation Act by restoring a constraint on the size of government, a constraint that the Democratic leadership in the Congress destroyed by creating special interest groups who benefit from higher taxes on the general population. The Fiscal Integrity Act would put a halt to the mushrooming national public debt by requiring a balanced budget. It would put a halt to the government taking an ever greater percent of national income in taxes—from taking 54 cents out of every dollar by 1985—by requiring, over a 20-year period, a net reduction of 7.5 percent in government expenditures as a percent of national income.

The Fiscal Integrity Act is pro-taxpayer because it stops the government's ability to continually increase taxes on productivity through inflation, and it stops the government's ability to continually take a larger percentage of the taxpayer's income. Together, the Jobs Creation Act and the Fiscal Integrity Act restore the productivity of the economy and the people's claim to what they produce.

BIG BROTHER

BIOGRAPHY

of

The Honorable William M. Ketchum
California

Presently serving his second term in the U.S. Congress, Bill Ketchum represents the 18th Congressional District of California.

Born in Los Angeles on September 2, 1921, Ketchum began a farming career in Grass Valley, California. In 1956, he purchased a ranch in Paso Robles where he served twice as President of the San Luis Obispo County Farm Bureau.

His political career began as a representative in the California Assembly (1966-1972) before coming to the Nation's Capitol in 1973.

During the 93rd Congress, he was a member of the House Interior and Insular Affairs Committee, the House Science and Astronautics Committee, and the District of Columbia Committee. He also served as Minority Whip of the Interior Committee's Water and Power Resources Subcommittee. Early in the 94th Congress, Mr. Ketchum resigned his previous Committee positions in order to devote full time to membership in the House Ways and Means Committee. He also serves as a member of the Task Force on Energy and Regulatory Reform.

Among his many awards, Congressman Ketchum is the recipient of the Bronze Star and Purple Heart for his distinguished service in both World War II and the Korean Conflict. He was also the recipient of the Outstanding Freshman (Congressman) Award, the Good Government Award and the Watchdog of the Treasury Award.

Bill Ketchum and the former Lola Heegaard are the parents of two children and three grandchildren.

WHO'S THAT LOOKING OVER MY SHOULDER—AND WHY?

A CASE FOR REGULATORY REFORM
by
Congressman Bill Ketchum

Our country's Constitution provides for the delegation of governmental powers into three specific branches—Executive, Judicial, and Legislative. Some of the most brilliant minds in our nation drew up this plan, with good reason. But over time, increasing power has been usurped by what has become known as the *fourth* branch of Government. While Congress turned its back, the regulatory agencies—a power group unforeseen by our nation's founders—came to occupy a position of unparalleled power and influence in the United States. With a workforce of over 63,000 employees in 30 agencies, and with literally trillions of rules and regulations in its control, this fourth branch of government has lately become a sad fact of the American way of life.

How did this shameful situation develop? It did not happen overnight. It was allowed to develop by the only government agencies that could have prevented it—the three traditional branches of government. We intend to point out the evils of our present condition, to examine attitudes toward it, and to recommend ways to put an end to it as soon as possible.

Our branch, the "Reform Congress" is largely responsible for the neglect of this primary issue. When before have we witnessed the spectacle of Ralph Nader and the U.S. Chamber of Commerce on the same side of one issue? And still Congress has failed to act on the vital issue of Regulatory Reform. The elected representatives of U.S. citizenry have recklessly failed to address the fact that these citizens overpay an estimated $2,000 per year per family in inflated regulation-era prices. Only if we act *now* with responsibility and forcefulness, can we avoid taking the nation beyond the point of no return in the name of "protection."

Congress, the servants of the democratic process, is about to destroy one of its fundamental concepts: the free enterprise system. We have interpreted our role of legislators to be one of nursemaid to the citizenry, and in doing so have very nearly smothered the baby under too many blankets. Syndicated columnist James J. Kilpatrick has aptly defined the current situation:

> Within the Congress . . . there develops what John Randolph called the legislative itch. On the body politic a rash is seen; it must be scratched. Statutes tumble upon statutes . . . and these laws must be administered . . . interpreted, construed, amplified, extended and enforced. Enter the regulator. He is a decent man but his passion is to regulate. It becomes a consuming passion.

It must be admitted that the causes are usually considered just: environmental conservation, job safety, antimonopoly, consumer advocacy. But what has happened to the ideas of self-regulation by business, employee accountability, and free market economics? Congress pays lip service to these laudable ideals, then casually passes legislation and creates more regulatory agencies that nullify these concepts. Congress must wake up before the baby smothers altogether.

Congressional ineptitude is amply demonstrated by the passage of legislation mandating the creation of an Agency for Consumer Protection (see Vote 2 in Table I). Fully 75 percent of the American people registered their opposition to this "protective" device. *They* saw it for its true worth: another layer of federal bureaucracy, subject to minimal accountability, capable of producing tons of memos and paperwork, capable of intruding into the lives and affairs of the American public—but incapable of actually protecting the American consumer. A confounding task indeed: just which of the 231 million American consumers would the Agency choose to protect? And from what? Laws already exist to protect buyers from force and from fraud and to prevent dishonest business transactions—or at least to provide retribution against dishonesty. The proliferation of regulatory agencies is unnecessary. Instead of facing up to the nightmare we have created and perpetuated, Congress has chosen to shrug off the responsibility. It's time to take some action.

We've all heard "horror stories" arising from federal activities in the name of regulation and protection. I cite just a few of these outrageous facts and figures here—not in the name of sensationalism, but to catalog distinct situations in which Congress can and must assert its remedial legislative authority. Interior bureaucratic reform has become a laughing matter. Abolition of federal regulatory agencies is politically impossible. Therefore, the legislators must do the job: Draft and pass legislation addressing the country's ills.

Protection From What?

The Consumer Product Safety Commission (CPSC) was created by Congressional fiat in 1972. The Commission has jurisdiction over a mind-boggling number of consumer products—everything from bicycles to diapers to slide projectors—and until recently, the absolute autonomy of this agency has wreaked havoc throughout the retail and consumer communities. In its zeal to protect against "unreasonable risk of injury" the Commission publishes mandatory standards. Although only one set of standards has yet been promulgated, one hundred such narrow rulings are foreseen by the target date of 1982, designed to save us from the evils of book matches, TV sets, and pot holders. Unpredictably, the one existing set of standards undertakes to carefully define the proper use and installation of swimming pool slides (at the request of the National Swimming Pool Institute). It seems irrelevant to comment on the effectiveness of a sign reading "Look out for people and objects below," when the children who use the slide cannot read.

In terms of costs of these brilliant standards, the figures are outrageous. Consider the cost of $142,000 for a study of bathtubs, the conclusion of which reads: "Slips and falls are by far the most frequent type of bathtub accident."

Power lawn mower requirements if effected could increase the cost of a $100 mower to $186 and might put 25 manufacturers out of business. How about dangerous dolls? In Los Angeles, the CPSC confiscated 80,000 of the Bradley Import Company's doll inventory, because the dolls had pins in them. Confiscation caused a Christmas-order season loss of $600,-000. But these dolls were collector's items, never intended for a child's toy. Is this kind of regulation justified?

Currently, the CPSC operates with a staff of 1,024 and a budget of $42.8 million. The fiscal year 1977 request is for $54.8 million to employ 1,226. These facts and figures say one thing to me in a very loud voice: Investigate. Are these activities worth $54.8 million or $42.8 million—or even two cents? Is this a federal matter at all? Congressional oversight committees—with the help of Federal Trade Commission specialists and manufacturer cooperation—could perform the same function. This generation has opened the door to consumer scrutiny and skepticism; is a special federal policeman any more than an insult to the consumer's intelligence (as well as a blight on their pocketbooks and an invader of privacy)? These issues must be answered by Congress immediately.

Another area of regulatory excess is the communications field, handcuffed since 1934 by the Federal Communications Commission (FCC). We have only recently become painfully aware of this agency's powers by implementation of the TV "family hour." Instead of attacking the issue of poor and deleterious programming, the FCC chose the "cosmetic approach." While this fiat may seem innocuous it does have ominous overtones. What is in fact involved are serious infringements upon our Constitutional rights. The FCC has intruded upon the individual's freedom of choice and the media's freedom of the press. Such blindness should not be tolerated.

Moreover, in the name of protection, the FCC has seriously retarded technological advances that could improve the quality and quantity of broadcast programming while lowering its costs. In its approach to the proposals concerning cable and pay TV the FCC is effectively fostering the unprecedented monopoly of the air waves that the three major networks now enjoy. Congress must see that the Commission it created more than 40 years ago needs revamping. Network profits rose 21 percent in 1974; certainly the industry can now stand on its own. Moreover, if free market economics were allowed to operate, and competition in cost and broadcast offerings were stimulated, the quality of this popular form of national entertainment would certainly improve.

It is the duty of Congress as makers of the laws of the land to see that the rules of the open marketplace prevail. The FCC must recognize right of entry to the many small new communications companies that offer specialized services at substantial savings. The FCC must allow entry to new technology and systems—not to delay for 11 years the launching of an international communications satellite designed to cut data transmission costs and long distance telephone rates. Examples like these should be carefully investigated by Congress to prevent their repetition. Autonomy in these agencies is frightening, especially when it becomes apparent that protection is often being extended to special interest groups, not to the consumer.

The Civil Aeronautics Board (CAB) is yet another case in point. Granted broad authority in 1938 to set rates and fares for commercial air transport, the CAB seems to have lost sight of the consumer in its zealous industry promotion. But the elected officials in Congress are the voices of the consumer; Congress must act to discourage these powers. For example, CAB rejected a British company's 1974 application to fly between London and New York City for $125 one way. Why? "Unfair competition" to American airline companies. But it seems to me that such service is indeed the very fairest of competition, offering a real choice to the consumer. Who is the CAB protecting?

The wonders of modern living are due in large part to the achievements of big business, through research enabled by investment of profit dollars. Government controls have only discouraged technological advances. Government's regulatory dabblings are becoming increasingly counterproductive. By driving up prices, driving away competition and small business, and jeopardizing free enterprise, regulation does nothing but harm the consumer. Why does it cost $44.37 to fly 334 miles from Chicago to Minneapolis and only $20.75 to fly 337 miles from Los Angeles to San Francisco? Because Pacific South-West airlines, the California carrier, is exempt from CAB regulations since it operates intrastate. In general it has been estimated that CAB regulations elevate air fares from 40 to 70 percent on 250-mile flights, from 75 to 100 percent on flights of 250 to 1,000 miles, and about 100 percent on trips of more than 1,000 miles. Why?

The CAB and the airline industry maintain that airlines need high fares to cover losses on unprofitable routes, and approximately 372 of the 994 domestic nonstop routes are considered unprofitable. But are these judgments justified? James Miller, of the President's Council of Economic Advisors, feels that if major airlines abandoned these "unprofitable" routes, most of the abandoned routes would be eagerly adopted by commuter airlines that are exempt from CAB regulations. Who benefits from the fact that no new major carriers have been certified since 1938? Not the consumer! Or from a situation in which through mergers and acquisitions the total number of trunk lines and local carriers has dropped from 33 in 1946 to 20 in 1975—with no observable economies for enlarged operations? Certainly not the consumer.

But, surprisingly, the industry isn't winning either. CAB's repeated acceptance of the industry's proposed rate schedules and increases has backfired. In the first quarter of 1975, airlines lost $190 million. Consumers who can choose alternate modes of transportation have done so. They don't believe the sales pitch about the opportunity to turn the neighboring empty seat into an arm rest: *they* know who subsidizes that empty seat. If airlines were allowed to compete for prices, the consumer wouldn't have to pay for the sales appeal of pastel-painted aircraft, movie selection, complimentary hors d'oeuvres, and the like. Unless serious investigatory moves are initiated and meaningful legislative reforms enacted, the CAB will price this marvel of technology right out of the sky!

ICC: Friend Or Foe?

Another ogre in need of Congressional censure is the Interstate Commerce Commission (ICC). It is the ultimate anachronism in terms of "consumer protection." Indeed, carriage regulated by ICC has proved too inflexible and costly to efficiently serve the consuming public's needs. It has been estimated that ICC rules and regulations cost consumers $5-10 billion per year in terms of higher prices, not to mention the waste of up to 460 million gallons of precious fuel annually and the production of 150,000 tons of pollutants added to our already fouled air. This Commission is the perfect example of Congressional inattention. The world is a different place now than in 1887 when the ICC was established to protect customers and rail lines from discriminatory pricing. The rules applied to the interstate trucking industry in the thirties and forties are long outmoded—and we pay through the teeth for this regulatory senility. It's time Congress called to account these 2,000 employees and the $34 million budget.

The ICC is yet another example of consumer protection run amok. Contrary to its intended purpose, the ICC has become the protector of trucking industry moguls in a bastardized version of antimonopoly policies. The Commission has power to decide which trucks may go into interstate business. Entry rights are judged solely on the proof that established carriers lack the capacity to haul specific traffic. Considerations such as lower cost, faster service, or greater responsiveness to customers are dismissed by the Commission as irrelevant. In addition, the ICC has control over what a commerical trucker may or may not carry. Thus, when Quaker Oats started a pizza plant in Tennessee, trucks hauling tomato paste from California were not allowed to carry pizzas back. While the ICC cites the fact that this ruling gives more truckers jobs, it disregards the obvious corollary: Consumers pay for the second truck to carry what could have been loaded in the first. The upshot of this situation is that regulated truckers travel *empty* an estimated 30 percent of their miles.

"Gateway restrictions" have created ludicrous routing procedures preventing truckers from taking the quickest, most economical route in order to pass through ICC-mandated "gateway cities." And the incredible practice of allowing competing truckers to set rates high enough to sustain their least efficient colleague is flatly sanctioned by the ICC. Economists estimate that, were ICC regulations relaxed, prices of almost *everything* would be reduced by an average 0.5 percent. When frozen vegetables were removed from federal regulations in the 1950s, shipping rates dropped at least 20 percent.

Naturally, the government can exempt itself from its own regulations. Defense Department shipments between May and November 1972 cost $60.1 million for 3 billion pounds of freight by truck: *$36.6 million* less than the going ICC rates! Other branches of government have caught on to ICC rip-off. Why hasn't Congress?

If ever a picture of a reckless Congress were painted, these regulatory nightmares certainly should suffice! The Constitutional image of a system of checks and balances has given way to unchecked regulations and imbalanced favoritism. How can Congress continue to call itself representative of the people after having implicitly approved federal regulations costing buyers of 1975 new cars more than $3 billion? If there are those among us who still believe all these regulations *protect* consumers, they'd better reflect upon the case of the mandatory buzzer and harness systems. Over 40 percent of car owners have disconnected this annoying contraption, but none can avoid the large chunk of the $320-per-car cost for protective devices this item caused.

Regulatory Reform

The methods for reform are visible, waiting only to be implemented. The President is urging action through his Regulatory Reform Commission. Versions of a Regulatory Reform Act have been introduced in both Houses. The Senate measure (S.2792) outlines a careful five-year time plan for acceptance of comprehensive reform plans in five economic areas with the threat of *abolition* of specific agencies and regulations unless reform legislation is enacted. The House version, H.R. 11026, introduced by Mr. Archer, grants veto power to Congress over all federally promulgated rules and regulations. (See proposal G in Table II.) Others have called for expiration dates to be written into all legislation, so that reflex action repassage will come to an end. The suggestion has been made for performance standards to be defined in every new program, as a guideline to check on its success or failure. On a simple level, the bright attorneys and rule makers of the various agencies might be required to spend some time in the field, actually dealing with some of the bureaucratic snarls they have imposed.

All of these concepts deserve serious and prompt attention. The key word is oversight; heretofore a mere perfunctory step in Congressional Committee function. The hours and days spent in oversight hearings lead to one lone item: the neatly printed transcript of all that has transpired. Congress is squandering a most valuable resource. Regulatory reform begins in Congress, and the people must demand significant and realistic solutions to the problems uncovered during oversight hearings. Moreover, these solutions must be timed right to apply effective remedies where and when needed.

Zero Agency Growth

Let's aim for Zero Agency Growth (ZAG) in Government. Let Congress adopt a standard whereby every new regulation or regulatory agency it approves will be matched by the abolition of one outdated regulation or agency. Thus, while we attack the problem of comprehensive reform of existing regulatory structures, we will not continue to pile up new and conflicting regulations.

Dr. Paul MacAvoy, of the President's Council of Economic Advisors, has outlined a scandalous picture of Congressional ineptitude. In his speech at a recent Conference on Regulatory Reform, Dr. MacAvoy said, in part:

Many agencies were created by, and continue to operate under, misdirected or misguided legislation. In some cases, the mandate has been so constraining as to make the impact of administrative change, reorganization within the Commission, negligible. . . . In other cases, the legislative mandate has been so vague that regulatory agencies have been virtually unconstrained. When the legislative mandate is vague, practices usually reflect incentives offered commissioners and they become quite susceptible to interest group pressures. At other times, the practices of the commissions under a vague man-

58

date deflect case-by-case decisions in other regulated industries as imposed on them by the Appeals court.

This, then, is the situation—for which a reckless Congress must take the greatest share of the blame. It is a situation that Congress alone can correct. The attack must be all-encompassing and immediate if it is to be effective. It is a sad fact indeed that it has taken the shocks of inflated price levels and economic disarray—borne by the American citizenry—to remind us of the free market foundations upon which this country is based.

Thomas Jefferson would be distressed at the distance we have come from "a wise and frugal government which shall restrain men from injuring one another (and) shall leave them otherwise free to regulate their own pursuits." Distressed because this distance is measured not in terms of progress, but in terms of serious regression. At this momentous point in our nation's history, we are very near destroying the foundations upon which it was so carefully built. It is our duty to decide upon a well-defined legislative program for across-the-board regulatory reform. This pressing issue must be a major concern as we elect members of the Congress. If we choose instead to shirk this responsibility, we may very well be forcing the demise of all Constitutional freedoms now treasured by the American people.

BIOGRAPHY
of
The Honorable Robin L. Beard, Jr.
Tennessee

Robin Beard, Jr., is in his second term in Congress representing the Sixth District of Tennessee.

Born in Knoxville, Tennessee, on August 21, 1939, Mr. Beard was raised in Nashville, attending the Montgomery Bell Academy. He graduated from Vanderbilt University in 1961 with a B.A. degree in History and a minor in political science.

After two years as associate director of Alumni Development at Vanderbilt and two years in private business, Mr. Beard entered politics with the campaigns of Maxey Jarman and Winfield Dunn. Under Governor Dunn, Mr. Beard, as State Personnel Commissioner, computerized the entire state personnel system and established an Affirmative Action Program to insure increased opportunities for minority persons in state government.

In 1972, Robin Beard ran for Congress and defeated fourth term Democratic Congressman William Anderson. He was re-elected in 1974 in a traditionally Democratic district in the midst of a national Democratic landslide.

Serving on the House Armed Services Committee and on the Post Office and Civil Service Committee, Congressman Beard has worked vigorously for a strong national defense, an economy free of governmental interference in private enterprise and was the principal author of the first comprehensive OSHA reform bill.

Robin Beard and his wife, the former Catherine Rieniets, live with their two children on a thirteen-acre farm in Franklin.

OSHA: THE BUSINESSMAN'S BURDEN
by
Congressman Robin L. Beard, Jr.

The energy and imagination of the American business community has been the driving force behind the economic success of our nation's free enterprise system. Yet today the business community is being slowly strangled by government red tape and regulation. The proliferation of government "watch-dog" agencies has had a crippling effect on the economy because their influence has resulted in lost jobs for the working man and higher prices for the consumer.

A prime example of government over-regulation is the Occupational Safety and Health Act (OSHA). When OSHA came into effect in 1971, it was praised as one of the most meaningful pieces of legislation since the Fair Labor Standards Act of 1938. At the same time it was severely criticized for being punitive rather than corrective.

Arguments to support this legislation generally center on job-related death and injury figures, with the implication that enactment of this legislation was necessary to stop the slaughter of American workers at the hands of insensitive and ruthless businessmen. Unfortunately, no thought was given to the fact that by any objective standard, the safety record of our nation's workforce is good and constantly improving. Figures compiled by the National Safety Council show that accidental "on the job" deaths per one hundred thousand population went from twenty-one in 1912 to seven in 1971. By 1971 the work force had doubled and the production level was seven times greater than in 1912.

Supporters of the original legislation believed that if the federal government were to take over the entire effort to ensure worker health and safety, the result would somehow be better than if these programs were left to state and local governments or to private enterprise. But what was not considered was the obvious fact that business has a very practical economic stake in promoting the health and safety of its workers; accidents and lost time are costly to business.

There is no question that the reduction of work-related death, illness and injury is a laudable objective. Indeed, the intent of the Occupational Safety and Health Act of 1970 was commendable. We shall see whether this goal has actually been achieved to any degree, or whether the federal bureaucracy managed to distort the original intent by establishing harsh and irrelevant rules and regulations. With a morass of hastily conceived and inappropriate standards, OSHA has become a severe burden on business, an administrative nightmare, and an enemy of the workers it was intended to protect.

What exactly is wrong with OSHA? The most frequent complaints concern regulations promulgated by the Department of Labor, the way in which the Act has been administered, and the Act's punitive rather than remedial approach. Let's take a closer look at the OSHA legislation.

Standards

OSHA establishes procedures whereby the Secretary of Labor promulgates federal standards for on-the-job health and safety. During the two years following the effective date of the Act, the Secretary was to write "national consensus standards" that would become effective as *interim* National Occupational Health and Safety Standards. This process has resulted in many standards that have the force and effect of the law but that are actually inappropriate and out of date. In fact, some of these standards were even out of print at the time they were incorporated as interim standards under the law.

The national consensus standards evolved in an interesting way. To define those standards, interested parties reached substantial agreement after taking divergent views into account. But who are those "interested parties"? Some are industry representatives: (Because the small businessman had little representation, there was virtually no input by small businesses.) The interested parties also included special interest groups more concerned with the safety of property than with the health and safety of workers. In many cases, standards were developed as *minimum* industry standards for equipment and systems in which the member organizations had a monetary interest. Some were representatives of private organizations with unrealistic ideas about employee health and safety. One of the many hastily incorporated "interim standards" included a prohibition against ice in drinking water—presumably a holdover from the days when ice was taken from rivers and therefore might be highly contaminated.

Inspection and Enforcement

In addition to setting and promulgating standards, the Secretary of Labor is also responsible for the enforcement of those standards. The Act provides powers to investigate and to inspect. Inspections are conducted without advance notice to the employer. In fact, the Act specifies that anyone who gives such advance notice without authority to do so may be subject to a maximum fine of $1,000 and a six month imprisonment.

The restriction against advance notice is indicative of the punitive approach of the Act. Businessmen rightly complain that the drafters of the legislation for OSHA have regarded them as criminals who must be secretly approached and caught in the act. Further, employers are not able to receive help from the Department of Labor in complying with the Act. If an inspector appeared at the place of business for any reason, he would be obligated to issue a citation for any alleged violation found during that visit. That citation and the penalty attached are binding unless contested within 15 working days. Then it becomes a final order and cannot subsequently be repealed.

The 15-working-day time frame is totally inadequate. For example, the case of an electrical contractor was cited in testimony before the Environmental Problems Subcommittee of the Small Business Committee. After citing the contractor for alleged violations of OSHA the inspector admitted he was in error. Even though there were no violations after all, the only way to correct the error was to contest the citation. When the contractor informed the Department of Labor of his intention to contest, the Department sent him a package of highly technical material. The contractor wrote requesting a clarification of the material and the Department replied by notifying him that the 15-working-day period had expired! The contractor was now liable for the fine assessed.

If an employer contests a citation within the 15 days the issue is heard by an examiner at the Occupational Safety and Health Review Commission. Only then can an employer take the matter to court. But even then, provisions for judicial review are sharply limited. No trial by jury is provided. The court does not conduct a trial *de novo*, but confines itself to the record of the Review Commission. No new objections can be raised that have not been raised before the Review Commission (except in extraordinary circumstances) and the Commission findings of the facts are generally conclusive.

Contesting a citation takes time and money. Many employers, though believing an imposed fine to be unjust, pay the fine without objection, finding it financially impossible to hire an attorney to contest the case through the Review Commission and perhaps in the courts.

Effects On Small Business

Enforcement of OSHA has created hardships that have crippled and even killed some small businesses. It has inhibited new starts in many business fields.

... A businessman in Illinois quit his excavation business—a steady profit maker until OSHA regulations came along. He concluded that the hundreds of thousands of dollars that he would have to spend to fulfill OSHA requirements would not have been enough. He stated, "It just looked like there would be no end to spending money. If I had fixed one thing, they would probably have found something else."

... Voicing the frustration felt by many small businesses, an Iowa furniture store manager said, "I want to comply, but I have got to keep making a living."

... An Illinois businessman said, "If an inspector walks in here I would probably just hand him the keys and go home. It would be giving up a lot, but it is not worth the worry and frustration."

For those who stay, OSHA adds tremendously to the cost of doing business. It has been estimated that the cost of business in general has increased 10 to 30 percent as a result of OSHA regulations. An example of the high cost of such government intervention is cited by Professor Murray L. Weidenbaum in his recent study of government-mandated price increases. A study commissioned by OSHA estimates that "it will cost American industry an aggregate of $13.5 billion to bring existing facilities into compliance with the current OSHA noise standards of 90-A scale decibels. If the more stringent standard of 85dbA is adopted as recommended by the National Institute for Occupational Safety and Health, the compliance cost is expected to increase to $31.6 billion." *Engineering News Record* reported in August 1972 that OSHA regulations mandated an increase of $4,315.00 in the base price of a new Caterpillar D-9 tractor. Clearly it is the small businessman and the consumer who bear the brunt of this cost increase.

The Occupational Safety and Health Act needs substantial revision. Testimony during Congressional oversight hearings, and debate over amendments offered to the Labor-HEW Appropriations bill indicate that even some of the strongest advocates of the Act admit certain deficiencies. The current makeup of Congress suggests that no action is likely to be taken toward real reform of existing OSHA legislation. Although 90 or more bills were introduced in the 93rd Congress to amend or repeal the Act, not one was moved out of Committee. In the 94th Congress, a similar number of bills are aimed at improving OSHA or repealing it altogether. They are also likely to die in Committee. I am afraid that this is due chiefly to the disinterest of the majority.

I introduced legislation outlining a comprehensive reform of the Occupational Safety and Health Act. This bill (H.R. 7836, see proposal H in Table II) contains over 25 reform provisions, including abolition of the OSHA Review Commission permitting a contest to go directly to the courts; a "grandfather clause" for equipment replacement except in extremely serious situations; extension of the time allowed for notice on intent to contest; and a provision for the use of alternative equipment and procedures not specifically provided for in the standards, if they afford adequate protection.

Eight bills in the 94th Congress are aimed at outright repeal of the OSHA law. Does your Representative appear as a co-sponsor of any of this legislation?

Because there is such a remote possibility that repeal or reform bills will move out of Committee, some Members have chosen the tactic of attempting to amend the Labor-HEW Appropriations Bill (H.R. 8069) to effect some relief. Unfortunately this approach is indirect and is far inferior to an amendment to the OSHA law itself. Amendments to appropriations bills require renewal and are, therefore, less permanent. Efforts to amend the Labor-HEW bill have centered chiefly on the relief of small businessmen. During the 94th Congress, for example, the House of Representatives rejected an amendment to H.R. 8069 that would have exempted employers of 25 or less individuals from first-instance sanctions for OSHA violations (See vote 11 in Table I). This amendment was designed to encourage the small businessman to seek out and correct violations without fear of receiving a citation while trying to determine how to comply with the Act. Although this amendment was rejected by the majority, the list of those who supported the amendment on the floor will give a fair indication of who looks with sympathy on the burdens of small businessmen.

After Legislation—What?

The problem we are addressing here is not common to OSHA alone. Congress has had a tendency to resolve problems by massive legislative steps. It then assumes the problem has been resolved and goes on to other business. Seldom if ever does the Congress pass legislation, allow it to be implemented for a time, and then make a comprehensive and critical review of the success of that legislation. OSHA is an outstanding example of our failure to take even this remedial approach when it is clear that reform is necessary. We entered into this legislation in order to prevent job-related injuries and deaths. Yet we have failed to ask the question, "Is OSHA accomplishing that task?" A related question might be, "What are the costs to the American people, and can those costs be reduced without increasing the number of job related injuries?" It is these kinds of questions that we must raise if we intend to be responsive to the needs of the American public. This is a part of our legislative responsibility that has long been neglected.

The key to diffusing overbearing federal legislation such as OSHA and to preventing passage of similar legislation in the future lies in the hands of the voters. Unfortunately most citizens are unaware of the kind of impact this legislation has on their lives. Over-regulation fuels inflation, forces increased unemployment, and is an abrogation of the spirit and ideals this country has always stood for. It is important that we note that our forefathers envisioned a country in which personal freedom was paramount while government controls were reduced to an absolute minimum. In recent years, legislation like OSHA has moved us in the opposite direction. We have been diminishing the freedom of our cities while trying to regulate every facet of our lives.

BIOGRAPHY

of

The Honorable William F. Goodling
Pennsylvania

William F. Goodling, who succeeded his father George A. Goodling, in representing the 19th District of Pennsylvania in 1974, entered Congress after a career in education.

Bill Goodling was born in Loganville, Pennsylvania, on December 5, 1927. He attended high school in York and college at the University of Maryland. As an educator, Mr. Goodling held various positions including that of School Board Director for the Dallastown District from 1964 to 1967 and Superintendent of Schools for the Spring Grove District from 1967 until his election in 1974, to the 94th Congress. He also served in the United States Army from 1946 until 1948.

In Congress, Representative Goodling serves on the Education and Labor Committee where he is able to lend his experience in teaching to responsible legislation in education. He also serves on the Select Committee on Small Business.

Mr. Goodling and his wife, the former Hilda Wright, have two children.

THE DISARMING OF CITIZENS
by
Congressman William F. Goodling

Congress, on the two hundredth anniversary of our nation's birth, has become increasingly disdainful of some of the rights and liberties for which the colonial Americans fought. Among these rights now threatened is one written into the Constitution—the right to bear arms.

Without much evidence to show that gun control would reduce crime, some Congressmen advocate that the Second Amendment be forgotten. Scores of anti-gun bills have been filed in both the House and the Senate. They range from measures calling for outright confiscation, to federal registration, to severe cutbacks on federal firearms licenses.

One of the most popular versions in both houses of Congress would prohibit the importation, manfacture, sale, purchase, transfer, receipt, possession, or transportation of handguns. The only exceptions would be members of the Armed Forces and law enforcement officials. The Secretary of the Treasury would be empowered to decide whether anyone else would be authorized, specifically mentioning his discretionary power to exempt professional security guard services that are licensed by the state in which the handgun is to be used.

Other legislation goes even farther by requiring the national registration of all firearms, in addition to the other prohibitions. As if that is not enough, some proposals would grant the government the power to establish minimum standards for licensing the possession of *all* firearms—not just handguns.

Proponents of the various gun-control schemes consistently resort to a few arguments that they hope will seem so compelling that we would fail to examine them more closely and realize them for what they are—sensationalism and half-truths.

They argue that if the guns were confiscated there would then be less crime. They also contend that many shooting incidents arise from family quarrels that are definitively settled by quick recourse to a gun. And they suggest that easy access to a gun increases the chance of an impulsive suicide.

Taken simply, or together, and supported by statistics that

tell only one side of the story, these arguments can sound convincing especially when coupled with an explanation that the Second Amendment does not really give everyone the right to bear arms, because it was meant to apply only to those in the militia or, as some would like to believe, the National Guard.

Gun Control and Crime Control

Proponents of gun control suggest a correlation between gun control and crime control. It is simply not the case. We have only to look at New York City, which imposes the strictest gun controls in this country. Despite such legislation, that city has one of the highest rates of murder by firearms. Overall, in New York City the rate of murder and non-negligent manslaughter in 1973 was 17.5 per 100,000 inhabitants. For the same year, the rate in Portland, Oregon, was 5 per 100,-000. If gun control has anything to do with crime control, one would expect the reverse to be true. Portland has not adopted New York City's gun restriction and yet experiences a far lower criminal homicide rate.

It seems obvious that the crime rate in a given area has little to do with numbers of guns or the controls exercised over their ownership. According to the FBI, crime rates are determined by such factors as population numbers, makeup, density, economic status, and education. Thus, it should not be surprising that the National Commission on Causes and Prevention of Crime has concluded that increases in the crime rate occur for reasons unrelated to home firearms possession.

Those who advocate gun control as a means of suppressing crime may well get exactly the wrong result. It is distinctly possible that confiscation of guns may serve only to increase the crime rate. The criminal intending to burglarize a home or store would hesitate, knowing the likelihood of encountering an owner in the possession of a firearm. However, given increased assurances by gun-control legislation that the owner would be defenseless, it would be possible to find ourselves with an appalling increase in theft, assault, and armed robbery.

If it were possible to confiscate every single gun in this country, the crime rate in my opinion, would not decline correspondingly. The same would hold true if we were to succeed in confiscating every single knife, blackjack, and axe. But it is absurd to suppose that owners of unregistered guns would surrender them. It stands to reason that if some persons are willing to break the law by using a gun to rob or murder, the last thing they would do is turn the gun in—especially since they intend to make use of it in their sinister line of work.

In fact, the Supreme Court has ruled in *Haynes vs. United States* that people illegally possessing firearms could not be compelled to turn them in, because that would violate their Fifth Amendment right against self-incrimination.

The only realistic expectation if handguns are confiscated is that there will rapidly develop a bigger black market and, after people are no longer allowed to protect themselves, an increase rather than a decrease in crime. In all likelihood, confiscation of guns would not only fail to bring about any reduction in the crime rate, but would be as impractical as trying to enforce prohibition.

A good example of what we could expect from nationwide gun control is Baltimore's Operation Pass. The little experiment was both costly and deadly. It was a bounty program in which the city paid $50 to everyone who turned in a gun and $100 for each tip leading to the confiscation of an illegal firearm.

The program ended at a cost of $675,000 to the city's taxpayers, and succeeded in collecting only 13,500 firearms. Despite this considerable expenditure, it was estimated that only ten percent of all firearms were turned in. Baltimore's own police commissioner was forced to admit that during the first 39 days of the program the number of gun-related murders rose more than 50 percent. From a rate of one murder every two days involving a gun, the city suffered three gun murders every four days.

The American people understand that the willful criminal is the real cause of most violent crime—not the gun. They also understand that the tide of crime—the terrible threat of violence to our people—will not end until the prevailing attitude of those who refuse to reckon with that simple fact is changed. We should all be very concerned about the criminal use of firearms and we need legislation that will deal harshly with it. Mandatory sentencing is a step in the right direction, because the answer to the criminal use of firearms is not in gun prohibition, but in changing the way in which we deal with the people who commit crime.

All of us would like to see crime reduced. But we need to be reasonable and practical when we assess the causes of

71

crime, not emotional. The fact of the matter is, guns do not usually kill people unless people pull the triggers; any more than the presence of alcohol makes people alcoholics unless people drink it; or the presence of drugs makes people commit suicide unless someone willfully takes an overdose. Ultimately, people, not society or some inanimate object, are responsible for what goes on in this world.

The Right To Bear Arms

The advocates of gun control are consistent to a point— they always do their best to discredit the Second Amendment. In fact, as of this moment, it is the position of some in the federal government that the Second Amendment does not protect the right of individual citizens to keep and bear firearms. This is certainly not the position of a majority of the American people.

According to a recent poll, 78%; of the American people believe that the U.S. Constitution gives them "the right to keep and bear arms", and 73%, reject the notion that this right pertains only to the National Guard.

An assistant U.S. attorney in Indiana ruled in 1973 that "the Second Amendment does not apply to private citizens as an individual right." The Second Amendment specifically says: "A well-regulated militia, being necessary to the security of a free state, the right of the people to keep and bear arms, shall not be infringed." The advocates of gun control claim that "militia" actually applies only to the National Guard. The claim is dubious if only because the Second Amendment existed before there was a National Guard.

Note carefully the language of the whole constitutional sentence. The first part supplies a reason, and the second part unequivocally guarantees a right to bear arms. The first part is a dependent clause, but the second is independent and stands alone as a complete thought: *the right of the people to keep and bear arms, shall not be infringed*. If the logic were reversed, and the dependent first clause had to do with bearing arms, the gun control advocates might have a case. In that instance, the Constitution would read, "The private ownership of firearms being necessary to the security of a free state, the right of people to form into a militia shall not be infringed." But the logic is clearly in the other direction: the Founders intended that citizens would have the right to bear arms, and cited the militia as the most important reason.

If it were otherwise, they would have reversed the two clauses.

The truth is that a basic right of the people to have arms for their own protection against harm from others and from abuse by their own government was a part of the English Common Law, which is the foundation of our law. Late Seventeenth Century writings clearly indicate the recognition of such a right in England.

The chief question on the Second Amendment debate is whether the right to keep and bear arms is individual, meaning that such a right applies to each person; or collective, that is to say, that such right applies only to a select group. The gun control advocates claim that the only group so authorized is the "militia" and that the individual has no such right. This is a tenuous point. Keep in mind that at the time of the Second Amendment's passage each colony had its own militia, which included *all* able-bodied men between certain ages, 16 and 60 or 18 and 45, depending on the place and the time. In fact, upon the demand of their colonial government they were required to appear for duty and bring their own weapons. Obviously, bearing arms was not simply a right, but a duty.

Senator Barry Goldwater of Arizona pointed out in the December 1975 issue of *Reader's Digest,* that "the Founding Fathers conceived of an armed citizenry as a necessary hedge against tyranny from within as well as from without, that they saw the right to keep and bear arms as basic and perpetual, the one thing that could spell the difference between freedom and servitude."

Gun control advocates also claim that the Second Amendment prohibits *only* the Congress from infringing on the people's right to keep and bear arms, and that it has no application to the state legislatures. If that is the case, it follows that they should abandon these Congressional attempts to impose gun control on the entire nation and instead leave the matter to the states. In recent years the Supreme Court has increasingly applied some of the prohibitions of the Bill of Rights to the states as well as to the Congress, which is why they want to override the Constitution altogether on the gun control issue.

Of course, it is conceivable that the Supreme Court could hold that the Second Amendment applies only to Congress and not to the state legislatures. Nonetheless, 37 states have constitutions providing the right of the people individually to keep and bear arms.

It should be obvious that those people and states who insisted upon a Bill of Rights—including the Second Amendment—as part of the Constitution really intended to preserve (indeed, took for granted) an individual citizen's right to possess arms for hunting, for his own defense, and for the defense of his community. Americans who ratified the Constitution and adopted the Bill of Rights did not establish a system of law which would eventually deprive them of their privately owned firearms! It is safe to say that, if the Constitution had restricted the use of firearms, the Constitution would never have been ratified.

The Second Amendment never implied federal jurisdiction over firearms. The Bill of Rights emphasized state control of individual freedoms in sensitive areas. The Bill of Rights excludes federal powers in these categories; it does not invite meddling. Why would there be an amendment giving the federal government power to regulate a militia when the same document (Article 1, Section 8) has already given the federal government authority to "raise and support armies"?

Therefore, by the very fact that the Constitution never granted the new federal government power to regulate ownership of unconcealed arms, and by the fact that the Bill of Rights reserves to the people and the states *all* powers not specifically granted to the central government, it is obvious that the constitutional case against federal anti-gun legislation is very strong.

Some Members of Congress have listened to the argument that we need gun control because of a rising crime rate, and their response has been reasonable. They understand fully the ineffectiveness of gun control as a deterrent for crime. These predominantly conservative Members have been searching for ways to get the criminals off the streets and make it safe, once again, for our citizens—old as well as young, infirm as well as healthy, poor as well as rich—to work and live in our society without the constant fear of being physically attacked and threatened.

Sure And Swift Punishment

Many Congressmen have introduced legislation aimed at providing mandatory sentences for criminals carrying firearms while committing a federal crime, such as H.R. 6056, authored by Congressman Robin Beard of Tennessee.

A similar approach, proposed by Congresswoman Holt of Maryland in H.R. 524, requires imprisonment for not less than five or more than ten years for using or carrying a firearm during the commission of a felony. For the second or subsequent conviction imprisonment would be for a minimum of ten years up to life imprisonment. This bill would also prohibit the court from suspending the sentence or giving a probationary sentence, nor could this term of imprisonment run concurrently with any term of imprisonment imposed for the commission of the crime itself (see proposal I in Table II). Both of these proposals are aimed directly at those individuals who misuse guns. These proposals do not attempt to register, license, or in any way ban guns for citizens who have no record of using their guns for unlawful purposes.

Instead of instituting gun control and thereby jeopardizing innocent citizens, we should be instituting sure and swift punishment for the most heinous of crimes. If potential criminals were assured that their deeds would result in swift, harsh, and irrevocable punishment, they would think twice before they trampled on someone else's rights. The eminent criminologist James Q. Wilson argues that sure swift punishment—rather than increasing severity—is the key to crime control. And that requires major court reform and revision of trial procedures so that the guilty do not escape conviction on technical grounds.

It is time to bring justice into our judicial process. Few people would argue with the view that justice is denied if an innocent person is convicted. Fortunately, that does not happen very often. But justice is also denied if a person who commits an offense is allowed to go free, and such cases routinely occur in every court in the country. In fact, in numerous instances known criminals have been set free simply because complicated rules of evidence have seriously marred the American criminal justice system.

The Supreme Court ruled in 1914 that illegally obtained evidence should be excluded from a federal criminal trial. Since that time, the Exclusionary Rule has been expanded, based on arguments by defense attorneys and philosophical opinions of judges. Now it includes any error in searches and seizures, confessions, lineups, and identifications. Congressman Steiger of Arizona has introduced a bill, H.R. 5628, which would provide a reasonable alternative to the existing rules of evidence in federal criminal proceedings. By reforming the inflexible Exclusionary Rule we can avoid many situations which free criminals on technical grounds and punish society and the victim by excluding the evidence of the crime. Steiger's bill would go a long way toward restoring public confidence in our courts—confidence that has eroded because arbitrary application of the Exclusionary Rule often allows an obviously guilty man to go free. The Exclusionary Rule has not fulfilled its extended purpose and the cost to society has been unwarranted. It will be interesting to see if any of the advocates of confiscatory gun control would be willing to support legislation aimed at criminals instead of law-abiding citizens.

The time has come for all Americans to stand up and let their government officials know how they feel about crime and how they feel about gun control! We know that our Founding Fathers meant for "the right to keep and bear arms" to be preserved and we know that it is still one of our inherent rights as American citizens today. We have also learned that when people in high places tell us that gun control is needed to control crime, we are listening to bureaucrats with an instinct for absolute power and a distrust of the American people. The only proper way to inaugurate gun control is to enact and ratify an amendment repealing the right to bear arms. But proponents of gun control, knowing the certain death of that amendment, are trying to impose their will on us through back-door tactics. They must be resisted by all citizens who treasure their rights and liberties.

BIOGRAPHY
of
The Honorable Sam Steiger
Arizona

Sam Steiger, born March 10, 1929, resides in Prescott, Arizona. He holds a bachelor of science degree in animal husbandry from Colorado A & M.

While serving as a tank platoon leader in Korea, as a first lieutenant in the U.S. Army, Representative Steiger received the Purple Heart and the Silver Star.

From 1960 to 1964, Representative Steiger served in the Arizona State Senate representing Yavapai County, and in 1965 spent several months in South Vietnam as a combat correspondent for the Phoenix Gazette and Prescott Courier newspapers. In 1966, he was elected to the 90th Congress and has been reelected to each subsequent Congress.

Congressman Steiger represents Arizona's Third Congressional District and is a member of the Interior and Insular Affairs Committee and the Government Operations Committee. He is the ranking Republican member of the Public Lands Subcommittee and the Government Information and Individual Rights Subcommittee.

Representative Steiger, a nationally-noted opponent of federal intervention in land use planning, is the recipient of "The Legislator of the Year" award presented at the 1975 Conservative Political Action Conference for his "significant contribution to the conservative cause in America . . . especially for his invaluable leadership in the defeat of the federal land use bill."

He is married to the former Lynda K. Spencer of Yuma and is the father of three children.

BUREAUCRACY: PATERNALISM ON
THE POTOMAC
by
Congressman Sam Steiger

There are very few absolute truths, so existing ones are well known. It may be presumptuous of me, therefore, to share with you the following as an absolute but it is.

When individuals are confronted with a problem they cannot solve, or when they seek to attain a goal that is beyond reach, and they allow government to assume the mission, two results occur: (1) the government structure formed to accomplish the task spends more time on justification of the structure than on the task: (2) the longer the structure exists, the less effort is spent on the mission and the more effort is expended in the care and feeding of the structure.

I call this Steiger's Law. It's true of entities other than government; government, however, is the most visible and viable sinner. The federal government is clearly the greatest, most unswerving devotee of these truths.

As we approach our Bicentennial, it must be recognized that the federal government, as designed by the framers of the Constitution, has developed into a complex of myriad and independent structures that by no stretch of the imagination resemble the Republic's original design.

The federal government, particularly in the past two decades, has managed to evolve into this series of structures not through any schemes or plans but as a reaction to another absolute truth. This truth states that where there is a vacuum of power, someone or something will always fill it.

I shall attempt to trace the causes of the present situation, which has led us to this total capture by our own structure.

From colonial times through the first third of this century the tasks of our government were limited, concerned only with the means of survival. As the nation grew, affluence and a growing sophistication developed. This sophistication saw merchandising of candidates, with aspirants for federal offices selling the notion of federal services in areas that previously had not been viewed as federal responsibility. The sheer volume of this largesse from Washington so engulfed us that we were unaware of the enormity and consequences of our willingness to be seduced.

We are now in the second generation of Americans who

see nothing incongruous about federal involvement in the qualitative judgments of individuals. Secure in their receipt of food, shelter and clothing they not only demand federal succor but choose to substitute federal judgement for their own. In the course of this evolution Congress ceased to function in even the limited capacity decreed by the Constitution and thus became the best example of Steiger's Law. That is, Congress is so totally involved in maintaining its own structure that it has abandoned its constitutional mission.

After many years of indifference and malfeasance, we are now beginning to hear this theme of too much bureaucracy from some strange quarters—liberal Democrats. For example, a famous Senator from a large eastern state recently declared, "There is a very serious kind of rethinking of the best way to meet the human needs of our society. Over the past few years, many have come to see that one of the greatest dangers of government is bureaucracy."

Was this Senator James Buckley, Conservative-Republican of New York? No. It was Senator Edward Kennedy, liberal Democrat of Massachusetts.

Another prominent Senator recently told his colleagues, "The liberals have to reevaluate their posture. Each program looks good, but you put 100 of them together and the results are more negative than positive. The federal bureaucracy is just an impossible monstrosity, you can't manage it, there's no way to do it."

Was this Senator Barry Goldwater of Arizona? No. It was Senator Gaylord Nelson, liberal Democrat of Wisconsin.

A New England governor has just announced, "The liberal Democrats are going to have to admit that they've made some huge mistakes creating this maze of federal programs that just breeds inefficiency and frustration. It's a disgrace. Some of the federal programs I've worked with as Mayor and Governor border on criminality. You put $1,000 in one end and the people don't get six cents out the other end."

Was this Republican Governor Meldrin Thompson of New Hampshire? No, it was Democratic Governor Philip Noel of Rhode Island.

In the last year, similar statements have been made by Senator Edmund Muskie, the Democrat's vice-presidential standard bearer in 1968; by newly-elected governors Jerry Brown of California, Michael Dukakis of Massachusetts, and Hugh Carey of New York; and by George McGovern's former campaign manager, Senator Gary Hart of Colorado, among many others.

The reason for this relatively new concern among leading "liberal" Democrats is the plain and simple fact that the bureaucracy has grown so large, so unwieldy, so inefficient, so wasteful, so counterproductive—in many cases, so disastrous—in recent years that even the most confirmed believer in the power of government to do good is downright alarmed.

In December 1975, *Newsweek*, which had previously not been known as a die-hard opponent of government economic planning and social programs, devoted a major cover story to the increasing problems caused by "Big Government." The cover was a cartoon of a bloated Uncle Sam.

As the authors of this article pointed out, "With a combined Federal, state and local workforce of 14.6 million people and a total expenditure of $523.2 billion, government on all levels now accounts for 37 percent of the Gross National Product ... as against 12 percent in 1929." The largest increase in the bureaucracy, they add, has been the "astronomical [growth of] Federally funded social programs and the state and local governments that must administer them."

My good friend and colleague, Congressman George Hansen of Idaho, recently told a state convention of the Idaho Farm Bureau:

> "Big Government" has become a gigantic rip-off—a rip-off of personal, local and states' rights and a rip-off of half a person's take-home pay, not to mention government-imposed compliance costs and fines passed on to the consumer. The federal government has taken away so much authority and responsibility from the private sector and from state and local government that it is smotheringly powerful and yet on the verge of bankruptcy. Federal laws and regulations have become a monstrous intrusion on personal rights and seriously threaten to destroy the family farm, close up the small businessman, and bankrupt the taxpayer and consumer. OSHA, EPA, and a whole bagful of regulatory agencies are saddling people with costs and abuse that is totally foreign to the American way.
>
> The current tax bill is 44 percent of the average person's income for all types of taxes, not to mention the $80 billion deficit in this year's federal spending which creates

81

an additional inflationary tax that everyone pays at the marketplace. Casper Weinberger, who recently stepped down as Secretary of Health, Education and Welfare said, "If these programs continue growing for the next two decades at the same pace they have in the last two, we will spend more than *half of our gross national product for domestic social programs alone by the year 2000.* In other words, when the century turns, half the American people will be working to support the other half."

The sprawl of the bureaucrats in the past 15 years is almost impossible to comprehend. In that time period 236 new federal bureaus, departments, or agencies have been organized while only 21 have been phased out of existence. There are no less than 1,250 federal advisory boards, committees, commissions and councils, most of which meet infrequently and do little work but serve as easy sources of patronage. They do, however, cost the taxpayer at least $75 million a year.

It is almost impossible to terminate any bureaucracy once it is set up. For instance, as UPI reporter Don Lambro points out in his valuable book, *The Federal Rathole*, we are still supporting two commissions set up to protect us against the WWII Nazis! Other commissions have such titles as "The Interdepartmental Screw Thread Committee" and the "Panel on Review of Sunburn Treatment."

It is inevitable in such a situation that a tremendous amount of wasteful and needlessly confusing duplication should exist. The advocates of the often-proposed new Agency for Consumer Protection (it could not be called the CPA because those initials are already taken!) had to be continually reminded that no less than 50 federal agencies and bureaus are already engaged in consumer protection.

Seven separate federal programs provide funds for out-patient health centers; 11 separate programs provide funding for child care; 14 independent units of the vast Department of Health, Education and Welfare administer as many separate programs for education of the handicapped. No less than 25 different services, bureaus, or offices of a dozen different departments finance research on water pollution.

At the same time that the Surgeon General's Office is requiring every cigarette packet to warn that they are "dangerous" to our health the Department of Agriculture finances a study of Oriental tobacco for "improving the quality of American cigarettes."

With all this confusion and duplication it is little wonder that more and more experts in the fields involved are concluding that the widespread federal social programs (which account for most of the increased bureaucracy) are simply not doing the job for which they were intended. That is, they are not really helping the needy in any effective way. What these programs do very well is provide highly-paid jobs for more and more bureaucrats and lackeys. When Daniel Moynihan, a liberal Democrat from New York who is now United Nations Ambassador, examined the poverty program he concluded that most of the money went for salaries of highly-paid professional social workers and administrators and that the poor saw relatively little of the huge sums spent. It is no accident that the two richest counties per capita in the United States are the Washington, D.C. "bedroom" counties of Montgomery, Maryland and Fairfax, Virginia which are heavily populated by high-salaried government officials.

Although the bureaucracy in large part can accomplish little good, it can and does effect much harm to many citizens. Thousands of small businesses, which provide jobs for hundreds of thousands of citizens, are being literally forced out of business by the growing costs of government paperwork. So bureaucracy provides jobs for bureaucrats but at the same time destroys countless jobs in the private sector.

For example, there is a single Labor Department form, called EBS-1. It requires a 31-page detailed report from all employers offering pension plans for their employees. To fill out the form correctly, the estimated cost is about $700 per employee. Now large business can absorb this cost by passing it on to the consumer—that's all of us—but many small businesses simply cannot afford to hire that many high-priced lawyers and accountants. So they choose not to make pension plans available to employees.

The total cost of paperwork generated by big government is estimated to go as high as $40 billion a year—about $800 a year for the average American family. If that amount were added to salaries, the families could doubtless spend that money in far more economically productive ways. Almost 5,-300 different forms are employed by the federal government today. *Ten billion sheets of paper* flow through federal offices annually. This quantity of forms would fill up 4 million cubic feet of space.

Congress cannot evade—indeed it must accept—much of the blame for this state of affairs. At least one hyperactive Representative has introduced an average of two bills a day during the 1975 session. As of July, 1975 more than 8,000 bills had already been introduced in the House for this 94th Congress. This does not count 502 resolutions, 476 joint resolutions, and 291 concurrent resolutions.

We find ourselves on a treadmill—as soon as anyone sees anything wrong anywhere, he wants to pass a law; very often a law is passed, followed by hundreds of regulations issued by the various concerned bureaucracies (many duplicating, some even contradictory). Then the new laws and regulations create new problems so a cry goes up for yet more laws! And so the process continues.

The *Federal Register* is a U.S. Government daily publication listing all the latest rules and regulations promulgated by the thousands of federal agencies in order to implement their interpretations of the laws of Congress.

During the 1960s the total *Registers* for one year came to about 15,000 pages. As late as 1970 an annual collection still came to only about 20,000 pages, in small type. Yet in four years time, this massive compilation had grown to more than 46,000 pages of rules and regulations, including more than 20,000 regulations of all conceivable shapes and sizes. In 1975, we may expect well over 50,000 pages, including more than 25,000 separate regulations.

As Congressman Edward Hutchinson of Michigan recently phrased it,

We are heading toward a society in which the individual is allowed increasingly less control over his or her daily life. Important decisions on how best to do business, how to grow crops, how to shop at the supermarket, how to travel, how to educate one's children, in short how to live, are being usurped by the government which sees no limits to its powers.

In the last year, a majority of Congress has unfortunately taken several more steps to strengthen this dangerous trend. The House approved, by a vote of 288-119 (see vote 12 in Table I) a bill to "de-Hatch" federal employees and allow them to engage in active partisan politics (a practice long barred by the Hatch Act). This bill (HR 8617) was opposed by me and many of my good friends and colleagues, but on this issue we did not prevail and the civil service will now become increasingly politicized and politicized, moreover, toward the left.

I also opposed HR 2559, passed by one vote (214-213; see vote 1 in Table I) on July 30, 1975. This bill (Executive Level Pay Raises) gave Members of Congress (as well as senior civil servants) automatic cost of living raises every October 1; besides obviously contributing to the inflationary spiral this bill insures that Congressmen will be exempt from the ravages of inflation and will be spared the responsibility of voting themselves future salary adjustments. As Rep. E.G. Shuster, Republican of Pennsylvania, put it, "The American people would be better off if Congress got a pay decrease when the cost of living went up and a pay increase when the cost of living went down."

By including itself in a growing bureaucracy, now automatically costing us more every year, Congress has done itself and the people a great disservice. One of the few checks on the expanding bureaucracy has thus been weakened.

What can be done to reverse this growing trend so dangerous to both American economic life and liberty itself? My colleagues and I have been working hard to implement a number of reforms that will limit the bureaucracy and make it more responsive to citizens and their elected representatives.

• Every law creating a new agency or a program ought to have a termination date expressly written in—three or five years—so that Congress can then reevaluate that program and decide on the basis of experience whether it should be terminated, drastically reformed, reduced, or continued, if it *is* doing a good job.

• A system of "zero based" budgeting should be adopted so that agencies will be required to justify every cent of every request they make when they appear before Congress.

• My colleague Congressman Del Clawson of California has introduced a bill (HR 8231; which to date has over 90 co-sponsors, including myself) which would provide for a Congressional veto over executive branch rule making. (See proposal G in Table II.) This bill would go a long way toward bringing the bureaucracy once again under the control of the people and would end the dangerous practice of an unelected civil servant making laws that affect millions of people.

These are just some of the much needed steps which we can take to bring this monster under democratic control. We have a difficult task before us—to reduce a trend of 40 years—but with the will, we can do it. We will have to do it, if democratic government is to survive.

The siren call, "Let the Feds do it for you," absolutely must be resisted and rejected.

BIOGRAPHY
of
The Honorable Edward J. Derwinski
Illinois

Edward J. Derwinski has represented the Fourth District of Illinois in the U.S. Congress since his election to the 86th Congress in 1958.

A native of his State, Mr. Derwinski was born in Chicago on September 15, 1926. He attended Mt. Carmel High School and graduated with a Bachelor's Degree in history from Loyola University.

Prior to his entry into national politics, Mr. Derwinski served as a State representative and as a member of the Illinois-Indiana Bi-State Port Commission.

Congressman Derwinski has been a member of the House Committee on International Relations since 1963 and serves on the Subcommittees on International Organizations and Oversight. He is the Ranking Minority Member of the House Post Office and Civil Service Committee, on which he has served since 1961.

As an acknowledged expert in Congress on international organizations, Mr. Derwinski has represented the United States in many international conferences. He was Congressional delegate to the United Nations in 1971 and to the Mexico-U.S. and other international parliamentary conferences.

Ed Derwinski was selected by the Chicago Junior Association of Commerce and Industry as one of the "Ten Outstanding Young Men" in the Chicago Metropolitan Area in 1959 and again in 1961. He is a member of the American Legion, Amvets, Catholic War Veterans, Kiwanis, Knights of Columbus, Moose, Polish National Alliance, and Veterans of Foreign Wars.

Congressman and Mrs. Derwinski (the former Patricia Van Der Giessen) have two children, Maureen Sue, 15, and Michael, 9.

POLITICS AND THE CIVIL SERVICE:
A NEW SPOILS SYSTEM
by
Congressman Edward J. Derwinski

It is comparatively easy to hypothesize a variety of altruistic motives for protecting the rights of our Federal employees. Following that scenario, the Democratic majority has conjured up visions of Federal employees toiling as "second-class citizens." While the legislative response has been a political hodgepodge, there has been no deviation from the real objective: emasculation of the system which does, indeed, protect Federal employees from coercive political pressure.

At a time when public polls reflect the fact that many Americans hold their government in low esteem, it is reckless to consider legislation which will further erode public confidence. The public has a right to expect impartial service from its Federal employees. That is what the Federal merit system is all about. That is why it was established in 1887, when it was recognized and accepted that political pressures did compromise the effectiveness of the Federal Government and the faith of the people in their government.

In 1939, Congress passed the Hatch Act to provide additional insulation against political pressure. The 1939 legislation was entitled "An Act to Prevent Pernicious Political Activity." I think, on the basis of 37 years of experience, it has been demonstrated that the best way to prevent improper political activity on the part of Government employees is to give them the positive assurance contained in the 1939 Act. The 1939 law makes it clear that a Federal employee is to be rated on the quality of service he or she renders the government. Tenure is not dependent upon skill in pursuing votes, contributing or soliciting funds or openly supporting a political candidate or party.

The Hatch Act has for 37 years protected Federal employees from pressure and coercion, that they otherwise might be subject to, to engage in political activities.

In my judgment, civilian Federal employees, career employees who do not owe their appointments to any political party, do not need to curry the favor of any political party to receive a promotion or assignment. They need the protection of the present law.

One point that was raised in debate in the House and which

deserves attention is that the Hatch Act somehow deprives individuals of their constitutional rights. This charge falls from lack of evidence. The Hatch Act has not been vigorously challenged in the courts and one Supreme Court ruling on the subject upholds the Hatch Act.

In United States Civil Service Commission v. National Association of Letter Carriers, the Supreme Court recently sustained the constitutionality of that provision in title 5, United States Code, which prohibits Federal employees from taking an active part in political management or in political campaigns, the very provision H.R. 8617 wishes to repeal. (See vote 12, Table I)

The court held, in sum, that Congress has the authority to regulate various political activities of Federal employees and that such regulation is not barred by the First Amendment or any other provision of the Constitution. In overruling constitutional objections, the Court said:

"It seems fundamental in the first place that employees in the Executive Branch of the Government, or those working for any of its agencies, should administer the law in accordance with the will of Congress, rather than in accordance with their own or the will of a political party. They are expected to enforce the law and execute the programs of the Government without bias or favoritism for or against any political party or group or the members thereof. A major thesis of the Hatch Act is that to serve this great end of Government—the impartial execution of the laws—it is essential that Federal employees not, for example, take formal positions in political parties, not undertake to play substantial roles in partisan political campaigns and not run for office on partisan political tickets. Forbidding activities like these will reduce the hazards to fair and effective government. . . .

"There is another consideration in this judgment: it is not only important that the Government and its employees in fact avoid practicing political justice, but it is also critical that they appear to the public to be avoiding it, if confidence in the esteem of representative Government is not to be eroded to a disastrous extent."

The impetus for this repeal has come not from the general public, but from leaders of Federal employee unions affiliated with the AFL-CIO. It has not come from the rank and file Civil Service employees. The reason is simple. Enactment would substantially increase the influence of Federal and Postal bosses over the Congress.

Dr. Nathan Wolkomir, the President of the National Federation of Federal Employees, charged that organized labor's interest in the bill "is nothing more than the old AFL-CIO pitch for muscle and power. It's a move for money and organizing influence." I agree.

Hearings produced no evidence that any but a small minority of Federal employees at any level of Government favor the repeal or emasculation of protections they enjoy under the "Hatch Act". This obviously shows that these employees are displaying better judgment than their so-called leaders, and we in the Congress should be listening to the employees rather than self-appointed bosses.

The observation has been made by some that the Federal workforce is somehow different in character and sophistication today than it was in 1939 when the Hatch Act was enacted. Even if this were so, it is no valid reason to tear down the protections that have helped insure an impartial government civil service for the past 36 years.

Actually, the potential for abuse of the system today is far greater than it was in 1939. For example, it is estimated that in 1939, there were 920,000 Federal employees as opposed to 2.8 million today; the total budget in 1940 was $9.5 billion as opposed to $324 billion in 1975; public assistance—welfare and government payment to individuals totaled $1.5 billion in 1940 while in 1975 the estimate is close to $147 billion; the average salary of a Federal civilian employee in 1939 was $1,871 as opposed to $14,480 today; and in 1939 there were 777,300 Federal civilian employees outside of Washington, D. C., whereas today we have 2,367,983 Federal civilian employees assigned through the country out of Washington, D.C.

We would be ill-advised to turn our backs on the political history which preceded the Hatch Act. To repeal it is to be blind to history.

Finally, one should take a brief glimpse at the effects of union control on foreign nations. Italy, Great Britain, and Argentina have allowed the unions to effectively destroy the economies of each of their respective countries. Great Britain was brought to its knees in recent labor negotiations with employees in the nationalized coal industry. It should be remembered that these employees are public employees.

In Italy, there was a crippling postal strike which resulted in the destruction of tons of mail. In Argentina, there still is a power vacuum because of union pressures to which the government acceded to head off another revolution.

The United States has been spared this union abuse of power by insulating its Federal employees against political blackmail by the unions.

The reckless Democrat majority, in its actions affecting Federal personnel, has disregarded the taxpayer completely. Their obvious interest is to expand political power. This is against the best interests of Federal employees, against your best interests as a taxpayer, and it is against the very concept of our American political system.

SOCIAL SERVICES

BIOGRAPHY
of
The Honorable Philip M. Crane
Illinois

Philip M. Crane of the 12th District of Illinois first entered Congress in a special election for the vacated seat of Donald Rumsfeld on November 25, 1969.

Born in Chicago on November 3, 1930, Mr. Crane attended Chicago public schools and received his BA in history from Hillsdale College. He then studied at the University of Vienna and the University of Michigan and received an M.A. and a PhD from the University of Indiana.

Congressman Crane served in Europe with the U.S. Army (1954-1956) before beginning his teaching career. After three years at Indiana University, he joined the faculty at Bradley University in Peoria where he was Professor of History from 1963 to 1967. Before his election to Congress, Mr. Crane was director of schools at Westminster Academy in Northbrook, Illinois.

Active in party politics, Philip Crane served as Illinois Research Director for the 1964 Goldwater candidacy. He is also the author of *The Democrats' Dilemma*, a book published in 1964, and *The Sum of Good Government*, published in 1976.

A founding member of the Republican Study Committee, Rep. Crane is also a member of the advisory board of the Young Americans for Freedom, and a director of the Intercollegiate Studies Institute and the American Conservative Union.

The son of a physician, Philip Crane takes an intense interest in health care issues and is a member of the subcommittees on Health and Social Security of the House Ways and Means Committee. He also serves on the Republican Policy Committee Health Task Force.

Congressman Crane and the former Arlene Catherine Johnson, married on February 14, 1959, have eight children.

LET'S NOT WRECK AMERICAN MEDICINE
by
Congressman Philip M. Crane

Advocates of a nationalized medical system, despite differences in their specific proposals, have one thing in common. They have all tried to prove that the existing system of private practice is faltering.

Those who tell us that there is now a crisis in American health care believe that if they say it often enough it will become true. The facts, however, tell a far different story.

Under our current medical system, the health of the American people has been steadily, often dramatically, improving. In 1900 the life expectancy of the average American at birth was 49.2 years; today life expectancy is more than 70 years. One-fourth of the babies born in 1850 died before the age of five; one-fourth of the babies born as late as 1900 died before the age of 25; three-fourths of the babies born today can expect to live to at least age 62. Of every 1,000 infants born alive in 1900, approximately 125 would not survive one year. Today, the annual infant mortality rate is 18.5 per thousand—an improvement of more than 350 percent. Moreover, this rate is superior to that of the Common Market countries where the ratio is over 20 per thousand.

Tuberculosis and polio have been practically wiped out. Open-heart surgery is almost commonplace. The death rate from cancer of the uterus has been reduced by half in the last thirty years. Medicine has been progressing steadily, sometimes spectacularly. Men and women throughout the world—many in countries with long-standing socialized medical systems—look to our private researchers and doctors to find a cure for cancer as they found a cure for polio and other fatal diseases. This is a sign of success, something which those who would scuttle private practice totally fail to recognize or acknowledge.

An example of the tendency to ignore the success of non-governmental health care is a recent attempt to manipulate the number and type of first-year residencies available to medical students in the United States. This effort was based on the assumption that residencies in the primary care specialties were diminishing and must be encouraged by government. The legislation involved certain provisions of the Health Manpower Act, also known as H.R. 5546. Fortunately Congressman James T. Broyhill (Republican, N. Carolina) pointed out the fallacy of the assumption and was able to get the offending provisions deleted from the Act in a vote of 207-146 (see vote 13 in Table I). Congressman Broyhill stated in his arguments:

—In the last five years the number of first-year residencies in these primary care fields has increased from one percent to 10 percent of the total. There is every reason to believe that this increase will continue at this rate and it is estimated by 1980, 50 percent of the first-year residents will be in this primary care field.

So I see no reason to set up this bureaucracy to make these decisions. I see no reason to arbitrarily stop the trend that is already going on.

I would urge that Members support my amendment to strike this unwise section of the bill.

Those who advance the idea of crisis in American health care argue that government intervention is necessary because we have a shortage of doctors. Somehow, they say, government control of medicine will ease this shortage. Unfortunately, most of the participants in the debate accept as a given the notion that a doctor shortage exists—and then argue only about the best way to deal with it. Their conclusion, however, is based on a false assessment of the situation.

Since 1965 the number of doctors has increased by more than 50,000, or approximately 17 percent. This rise has been roughly three times as great as the growth of population, and projections for the next decade indicate the same ratio of production of physicians over population growth. Yet much of the discussion about the alleged shortage of doctors has proceeded as if there had been no change in the situation.

It is also forgotten that the equivalent ratio of doctors to patients in a country such as Great Britain, which has had nationalized medicine for a generation, is one doctor for every 750 patients. That ratio is threatened by the large emigration of doctors from England, primarily because of serious political interference with the private practice of medicine. The same is true with regard to Sweden, and the doctor-patient ratio in the Soviet Union is far worse than in the United States.

The arguments presented by those who charge that a medical crisis exists—a crisis for which their own proposals are the proper remedy—usually conclude by citing high medical costs. With regard to this question, Marvin Edwards notes that:

> ... the plainest of all the misrepresentations advanced by foes of private medicine is the argument that something inherent in free enterprise keeps driving medical costs continually higher. The rise in costs is directly traceable, not to free enterprise, but to the interventions of government. The most obvious culprit is government-spawned inflation.

Consider some of the real data with regard to the relative increase in medical costs and the relative increases in other areas of the American economy.

The average price of a semiprivate hospital room has gone up dramatically. The reasons, however, are diverse. One is government-created inflation, which increases the cost of everything the hospital itself must purchase. Another reason is the fact that hospital workers have now become unionized and are demanding wage increases. In addition, construction workers are among the most highly paid in the nation. Further, the sophisticated new life-saving equipment used in modern hospitals is expensive even in noninflationary periods and it requires more staff to operate. Nurses are demanding better pay and better working conditions, and the burden and cost to hospitals has increased notably because of governmental programs such as Medicare and Medicaid. All of these factors—not the health-care delivery system itself—have driven medical costs ever higher.

The High Cost of Socialized Medicine

Would the socialization of American medicine, or one of the lesser steps in that direction, in any way lower the *real* cost of health care in the United States? The advocates of such programs imply that it would, although their real meaning seems to be that since individuals will pay for medical care *indirectly through taxes* rather than *directly* to the doctors and hospitals involved, it will *seem* like less. The result would, of course, be politically advantageous.

For an indication of foreseeable costs, using the figures produced by the Committee for National Health Insurance (the group responsible for drafting the legislation now being advanced by Senator Edward M. Kennedy), the plan's sponsors figure that for fiscal 1969 the federal government spent over $9 billion for all personal health programs. If their program had been in effect then, they say, it would have disbursed most of that amount and would have required an additional $6 billion from the general tax revenues.

But the costs of all government programs tend to rise significantly above initial estimates. Thus, an article in *The New Republic* by Washington health writer Mel Schechter states that Medicare alone, without any changes, needs more payroll taxes to meet a 25-year projected deficit of $236 billion in hospital-related benefits. This is a shocking overrun of nearly 100 percent.

Involving the federal government in direct control of medical care in our own country would, according to Ralph R. Rooke of the National Association of Retail Druggists, "produce an administrative nightmare, with federal officials ... working out contracts with 6,000 hospitals, 25,000 nursing homes, 700 visiting nurse groups, and, later, with 208,000 doctors and 55,000 retail pharmacists." The paperwork involved in processing the millions of resulting claims "staggers the imagination. An extremely large force of government workers would undoubtedly be required to do the job."

How Socialized Medicine Has Failed Abroad

In the end, would American health services be better served through government than under our current system? A report on the National Health Service (NHS) by Professor John Jewkes, who served on Britain's Royal Commission on Remuneration of Doctors and Dentists, concluded that "the average American now has more medical services than the average Briton and the gap between the two has been widening" since the inception of the National Health Service.

More and more Britons, according to the evidence presented by Jewkes, are seeking medical care outside of the National Health Service. These people are "ready to make sacrifices in other directions in order to enjoy prompt hospital and specialist treatment, free choice of consultant and private accommodation." To make things even more difficult, there is a massive exodus of doctors from Great Britain—their reaction against the regimentation of the National Health Service.

It seems clear that medical care would be far more costly under a nationalized system than it is today. If the experience in England, France, and Sweden is indicative, people would tend to overcrowd existing facilities. Writing in *Private Practice*, Dr. Klaus Rentzsch of Hamburg, West Germany, notes that while U.S. patients stay in the hospital about six to eight days on the average, "in Germany we have a twenty-four-day average hospital stay. The situation is comparable in every country with a total medical-care program such as ours."

In its issue of August 15, 1973, the West German newspaper *Bremer Nachrichten* discusses the long waiting lists for surgery in the semi-socialist medical system of that country. The paper notes: "Patients needing complex surgery are often forced to wait a matter of months or years. Many large hospitals have drawn up waiting lists. Heart operations involving the use of heart and lung machines, kidney transplants, tonsillectomies and fitting of false joints are often subject to long delays." Waiting lists of up to six months are looked at as "almost-normal" at large hospitals in Baden-Wurttemberg, the paper reported. In Hamburg, for example, there is a waiting list of about 1,000 for operations involving use of the city's only heart and lung machine. One hospital in Stuttgart has a two-and-a-half year waiting list for patients requiring an artificial limb and in Dortmund the delay can be as long as three years.

The unfortunate fact is that, although advocates of government involvement in medicine tell us that it will decrease costs and improve quality, the evidence of our own Medicare and Medicaid programs shows precisely the opposite—that it will increase costs and decrease quality, not unlike our experience with a government-run postal system.

Great Britain has adopted a system of socialized medicine. It can serve as an example of the deterioration of medical care and increase in medical costs that would befall the United States were such a program to be adopted. In December 1950, less than three years after Britain's National Health Service went into effect, the Ministry of Health announced that 533,557 people were on the waiting list for hospital beds—100,000 of them in London. Shortly after NHS went into effect a group of health administrators informed the London Institute of Public Administration: "The public is adopting the attitude that because of the Welfare State they have no responsibility for their aged parents." As a result many of the aged who were mentally deficient or helpless were left without care and had to shift for themselves, since there was no room in the overcrowded hospitals.

Harold Gurden, a member of Parliament from Birmingham, has called for a public investigation into waiting lists for children to have ear operations. In 1969, Gurden said, fifty Birmingham children were going permanently deaf each year because they were unable to receive hospital treatment in time. The situation has not improved.

Medicaid In America

Let us look briefly at a Medicaid report to determine whether this program has been successful.

In New York "Fifty percent of the money spent on Medicaid went down the drain," according to an unnamed high-ranking Medicaid official quoted in the report. "Testimony disclosed the incredibly chaotic manner in which records were kept and Medicaid documents were processed for payment," the report said, asserting that dozens of examples of "widespread and flagrant abuses" had been discovered and charged that physicians had billed the city for services and performed inadequate work.

The jury said it had found patients' names forged by dentists on forms used to collect money from the city. Other patients were told to sign blank forms and physicians billed the city for work never performed. It also listed cases of Medicaid recipients passing their identification cards to relatives or friends otherwise ineligible to receive free medical care.

New York City *Daily News* reporter William Sherman wrote a series of articles concerning Medicaid abuses that was placed in The *Congressional Record* on February 21, 1973. Here are some highlights of the *News'* Medicaid probe:

Ping-ponging of patients from doctor to doctor in several privately-owned group medical centers where the poor are rammed through an often needless, but costly, labyrinth of X-ray exams, lab tests and dental care.

Cases in which doctors insisted that the patient fill prescriptions at a specific pharmacy even though Medicaid regulations demand that all patients be given a completely free choice of pharmacies.

A voluntary hospital that was paid $457,000 for care that city health officials later discovered centered on the use of drugs that were never approved by the federal government for human experimentation, much less for actual clinical treatment.

A deal in which optometrists and an optical company

collaborated in charging Medicaid about $800,000 for eye examinations and eyeglasses even though most of the glasses were declared to be unsatisfactory by the Department of Health.

Psychiatrists who bill the city for more hours than there are in a day—one for as much as 35 hours of consultation in a single day.

The unfortunate fact is that volumes could be written about Medicaid abuses in New York City alone. New York, it must be remembered, is not atypical. Similar stories have been told about Medicaid practices in almost every state and city in the United States.

In any consideration of the operation of the Medicaid program, it is incorrect to think that doctors and other providers of health care are the only ones, or even the primary ones, who take advantage of the system. Patients often view the Medicaid program much as they view the totality of the nation's welfare programs to which it is tied—as a means of obtaining the taxpayers' money for their own advantage.

The Medicare Experiment

Medicare has not only been a failure; it has been a costly failure. The entire Medicare experience has been one of constant actuarial error. According to Robert J. Myers, for 23 years the chief actuary of the Social Security Administration and now a professor of actuarial science at Temple University, disbursements for hospital insurance benefit payments and administrative expenses for the first three years of the program were $11.2 billion higher than the original estimates—an overrun of more than 41 percent.

Within five years after its adoption the nation's Medicare law was an acknowledged failure. Costs continued to soar as Congress hiked the price the aged had to pay to use the program. Administrative expenses—the cost of maintaining the massive health bureaucracy created by the program—totaled nearly half a billion dollars and had more than doubled in the first five years to almost $150 million.

If anything is clear about the American experience with the Medicare program it is the fact that costs have skyrocketed, and that the original estimates provided by "experts" concerning the projected cost of both Medicare and Medicaid have had absolutely no relationship to the real costs that have been encountered.

101

The Threat to Freedom

In addition to the fact that a socialized medical system is always more expensive and less efficient than private enterprise in medicine, implicit in such a system is a real threat to the freedom of doctors, patients, and druggists. Even without national health insurance we have witnessed serious infringements upon the traditional doctor-patient relationship. One of these infringements is found in the program of Professional Standards Review Organizations (PSRO).

This law requires that medical care be "standardized" for Medicare and Medicaid patients. Their doctors are forced to comply with a system of pre-set standards of medical diagnosis, treatment, and care in accordance with rules set by the Department of Health, Education and Welfare. In addition, the PSRO program eliminates the confidentiality that has always been inherent in the relationship of a doctor with patients.

Dr. Donald Quinlan, former president of the American Association of Physicians and Surgeons, says of this law,

A physician can be forced to turn over to federal employees all medical notes taken in his office or in a hospital, including the most confidential information about his patients. Likewise, it is planned to have massive detailed, computerized files on patients and doctors which will be instantly available to federal employees as an aid to the surveillance program and for such other purposes as the Secretary of HEW may provide.

Even patients who do not receive federal aid in any form will be subject to having their confidential records examined by government agents in an effort to establish "norms" of medical care. The PSRO examiner is able to search through a doctor's files and records without any court order or search warrant.

The Road to Euthanasia

The PSRO program may be only the beginning of government control of medical care. Far more serious dangers lie ahead. Consider what is being discussed in England, a country that has gone farther down this mistaken road than we.

In a June 1968 symposium on euthanasia, Dr. Eliot Slater, editor of *The British Journal of Psychiatry,* stated that even if the elderly did retain their vigor, they suffer from the defect of an innate conservatism. "Just as in the mechanical world, advances occur most rapidly where new models are being constantly produced, with consequent rapid obsolescence of the old, so too it is in the world of nature." (*The London Times*, July 5, 1968).

British Professor Glanville Williams recently presented the argument for euthanasia in front of millions on television, stating:

> At present the problem has certainly not reached the degree of seriousness that would warrant an effort being made to change the traditional attitudes towards the sanctity of life of the aged. Only the grimmest necessity could bring about a change [that] would probably cause apprehension and deep distress to many people and inflict traumatic injury upon the accepted code of behavior built up by 2,000 years of Christian religion. It may be, however, that as the problem becomes more acute it will itself cause a reversal of generally accepted values.

Lord Longford, who, as leader of the House of Lords, left the Front Bench to speak against an abortion bill, said he was shocked by the bill but far more so by what he thought lay behind it. To Professor Williams' statement, Lord Longford said, "So the execution time of the old people may not be so very far off."

The prediction was not inaccurate. In March, 1969, a voluntary euthanasia bill was introduced in the House of Lords. *The London Times* for March 24, 1969, opposed it on several grounds, including what it called "the slippery slope". "The progress of the law of abortion (where the legal grounds for destroying the fetus have expanded from the life of the mother, to the health of the mother, to the welfare of the children already born) confirms the suspicion that euthanasia once legally admitted would be similarly expanded."

Every area government enters involves serious limitation of individual freedom. Discussing in *Private Practice* the socialized medical system in West Germany, Dr. Klaus Rentzsch, who practices in Hamburg, notes:

> the more social security is guaranteed by the government, the greater becomes the control over social behav-

ior. One danger of a social security system guaranteed by the state is that personal freedom may be limited because the institution that has to pay for risks of health may demand that members avoid circumstances which may be a risk of health. . . . A system that gives free medical care and payment for income loss will, of course, try to keep things under control. But control in medicine is a bad thing. Such controls limit the doctor's freedom, his therapy, and even regulate how long a patient stays away from work. All systems of national health insurance believe in this control.

There is every reason for Americans to reject the idea of national health insurance. If we carefully consider the strengths of our private practice system and the availability of private health insurance tailored to each person's needs and resources, and compare it to the weaknesses of the socialized medical systems of other countries, and then review the failure of our own government programs such as Medicare and Medicaid, that conclusion becomes inevitable. Let us not in the name of "better health care" set in motion a series of events that will damage health care, impose heavy new taxes, and demolish more individual liberty.

BIOGRAPHY
of
The Honorable Clair W. Burgener
California

The election of Clair W. Burgener in the 93rd Congress in 1972 from the 42nd (now 43rd) District of California capped a distinguished career in community and state service.

Rep. Burgener was born on December 5, 1921, in Vernal, Utah. In 1941 he married Marvia Hobusch. They have three sons. Burgener obtained a B.A. in Liberal Arts from California State University at San Diego in 1950.

Cong. Burgener is currently serving in his sixteenth year of elected office. He had served in State government in both administrative and legislative capacities before coming to Congress.

The deep interest he has shown in his community is most clearly seen in his involvement in the training and education of the mentally retarded and the handicapped. He is a lifetime member of the San Diego County Association for Retarded Children, and has been honored many times for his work with the retarded, the neglected, the dependent, and the handicapped. He was Vice-Chairman of the President's Committee on Mental Rehabilitation, and was a member of the National Advisory Committee on Handicapped Children.

Clair Burgener has acted on his convictions by authoring legislation mandating special classes for trainable mentally retarded children in public schools, and by authoring the California welfare reform legislation of 1971.

A leader in legislating meaningful welfare reform in the California State Senate, Congressman Burgener is now a principal advocate of welfare reform in the U. S. Congress.

TAMING THE WELFARE PROBLEM
by
Congressman Clair W. Burgener

Few subjects cause such consternation to the taxpayer as the growth in our nation's welfare programs over the last 40 years. Indignant citizens read about the burgeoning expense and abuses, but conclude gloomily that little can be done.

Such despair is misplaced. With careful and analytical attention to the causes of spiraling expenditures and growing caseloads, and with the application of solutions that have proven successful elsewhere, welfare *can* be brought under control. Indeed, the pattern of increasing dependency and reliance on the welfare dole can be reversed. In the following pages we will outline the nature of the problem and will offer ways to reduce expenses while helping the genuinely needy.

In order to understand what needs to be done it is essential to understand where we are, where we have been, and how we got where we are in our journey toward welfarism in the United States. Knowledge of these kinds of program characteristics and a brief bit of history are crucial toward understanding how we can begin to reverse the welfare tide.

Evolution of a program. When the term welfare is used in this country it usually includes the categorical aids: Aid to Families with Dependent Children, Supplemental Security Income (formerly Old Age Security, Aid to the Blind, and Aid to the Disabled), food stamps (see next chapter), general relief or county assistance, and Medicaid. If we were to look at all of the income transfer programs in this country, however, we would discover a host of separate programs that provide cash or in-kind assistance to persons in need: free school lunches, free school breakfasts, special summer feeding programs, special supplemental feeding programs for pregnant or nursing women, free noon meals for the elderly, housing subsidies in a number of forms, fuel and transportation coupons in some areas, free social services, child care, mental hygiene services, numerous forms of free or reduced-cost medical care in addition to Medicaid—the list is almost endless.

This discussion will focus upon only one program: Aid to Families with Dependent Children (AFDC). Until recently, when its growth was surpassed by the food stamp program and certain quality control actions began to improve its administration, AFDC was spiraling out of control. It still remains in serious need of reform, as the following statistics will show.

The growth of AFDC. Since its inception in 1936, the AFDC program has grown at an incredible rate. Caseloads increased over twentyfold from December 1936 to December 1974. The ratio of children covered by AFDC to the nation's population of persons under eighteen years of age also grew substantially, from one in fifty to one in eight. Nationwide, just since 1960, the proportion has more than trebled. By February 1974 the ratio in a number of the country's large urban centers was even more alarming: Chicago and Detroit, one in five; New York and Newark, one in four; and St. Louis, Baltimore, Boston and Washington, one in three. It took 15 years, from 1940 to 1955, for the AFDC rolls to double. Ten years later the 1955 figure had doubled again and by 1970 those rolls had doubled once more.

Causes of program growth. A number of social factors have contributed to the startling caseload growth: the increasing difficulty of matching unskilled or low-skilled persons with available jobs, the high incidence of family desertion, the growth in illegitimacy, and the elimination of jobs caused by federal wage controls. On the other hand, however, a large portion of the explanation lies in the way the programs have been deliberately structured, the loopholes that exist, the way in which they are administered, and a sloppy lack of concern for those who truly need public assistance. Some of these failings can be remedied through aggressive and constructive action: those, for example, relating to desertion and child support.

How AFDC has evolved. Throughout the 1940s and 1950s AFDC was limited to the single-parent household, which received aid only when the family breadwinner was absent through death, desertion, or incarceration or was unable to provide for his family because he was ill or handicapped. In 1961 a significant liberalization permitted both parents to be present in the home; the family was eligible if the breadwinner worked less than 30 hours a week. This provision was optional, and about half the states have adopted it. In 1967 further liberalizations enabled persons to deduct certain amounts of outside earnings. In theory the deductions were to serve as a work incentive; in practice they have had the effect of keeping people on aid even while their own earning power reached significant levels.

Throughout this period both the Congress and the states, which share the AFDC burden in some ratio of federal and nonfederal funds, adopted program modifications that usually served further to liberalize the program. Special exceptions, deductions, exemptions, grant modifications, eligibility enlargements, and computational changes all have been piled atop the structure to permit more and more persons to qualify or to maximize their grants.

Significantly this has occurred within a system of very complex regulations in which apparently slight changes turn out to be very expensive. (A one dollar change in the AFDC program costs approximately $132 million nationally.) The system enables administrators to interpret the law and regulations so that benefits are maximized.

The California Experience

During my ten years in the California Assembly and State Senate I became increasingly concerned that welfare caseloads were rising without any relationship to what was happening in the economy. AFDC caseloads, for example, rose sharply throughout many of the prosperous years of the 1960s. More important, we were unable to take adequate care of those who were in legitimate need. In the 1960s, AFDC caseloads were escalating at the rate of 40,000 a month. There had been no direct increase in grants since 1958, although administrators had liberalized some provisions. By the time 1970 rolled around, California was facing insolvency if welfare caseloads were permitted to grow as they had been growing. A tax increase in 1971 was inevitable unless something was done. Neither financial juggling nor a previous tax hike had been able to keep pace with the voracious AFDC budget demands.

Governor Reagan, aware that this was one of the most crucial problems facing the state, took decisive steps. He appointed a task force of seasoned public administrators, management analysts, and attorneys to review the welfare program in California. That task force went through the federal Social Security Act, the state Welfare and Institutions Code, the HEW regulations, and the state regulations. It emerged with over a hundred separate legislative and administrative recommendations. The head of the task force was appointed Director of Social Welfare in January of 1971 and immediately began implementing the administrative portion of the changes. Concurrently, a series of bills were prepared which I introduced in the California State Senate as the Governor's Welfare Reform Act, which was enacted into law with bipartisan support.

In March of 1971, shortly after the administrative changes started, the graphs depicting California's AFDC caseload took a dramatic *downturn*. Instead of burgeoning at the rate of 40,000 a month, they started to sink at the rate of approximately 8,000 a month. They continued downward with minor fluctuations throughout the succeeding period—even through the recent recessionary and inflationary period. Caseloads elsewhere in the country showed continuing increases. Clearly something was working in California.

It has been estimated that, as a result of welfare reform in California, taxpayers in my state saved approximately $1.5 billion in the last four years—money they would otherwise have spent had welfare gone unreformed. Forty-two of the 58 counties were able to *cut* property taxes, largely because of welfare reform. But even more significant we were able to increase grants to the truly needy by almost 27 percent the first time around, in 1971. We included an annual cost-of-living increase. We have assured legitimate recipients of an increase of almost 50 percent above 1971 levels as a result of welfare reform.

This is what welfare reform is all about. The dramatic successes in California, it should be noted, occurred as a result of only those changes that were made in *state* legislation and regulations. Can the same thing be done in Washington? It can.

The Solution

Shortly after the start of the 94th Congress I joined with almost a hundred members of the House and Senate in introducing the National Welfare Reform Act, which contains 25 separate provisions that would reform the nation's AFDC program. (See proposal J in Table II.) It has been estimated that passage of this legislation alone would save from $1.7 billion to $2.2 billion annually—without accompanying administrative action that could also be taken at the federal level. Just as the California experience included an effort in both spheres, both should be undertaken in Washington.

This bill, the result of research efforts that have identified numerous possible improvements, would enable the California experience to repeat itself nationally: Persons who *should* be ineligible would become so, and the savings would cut costs and permit increased benefits for the truly needy.

110

The abuses we are trying to correct fall into five main categories: recipients with income, improper beneficiaries, utilization of resources, family responsibility, and work requirements. Let's examine each area.

AFDC recipients with income. Because of the absence of any gross income ceiling and as a result of manipulations of income exemptions and work-related expense deductions, persons with high amounts of outside income can remain on the rolls. A fully employed woman with two children and a monthly salary of $977 remained on the rolls in California, as did another with only *one* child earning $1109, and others with monthly earnings of $1110 and $1200 respectively. One survey in Los Angeles County showed that there were over 1600 persons, each earning $600 a month or more, receiving welfare. In Oregon, a family earned $11,000 annually and remained on public assistance. The solutions to these situations include: 1) insertion of a gross income ceiling that bears some relationship to family size and costs, 2) closure of loopholes through which exemptions and deductions are manipulated (*e.g.*, deducting work-related expenses before the $30 and one-third earned income exemption to prevent deduction of one-third of the work-related expenses twice, and making the four-month period during which earned exemptions are permitted a single four-month period), and 3) simplifying administration through a standard work-related expense option.

Improper beneficiaries of public assistance. Current laws and regulations are so loosely written that strikers, illegal aliens, persons who commit fraud, and persons who are legally adults with no children of their own can receive Aid to Families with Dependent Children. The National Welfare Reform Act would close a number of these loopholes by prohibiting aid to the *voluntarily* unemployed and strengthening alien and fraud-control efforts, by instituting a photo-identification card, and by conforming the definition of child with those in use in the states to determine the age of majority.

Utilization of resources. Welfare recipients can have substantial sums available in outside resources and still not be required to use them. They may live with other persons who are under no requirement to contribute to the needs of the family even though some of the welfare funds may be meeting their expenses. Even if they live with another welfare family, duplicate allowances are made for housing and utili-

111

ties. In litigation, legal aid attorneys, already paid by the tax-payer, may have costs awarded to them.

Current law provides that once a statutory limit of 10 percent of the caseload is reached, states may not make payments directly to providers of goods and services when recipients have demonstrably mismanaged their funds. Persons may elect public assistance over other forms of aid available to them. All of these areas can be reformed by requiring that recipients effectively use available resources or by eliminating all duplicate payments.

Family responsibility. Fathers who desert their families and fail to support wives and children are at the core of the problem. While amendments made by the Congress at the end of 1974 have significantly improved efforts to reach the absent father, much remains to be done. For example, the definition of continued absence is so loose that some military personnel qualify for assistance when they should be supporting their families. Military personnel, moreover, no longer are required to forward allotments of their pay to their families, a requirement that existed prior to 1973. Further, self-sustaining persons living with welfare families, such as step-parents, may claim the children of the family as deductions for income tax purposes when the "support" is not known or calculated in computation of the welfare grant. Present law has no uniform requirement that states apply sanctions against knowing and willful misuse of the grant. Finally, judges in some states waive a father's arrearages in child support as a condition to future payment, and individuals, knowing this, may build up a substantial backlog and then agree to pay in the future on the condition that the backlog be erased. The National Welfare Reform Act contains specific recommendations that would correct many of these abuses.

Work requirements. The question of work requirements is at the heart of an effectively run welfare system, so that persons may not opt for an indolent life at public expense. The nation's AFDC program can be significantly strengthened by insisting not only upon work registration, but also job search (presenting evidence of a given number of employer contacts), and community work programs (recipients work in public service jobs in return for their welfare check). The last of these is particularly important. Work registration alone in practice is often little more than a paper exercise. What is needed is a program in which 1) recipients secure job skills; 2) work is performed in the community that would otherwise go undone; and 3) it is clear to the able-bodied recipients that if such work is available they may not remain at home idle while they continue to receive their welfare checks. Through community work experience programs everyone benefits: the recipient, through the acquisition of work habits and skills; the community, in which such work is performed; and the children of the recipient, who see the breadwinner leave at a regular hour in the morning rather than remain home and have government checks come in like clockwork. (Here the term breadwinner refers to the unemployed parent in a two-parent household participating in the Unemployed Parent component of the AFDC program. In single-parent households, public or private employment would be conditioned upon the age of the children and the availability of suitable day care.)

The jobs need not and should not be demeaning. There is nothing degrading about such occupations as school crossing guards, library assistants, playground attendants, nurses' aides, or highway maintenance men. These are the kinds of public employment that can provide meaningful benefits to needy men and women. Moreover, they can be combined with job search so that the recipient is employed in community work only 80 hours a month (half-time), enabling him to pursue aggressive job search the rest of the time.

Specific and clear sanctions for refusal to register for work, look for jobs, or work for the public need to be included in a more comprehensive and standardized way in our nation's welfare programs. Too often, as with many of our criminal sanctions, the lag between offense and official action is so great that there is no clear tie between the two. For example, in the Work Incentive Training (WIN) program, the WIN participant is made ineligible only when he refuses to accept work or training, and then only after a 60-day "counseling" period. The provision encourages such persons to refuse to accept work or training and then to recant on the 55th day, because their grant continues through the "counseling" period and will continue if they agree to accept work or training at any point during that time.

The above discussion of the five main subject areas of the National Welfare Reform Act demonstrates, then, that there are ways in which welfare *can* be reformed and current loopholes can be closed. Certainly these are not complete; they are simply illustrative of the kinds of managerial and legislative improvements that can be made in the AFDC program that would save countless tax dollars.

Why has not the Congress undertaken such analytical reform? Why has not the Department of Health, Education and Welfare seized the initiative and proposed such changes? Generally, the answers lie in three areas: 1) throughout the past four decades, the nation's public assistance programs have been staffed by individuals devoted to getting *more* money, not less; 2) until the 1970s, managerial and fiscal analysts have been lacking and the kinds of analytical tasks described in this chapter have not been undertaken; and 3) many welfare professionals have been totally committed to enlarging welfare. We saw such a development emerge from HEW as the Family Assistance Plan. In the name of simplification and integration, aid would have been extended to the working poor, and more persons would have been added to the welfare rolls. Often, too, these expanded programs are offered in the name of equity, while this vague ideal is constantly redefined upward so that increasing affluence can never eliminate welfare and its bureaucracy.

Well, yes, one may say, it is possible to understand why the professionals in the field—from their point of view—have been seeking the kind of massive expansion that the guaranteed annual income or Family Assistance Plan represents. But why, in the meantime, do they not correct the existing program and close obvious loopholes? Here, the answer appears to be the vested interest of the welfare bureaucracies in expanding and perpetuating the existing morass.

Experience in California and elsewhere in the country has proven that when there is the will and the expertise to grapple with our welfare problems, significant reform can be achieved. It is reform that the nation's taxpayers sought long ago. Congress has the opportunity to enhance the nation's solvency by enacting the National Welfare Reform Act of 1975.

BIOGRAPHY
of
The Honorable William L. "Bill" Dickinson
Alabama

A native Alabamian, Bill Dickinson was born in Opelika, Alabama, June 25, 1925. He received his law degree from the University of Alabama in 1950 and had a distinguished career in the law in Lee County, serving as a practicing attorney and holding several judgeships, including four years as circuit judge of the Fifth Judicial Circuit of Alabama, before coming to the 89th Congress in 1964. He is a Navy Veteran of World War II.

In Congress, he is a member of the House Armed Services Committee, the Joint Committee on Printing, the Ranking Minority Member of the Committee on House Administration and serves as Assistant Minority Whip for the Southeastern United States.

Mr. Dickinson has received numerous awards for service as a civic and community leader. Each year that he has been in Congress he has earned the Distinguished Service Award from the Americans for Constitutional Action for his conservative and responsible voting record as well as many awards for his fiscal conservatism.

A leader in the battle against food stamp fraud, he has been active in attempting a general reform of the food stamp program.

FOOD STAMPS: GOOD INTENTIONS DISTORTED . . . OR HIDDEN INTENTIONS FULFILLED?

by
Congressman William L. Dickinson

The food stamp program began as a deceptively simple program of modest scope to enable low-income Americans to have adequate nutrition while utilizing some of our farm surplus. It has become a multibillion dollar welfare nightmare. Its original intent has become perverted. Surrounding the food stamp program and perpetuating its growth is the deliberately irresponsible attitude that one has a "right" to food stamps, regardless of income or ability to support oneself. This is true of other welfare programs as well.

Caspar Weinberger, when he stepped down as Secretary of Health, Education and Welfare (HEW), warned that at our present rate of expenditure 50 percent of the American people will be living off the other half by the year 2000. The message comes loud and clear from my district that those who are doing the supporting, as well as the truly needy, are increasingly angry that freeloaders are eligible for food stamps and many other costly welfare benefits. It appears that an outraged public, fed up with abuses of government giveaways, has finally cried, "Enough!" and is looking to Congress for leadership in reforming the food stamp program.

Let's take a look at why the food stamp program is not working and how conservatives in Congress are attempting to bring about desperately needed reform.

Welfare by Design

When the Congress of the United States moved from two pilot projects (1939-43 and 1961-64) to full-scale adoption of the Food Stamp Act as a national program in 1964, two primary justifications were offered. One was the alleged existence of hunger and malnutrition in the United States. The other was the agricultural surpluses to which new purchasing power could be directed. Each could be used to solve the other. Few imagined the degree to which the new food stamp program would turn into one of the largest income transfer programs known in the history of the United States.

The food stamp program duplicated existing programs by offering financial aid to large groups of people already eligi-

117

ble for aid in the form of Aid to Dependent Children, Old Age Security, Aid to the Blind, Aid to the Disabled, and many other social services. Further, it lacked all but one eligibility test contained in those programs—the test of income—and that test is patently easy to circumvent. I suggest, therefore, that the designers of the food stamp program knew exactly what they were creating: a package that would encourage dependence on government by a host of able-bodied people who would never otherwise have dreamed of applying for federal assistance. This new kind of income transfer was eventually to reach staggering proportions in the name of welfare.

In fiscal 1965 total expenditures for the food stamp program stood at $36.4 million. In just ten years expenditures had swelled to $5.2 *billion*. That represents an increase of over *14,000 percent*! In terms of participation the figures are every bit as astounding:

1965: 1 in 439
1967: 1 in 157
1970: 1 in 47
1973: 1 in 17
1975: 1 in 13

An alarming index of the extent to which this program is expansionist by nature is the fact that one in four Americans can now be *eligible* for the food stamp program. By no stretch of the imagination can it be argued convincingly that one in four Americans are in such dire nutritional straits that they require welfare aid in the form of food stamps.

How did we reach this point? What program elements and eligibility criteria encourage this phenomenon to occur unchecked? Let's examine some of them.

Expanded Eligibility

In 1971 a major shift occurred, and the eligibility formula was *directly* tied to what, in the judgment of the United States Department of Agriculture, was required for a "nutritionally adequate diet." This became an interaction of three things: a person's total income; that proportion which it is held he should spend for food; and the cost of a basic, or minimally nutritious, diet. For example, if the "Thrifty Diet Plan" as developed by the Department of Agriculture would cost $150 per month, and a person would normally spend 30 percent of his income for food (the figure cited in the Food Stamp Act), he would be permitted to have no more than $500 per month in order to qualify.

In the curious fashion which sometimes characterizes governmental decisions, however, 30 percent became something less than 30 percent and income became something less than gross income.

Exemptions and deductions are the key to this amazing concept of eligibility. Look at this list of items that need not be included when income is calculated.

- Federal, state, and local income taxes
- Payments into a retirement fund
- Social Security taxes
- Union dues
- Ten percent of earned income up to $30 per individual
- Some types of garnishments
- Losses due to disaster such as fire, theft, or flood
- Medical costs in excess of $10 a month, including Medicare and insurance
- Child or invalid care payments
- Child support and alimony
- Tuition
- Costs of shelter—including mortgage payments and interest, rent, utilities, property taxes, water and sewer, garbage, and telephone—that are more than 30 percent of *net* income

Assume a family has *gross* monthly income of $1,000. After making all of the deductions above, their countable income becomes only $400—well below the $500 limit cited above. What percentage of $1,000 would the "Thrifty Diet Plan" consume? Fifteen percent, not thirty. Purchase requirements (the amount the family must pay for the stamps) then are tied to net income and become a much lesser percentage of gross income than the 30 percent envisioned in the law.

What all this finagling achieves in the long run is that there is no gross income ceiling in the food stamp program. Any family that has sufficient deductions may qualify. Maintaining an expensive home and sending the children to expensive private schools help a family to qualify.

Assets are another critical element determining eligibility. A responsible public assistance program has realistic asset limitations built in so that non-needy persons cannot create a need for assistance through the purchase or retention of expensive items of real or personal property. Under income calculations of the food stamp administration all of the following are now exempt:

A home and lot "normal to the community"

One currently licensed vehicle used for household transportation and any other vehicles necessary for the employment of household members (of any value)

All personal effects, including clothing and jewelry

All household goods, including furniture and appliances

The cash value of all life insurance policies and pension funds

Any property which "is producing income consistent with its fair market value," or other property "essential to the employment of a household member; machinery, livestock, or land of a farmer; and goods, property, vehicles, etc., used by self-employed persons in their self-employment enterprise

Irrevocable trust funds, property in probate, and notes receivable "which cannot be readily liquidated"

Money which has been prorated as income for self-employed persons or students

Indian lands held jointly with the Tribe or land that can be sold only with the approval of the Bureau of Indian Affairs

Relocation assistance payments

Payments made to persons participating in programs sponsored by ACTION

Benefits received under the WIC program (Special Supplemental Food Program for Women, Infants, and Children).

It is clear that people can own homes and automobiles of virtually any value, expensive household furnishings, and jewelry—and still be eligible for food stamps. Clearly the issue involves a question of priority, and it would seem almost axiomatic that food should come first in a family's priorities, particularly when it comes to requesting government aid to meet expenses.

Other loopholes exist in this category: coupon allotments are adjusted every six months according to the increase in the cost of living, but purchase requirements are not; there is no prohibition against the deliberate rearrangement of assets in order to qualify; and welfare recipients are *automatically* eligible, even though in some high-grant states their total income might be higher than the maximum cut-off levels for food stamp purposes.

The result of all of the above: testimony before a Senate committee in 1975 indicated that 57 percent of the eligibles and 31 percent of the recipients had incomes above the poverty line in a 1974 study.

Loopholes: Who Benefits?

In addition to the basic deficiencies that have developed in the eligibility formula, a number of specific loopholes exist. There is no minimum age in the food stamp program; children may leave home, band together, and exist on food stamps. Isn't it time to question the wisdom of a governmental program that encourages children to leave home?

Work requirements are even more lax than those found in the Aid to Families with Dependent Children program. In the latter, those with no children under six are required to register for work. In the food stamp program, any caretaker with a child of *any* age is exempt from work registration—as are all students. Moreover, work "registration" tends to become a paper exercise, with no required job search or involvement in community work experience programs, two additional approaches which can be productive in enhancing the return of the recipient to self-support. Community work experience engages the recipient in public-related work for 80 hours a month, half-time. The recipient may use the remaining 80 hours to search for regular employment.

Unlike the eligibility criteria for most unemployment insurance programs, criteria for food stamp benefits allow applicants to voluntarily leave their previous employment without good cause.

Recent changes in the Food Stamp Act, make food stamps available to drug addicts and alcoholics in rehabilitation centers—and they are under no requirement even to register for work.

While this is troublesome enough by itself, a particular category of voluntarily unemployed persons often rely on food stamps: *strikers*. A Wharton School of Finance study has documented the massive use of food stamps by strikers in major steel, electrical, automotive, and other strikes in 1969-71 at a cost to the public of $240 million. The abuse of the system is one that I have personally tried legislatively to cor-

121

rect. On July 19, 1973, the House passed my amendment to the Farm Bill to prohibit the issuance of food stamps to strikers. However, the amendment was left out of the Senate version of the Farm Bill and a complicated parliamentary situation prevented me from offering the amendment to the compromise Farm Bill worked out in House-Senate Conference.*

I introduced the amendment not because I am opposed to organized labor, for I am not, but because the amendment is "pro-poor people." Food stamps should be issued to those who are poor and cannot help themselves, not to those who voluntarily choose not to work.

Food stamps for strikers destroy the balance necessary to maintain a true collective bargaining system. When we take taxpayer's dollars and use them to favor one side over another—to give one side an advantage over another—in a matter directly affecting the public and consumer, we are abandoning our principles of fair play and free enterprise. The collective bargaining system depends on pressure on both sides to negotiate a settlement, and if strikers are receiving enough public assistance—a great part of which is food stamps—to keep them from needing to go back to work, there is obviously not the same amount of pressure on the strikers as there is on the management.

If the government through intervention eliminates the pressure on one side, it eliminates the incentive to negotiate in good faith and thus prolongs strikes. Prolonged strikes mean higher wages at settlement and eventually higher prices and higher taxes. Therefore, we destroy the economic function of collective bargaining and throw the whole system out of balance.

This point was emphasized in a 1974 Supreme Court ruling on a case brought by Super Tire Engineering Company against New Jersey officials concerning welfare benefits for strikers. Although the Court did not decide the original issue of the legality of such benefits, it did rule that lower courts have jurisdiction in the case even though the strike in question was over. Justice Blackmun, writing for the six-to-three majority, said the lawsuit was still alive because the state law providing welfare benefits to strikers could easily influence

---

* For Congressional debate and three recorded votes on this issue, see *Congressional Record*, July 19, 1973, pp. H6322–H6334.

contract bargaining and union strength in the future. He wrote:

> It cannot be doubted that the availability of state welfare assistance for striking workers in New Jersey pervades every work stoppage, affects every existing collective bargaining agreement, and is a factor lurking in the background of every incipient labor contract.

Use of food stamps also leads strikers into other benefit programs designed to help the needy, not those voluntarily on strike. For many years, unions could not draw upon public funds to subsidize strikes. Today, when unions are better financed and more powerful than ever before, there is no need to increase union power by substituting public monies for union strike funds.

It is not my intention to see innocent people have difficulty in obtaining the food they need. I simply believe that the unions—rather than the public—should support strikers. After all, this is the basic justification unions have for charging dues to their members.

Additionally, the provision of public assistance to *this* group of voluntarily unemployed persons makes it extremely difficult to refuse aid to other types of voluntarily unemployed persons: those who live in communal settings and others who prefer simply to pursue a relaxed lifestyle at the taxpayers' expense.

College students represent a further problematic group. On the one hand, there is the natural inclination to aid poor students who require assistance in order to complete their higher education. Yet we find it curious that under the food stamp program "students" may register for school only half time and be under no requirement to register for work the other half or even in the summer. Moreover, their course of study need have no relevance to self-support whatever. Finally, however, we must come to the basic question: *Should the blue-collar high school graduate have to support with his taxes persons who opt for a higher education?* This is clearly unfair. The government already sponsors a multitude of scholarships, loans, and work/study programs that truly needy students can use instead of succumbing to the lure of welfare. But food stamps have replaced the once-valued tradition of working one's way through school.

Definitions of who may live together and collect food

stamps as a separate household are equally lax. A requirement of the current program indicates that persons must "buy and prepare food separately," but this is easily circumvented. Furthermore, it is unlikely that every refrigerator and hot plate will be policed. Individuals in a group-living arrangement can each receive a separate food stamp allotment as head of a household.

Other instances of fraud and misrepresentation abound. Food stamps are as easily negotiable as cash—and requirements for identification of users are minimal. As a result, the opportunities for counterfeiting, theft, and blackmarketing, as well as general fraud, become extensive. Investigators from all parts of the country testified to the manner and the incidence of fraud at Senate hearings late in 1975.* Moreover, in a system that spends almost $6 billion annually, we have no methodical system for determining when persons apply for food stamps in multiple jurisdictions or when they underreport their income. Emphasis throughout has been on *prima facie* eligibility and reporting methods, without careful and effective controls of the kind that are demanded in a program of this magnitude.

Finally, we have the absurdity of a multiplicity of governmental programs all designed to achieve the same end: adequate nutrition. The entire food stamp formula is predicated upon the receipt of a minimum or basic diet; yet the *same* family may also receive free school lunches, free school breakfasts, or free noon meals for the elderly under separate programs with no offset in their food stamp allotment.

How to Sell a Giveaway

The current food stamp law mandates an incredible level of outreach in order to inform persons of their possible eligibility for food stamps. Television and radio spots, newspaper advertisements, grocery bag stuffers, leaflets, and even full-time employees are funded through outreach provisions of the law. The current statute contains this startling mandate: States must "undertake effective action . . . to . . . *insure* (emphasis added) the participation of eligible households." *Reasonable* efforts to inform concerning public programs may very well be appropriate; ludicrous has replaced reasonable in the current food stamp program's outreach efforts.

_____
* See hearings of the Senate Agricultural Subcommittee on Agricultural Research and General Legislation, October 7-10 and November 17-20, 1975.

Reform

Almost without exception since the beginning of the program, food stamp amendments have further liberalized the program or created the loopholes described above. The Congress never formally considered a carefully developed reform plan until the first session of the 94th Congress, when such a plan was introduced. It remains to be seen how this Congress will deal with the reform issue and whether meaningful reform will be enacted.

On June 23, 1975, the National Food Stamp Reform Act (H.R. 8145, S. 1993) was introduced, with bipartisan cosponsorship in the House and Senate, which—at the date of this writing—now totals 100 Members in both houses. (See proposal K in Table II.) With 41 separate provisions for correcting the defects, it is estimated that the bill would save between $2.0 billion and $2.5 billion in taxpayers' funds. At the same time, *coupon allotments would be increased by approximately 29 percent—insuring that those with the greatest need in fact receive more adequate nutritional funding*. Liberal attackers of the measure have carefully avoided mention of this provision.

If the bill is enacted, the proposals contained in the Buckley-Michel National Food Stamp Reform Act will:

- Place realistic limits so that persons with high incomes will not qualify and thereby drain resources from a program that is to meet the needs of the legitimately needy
- Institute a food stamp formula based upon what the average American family, by size and income range, spends for food, eliminating the many complex deductions and exemptions
- Close numerous loopholes that permit the voluntarily unemployed to receive food stamps and others to manipulate the system
- Tighten work requirements so that the food stamp program does not subsidize idleness or serve as a substitute for gainful employment
- Simplify administration by basing eligibility on gross income and by linking with welfare administration
- Require recognition of multiple public benefits that go to the same family
- Direct additional funding to swifter processing of applications and to nutritional education

- Eliminate outreach program
- Improve cash and coupon handling methods to minimize opportunities for theft, loss, and misuse of federal coupons and funds
- Limit fraud through photo-ID cards, countersigned warrants, and earnings clearance and central clearance house systems
- Increase amounts paid to the truly needy, by 1) substituting the Low Cost Diet Plan for the Economy Diet Plan, raising coupon allotments by 29 percent and 2) reducing food stamp costs for the aged, with a $25 monthly income deduction

It is possible through the enactment of these long overdue reforms to *substantially increase benefits* paid to those who genuinely need nutritional assistance and to *realize significant savings* for the taxpayer. By closing loopholes, correcting defective elements of the eligibility formula, tightening work requirements, and curtailing opportunities for fraud and other criminal activities, the food stamp program can be restored to legitimate purposes.

Another Plan

Not long after the introduction of the National Food Stamp Reform Act, the liberals hastened to come up with a measure of their own. After writing an earlier bill to effect self-certification for food stamps, Senator George McGovern (D, S. Dakota) introduced a "reform" bill. Unfortunately this bill contains little in the way of control and much in the direction of liberalization.

The purchase requirement (that portion which the applicant pays to receive the bonus stamps) would be completely eliminated, thereby removing any insurance that the recipients' funds actually go for food and having a drastic probable *upward* effect on participation.

Although a standard deduction is included (as in the Administration bill, introduced later in the session), it is one of the most liberal of any bill yet introduced. It constitutes $125 a month for everyone and an additional $25 per month for the elderly. It would permit a household of four with income up to $10,000 to be eligible. In addition to the standard deduction of $125 monthly, the McGovern bill would exempt federal, state, and local income taxes; retirement payments; union dues; Social Security payments; any other mandatory deductions; and student loans and scholarships. Not only would these escalate the income ceiling of those who would qualify, it restores the kind of administrative complexity that everyone is trying to avoid; it is corrected in the Buckley-Michel bill through the use of a simple gross income ceiling.

Equally serious, the McGovern bill completely fails to address the many loopholes and problem areas that are effectively covered in Buckley-Michel: lack of minimum age, need for assets limitations, laxity of current work registration requirements, eligibility of the voluntarily unemployed, duplication of other government programs, and opportunities for fraud and other criminal activity.

Gross Income Ceiling

A key provision of the Buckley-Michel National Food Stamp Reform Act provides a gross income ceiling on recipients. That ceiling is the government's *poverty index*, $5,050 for a family of four. The poverty index figure was selected because the food stamp program's alleged purpose is to provide a nutritionally adequate diet to those persons *too poor to afford it themselves*. It should not be a giveaway supplement to persons who can feed their families if they only order their priorities—and who, if they have difficulty in meeting other required expenditures, have many other kinds of programs, public and private, on which to rely.

A key vote came on the floor of the House of Representatives on November 13, 1975, when Congressman Paul Findley (R, Illinois) offered an amendment to the supplemental Agriculture Appropriations bill to incorporate the poverty index limit provision of the Buckley-Michel bill for food stamp eligibility. Here was a key test to determine which Members of the House supported immediate action to curtail food stamps except to those most genuinely in need. The final tally showed 159 in favor of the amendment, while 230 continued to opt for the present runaway practice of no gross income ceiling at all. (See vote 14 in Table I.)

Here was an opportunity for the Democratic-controlled Congress to restore fiscal sanity to the food stamp program and to bring it back to its original purposes: to assist only those who, by the Government's own standards, are officially defined as poor. Of the 259 Democrats voting on the issue, *199* voted against the ceiling, saying in effect food stamps should continue to go to upper-income categories and to anyone clever enough to manipulate the loopholes. The very essence of the Buckley-Michel bill, the National Food Stamp Reform Act, is to close these loopholes, cut off high-income eligibility, and in fact increase benefits for the truly needy. The liberal establishment in Congress constituted the core of the 199. By their vote against the Findley amendment they made it clear their real concern is *not* for careful direction of resources to the poor: they would prefer to leave the floodgates open, spending with abandon to needy and non-needy alike. They are satisfied with a program that is spending at the rate of $6 billion after only ten years and that has made one in four Americans eligible.

Fortunately, the Buckley-Michel gross income ceiling remains one of the 41 items in the National Food Stamp Reform Act. The comprehensive reform package at this writing is now pending action in the Senate and House. The opportunity for effective action on the basic eligibility issue and many others critically important to the careful operation of a responsible food stamp program is still present. As tax resources become increasingly scarce, as competing demands are placed upon them, and as income transfer programs continue to spiral, it remains to be seen if effective action will be taken in the 94th Congress.

The taxpayer—aware of some of the problems in the food stamp program—can and should watch carefully.

BIOGRAPHY

of
The Honorable Barry M. Goldwater, Jr.
California

Barry M. Goldwater, Jr., came to the U.S. Congress from the 27th District of California after a special election in April of 1969. He currently represents the 20th District.

Born on July 15, 1938, in Los Angeles, Representative Goldwater attended the University of Colorado and Arizona State University, where he majored in business and marketing. He graduated in 1962 and settled in Los Angeles, eventually becoming a partner in the stock brokerage firm of Noble Cooke.

As the ranking Republican on the Subcommittee on Energy Research, Development and Demonstration of the Science and Technology Committee, Congressman Goldwater was an author of solar and geothermal energy legislation. He is also a member of the Committee on Public Works and Transportation.

On the national scene, the Congressman has emerged as a serious, effective voice in the protection of individual rights and personal privacy, and has authored several measures to protect the individual from privacy invasion. One of his bills, the Right to Privacy Act of 1974, was signed into law on January 1, 1975.

An advocate of free enterprise, the Congressman from California opposes any measure that would increase the power of the federal government or give the Executive Branch unnecessary power.

Barry Goldwater married the former Susan L. Gherman in March of 1972.

SOCIAL SECURITY:
GOING THE WAY OF NEW YORK CITY?

by
Congressman Barry M. Goldwater, Jr.

During the Great Depression, the Congress and the President founded the Social Security system for two basic reasons: to prevent destitution and a dependence on welfare among older Americans; and to create more jobs by encouraging retirement.

Like the tiny, appealing pup of dubious parentage, however, the Social Security system has grown to become voracious in appetite and impossible to manage.

More than $69 billion a year is paid to one out of seven Americans—the largest cash-disbursing system in the history of the world. Riddled with mismanagement, liberal social planners have brought this vital pension system to the brink of bankruptcy, much as irresponsible and incompetent politicians did to the city of New York.

The parallels are there. As with New York, the Congress and Social Security administrators have been deceiving the public, juggling the books, frantically hoping the crash will not come until *they* retire.

Contrary to an oft-stated and widely held belief, the Social Security system is *not* insurance or based on actuarial standards. It is *not* money set aside for a rainy day. Its benefits *are* being supplied almost entirely by the taxes of those *currently* employed. The pay-out of future benefits depends solely on future workers—some of whom are not yet born.

Since those who work today are paying for those now retired (and for their dependents and the disabled), the ratio of workers to recipients is crucial. In 1975, three workers paid taxes to pay one beneficiary of Social Security. In 2001, because of a declining birth rate and increased longevity, there will be only two workers for each beneficiary. Far off as 2001 sounds, it is but 25 short years away. What this means, of course, is that many of today's workers and all of their children will be affected by current Social Security mismanagement.

The increasing life span factor has not been put into proper perspective, either. Consider this: since people will

131

live, on the average, longer and longer, they will receive Social Security that much more time—which will mean ever-increasing taxes to pay for those lengthened benefits. The only alternative, if we continue the present system without reform, will be to reduce benefits directly or indirectly (raising the retirement age and allowing inflation to erode payments), or greatly increase wage taxes to make up the cash short-fall.

It's time to dispel yet another misconception. Those of us in the Congress who work for fiscal responsibility are *not* out to destroy or weaken the Social Security system. The exact reverse is true. We are trying to save it. We are trying to stop the silent tax of inflation that is caused by runaway, deficit federal spending. *We are trying to insure that everyone who paid their taxes for this system in good faith will reap the benefits in their later years.* The time to make sure the system continues to deliver on its promises 25 years from now is in the next few years. If we wait and just hope for the best, as New York City officials did, we will all wake up one morning to find the largest pension system in the world has gone bust —and a bleak retirement for many of our people.

Remember that the liberals who ran New York City kept telling us that future tax receipts would be much higher; and that the budget would be balanced. Then, whammo! No revenue increases transpired, some officials were secretly using capital construction funds to finance the day-to-day expenses of operating the city and no budgets were balanced.

Note that recent independent reports* all agree that the Social Security Administration has been similarly and unrealistically optimistic. The SSA has counted on a higher birth rate than now seems probable, and on a higher rise in real wages than now seems justified by the experience of the last decade.

Because of such serious miscalculations, some economists estimate that if the SSA cut off new beneficiaries at the 1974 level, but continued to collect taxes and pay benefits to those covered until the cut-off date, the system by year 2049 would be *$2.5 trillion* in the red (including market rates of interest compounded annually).

Even SSA defenders, such as former HEW Secretary Wil-

---

* The Kaplan-Weil Report to the Secretary of the Treasury (by two independent economists from Carnegie-Mellon University and Georgia Institute of Technology): the report of a Special Panel of the U.S. Senate Finance Committee: and the 1974 Report of the Social Security Administration's Trustees.

bur Cohen, admit that taxes will have to be raised 10-25 percent over the next 30 years to maintain the same level of benefits as presently exists. Most economists agree a rise of 50 percent in the payroll tax will be needed over the next 25 years unless the system is reformed soon.

Recently, the SSA admitted that the system would be almost $3 billion in the red for 1975, and about $6 billion in the red for 1976. SSA officials proposed to make up most of the deficit by dipping into the Social Security Trust Fund. In 1947 the Fund was supposed to be enough to finance the system for 17 years and six months. Recently, after almost 30 years of mismanagement, the so-called "trust fund" could pay benefits for less than nine months! Thus, raiding the trust fund is no answer. So much for the liberals' version of "fiscal responsibility" for the last 30 years.

A lack of reserves translates into higher payroll taxes. The maximum annual rate paid by employees will be $895.05 in 1976, on the first $15,300 of income. This is almost 20 times the rate of 26 years ago, when the maximum tax was $45 a year.

The payroll tax more than doubled from 1970-1975. According to U.S. Treasury statistics, a family of four with one wage earner making less than $9,057 now pays more in Social Security taxes than are paid in federal income taxes. This growth in Social Security tax has made it the second-largest source of federal revenues, higher even than corporation taxes!

The squeeze most Americans feel caught in these days can also, in great part, be attributed to the Social Security system. Martin Feldstein, a noted Harvard economist, recently pointed out that the cost of the system has had a major side-effect of reducing total private savings (and investment in the economy) by about 38 percent. The gross national product has been reduced by $120 billion in 1974. Wages, on the average, are now 15 percent lower than they would otherwise have been. Conversely, interest rates are 28 percent higher—resulting in less housing, fewer jobs, less prosperity for all Americans, and a watering down of the value of Social Security benefits.

Who is Hurt?

The group that will be hurt most by the present system is the young people now starting to work. In 1971 the Social Security Administration calculated that the maximum lifetime contribution of a person who began work at 18 would be $24,273. Benefits received could total $94,404.

But if that sum was invested very conservatively in the usual monthly installments and earned the modest interest of 5.5 percent it would grow to $107,983 when the person reached 65. If we add the employer's contribution (which, as we have seen, must be regarded in large part as a fringe benefit and part of an employee's total compensation) the sum would come to $215,966. For that amount the young worker could have bought a private annuity to pay him $21,804 a year beginning at age 65 or a total of $282, 362 over the life expectancy calculated by the Social Security Administration.*

According to this calculation, a young person could receive *three* times the pension benefits if he invested his Social Security taxes in a private pension plan. In addition, there would be no limit on how much he could earn after age 65. In some cases, depending on how he invested his money, he could have a sizeable capital sum to leave to his heirs upon his death. Since most Americans do not leave any sizeable estate to their children such a change in our national pension system would amount to a social revolution with far-reaching effects. Because of these facts, it is impossible not to conclude that Social Security is a very bad bargain for the young person today; indeed, it can only be called a financial disaster.

Righting the Wrongs

Simple changes in the law would correct many of the inequities in the present system. My colleague, Congressman Bill Armstrong of Colorado, has introduced the Social Security Reform Amendments of 1975 (H.R. 7595; see Proposal L in Table II). The bill, which I have co-sponsored, would make seven key improvements in the system:

1. It would *repeal the earnings limitation* for SS recipients. Those between 65 and 72 are now allowed to earn only $2,760 a year (1976 regulation) before their benefits are reduced by one dollar for every dollar earned above that amount. In other words, those who must work, or simply desire to remain productive, must pay a 50 percent tax on their earnings over $2,760—a tax bracket normally reserved for single persons with incomes over $50,000.

2. It would allow current recipients to *marry without pen-*

---

* These figures are based on 1971 Social Security costs which have, as we have seen, gone up considerably since then.

alty. Restrictive clauses curtail some benefits to those recipients wishing to marry. The only alternatives to a reduction in benefits are for a couple to deny themselves happiness and companionship, or to live together unmarried.

3. It would grant *equal treatment* to widows and widowers and for husbands and wives. A married woman who had a career often receives far less benefits, through her husband, than she would have had she remained single. More than 30 million working women in America must be accorded the same benefits for themselves and their dependents as working men receive.

4. It would grant an *optional exemption* for recipients 65 and older from paying further SS taxes. It hardly seems fair to tax a person's meager earnings after that person has paid in full for 30 years or more.

5. It would *repeal a particularly cruel provision* which requires a beneficiary's heirs to return a check if the beneficiary died before the check cleared. The new measure would allow a beneficiary and heirs full benefits for the last month of the beneficiary's life.

6. It would bring about a partial reform of the Medicare billing system, to *permit the system to make direct payments to doctors*. At the present time, a low-income beneficiary must wait to be reimbursed by Medicare, and this often places an impossible hardship on the person. Health of the beneficiary usually suffers as a result. I have some reservations about this provision, but feel it would be preferable to the present situation.

7. It would *eliminate the five-month waiting period* to receive disability payments under SS. The present system forces a sick or disabled worker to wait five months after he is unable to work before benefits can be received.

These reforms would not perfect an imperfect system. But they would go far in removing the daily irritants and frustrations many SS recipients experience, *as well as reduce administration costs by streamlining the presently awkward system.*

Can We Avoid Disaster?

The larger question still remains: How can we put the Social Security system on a fiscally sound basis and avoid cheating those who are currently receiving benefits and those who are paying into it? And, more specifically, how can we give greater value for money invested?

Be ready for the traditional liberal's answer: Raise taxes!

Use general treasury funds! Pump more money into the system!

Given the present system, however, only three other alternatives are open to us. First, increase the tax rate for contributions to the Social Security system. This obviously reduces the amount of take-home pay of every wage earner. Second, Congress can raise the taxable base from $15,000 a year to $25,000 a year. The problem with this solution was recently pointed out by Senator Long, Chairman of the Senate Finance Committee, who noted that there are just not that many Americans earning over $15,000 a year to make up the cash short-fall. It is even doubtful that a combination of an increase in the tax rate and the maximum taxable income would generate enough revenue to eliminate the deficit —because neither approach cures the basic flaws of the system.

The third alternative is to raid the Treasury—using general tax revenues to support the system. This approach has the political advantage of being the least financially painful device (for its financial impact might not show up in increased federal income tax rates) and it permits the Congress to avoid reforming the basic financial nature of the Social Security system. However, this would destroy the supplemental insurance character of the current pension system and make Social Security just one more aspect of the federal welfare program. I know our citizens emphatically do not want that to happen. *They want a system that is financially sound and that honestly gives them a value in benefits equal to the value they paid in—nothing more and nothing less.*

These approaches, because they seek only to make up short-falls in the cash reserves of the Social Security system are merely white-wash. They do not reform the system or remedy the real problem: more money now goes out than is taken in and this situation will get worse every year from now on. Raising Social Security taxes when done routinely as has been done for the last 20 years, exacerbates the real problem and adds more fuel to the fires of inflation.

Senior citizens must be allowed to receive the true value of their Social Security payments. I cannot emphasize this too strongly—my whole aim in approaching this problem is to *safeguard* the benefits of our older citizens. What I and many of my colleagues in the Congress question is increasing benefits to off-set inflation without doing anything about the causes of inflation. It's a vicious circle that must be broken.

The attempt to make up cash short-falls is at best a losing game. It neither compensates for inflation's erosion of the dollar nor solves the basic financial flaw of the system. The last five Social Security increases the Congress has voted have been rapidly swallowed by continuing inflation. Most Social Security recipients have gained nothing in real terms. Less real buying power and increased vulnerability to financial disaster has been the result for most. Without meaningful reform the Congress will be forced to vote one benefit increase after another, while raiding the general treasury to do it—thus ending the insurance program and running the risk of merging Social Security with welfare.

An interim solution may be found in the suggestions of Professors James Buchanan and Colin Campbell.* They suggest that the current deficit condition of the Social Security Fund could be eliminated by selling Social Security bonds. The bonds would total the amount of the current deficit and would earn interest at current commercial rates and would be applicable to the beneficiary's annuity account. This approach would eliminate constant raids on the Treasury. It would, if successful, start the Social Security system on the road toward sound actuarial operation. And, most importantly, it would force the Congress to face the Social Security question openly and squarely. I recognize such an approach would have to be thoroughly investigated, and all questionable aspects resolved before considering implementation. It does, however, represent a positive alternative to solve the short-range problem of sufficient funds. Of course, in recognizing such an alternative the Congress would have to admit that the Social Security system is in truly serious trouble.

Regarding proposals for a more permanent reform, I would suggest a reading of *Retirement Security Reform*, a book by two young economists, Charles D. Hobbs and Stephen Powlesland.** Their proposal, in my view, is an example of the kind of system we must institute if the present concept is to be salvaged.

They advocate restoring government to its rightful role as the protector of individual choice. The monopoly now exer-

---

* For a detailed discussion of these proposals see James Buchanan and Colin Campbell, "Voluntary Social Security," *The Wall Street Journal*, December 10, 1966 (Editorial Page). Buchanan has a longer discussion of their proposal entitled, "Social Insurance in a Growing Economy," in the *National Tax Journal*, December 1968, pp. 368-395.

** Institute for Liberty and Community, 1975, Concord, Vt.

cised over minimum retirement security funds by the SSA would be ended. The payroll tax (due to rise to a combined total of 12.10 percent in 1978) would be terminated, and the employee's and employer's contributions returned to the worker in the form of additional wages.

Every employee or self-employed person would then choose between investing in a government insured private pension plan* or in U.S. Retirement Bonds with annuity pay-off. Each worker would be required to invest 10 percent of his earnings or $2,500 annually, whichever is less. Bonds would be geared to the annual Cost of Living Index, and would be protected against inflation. They would have a lifetime annuity value at retirement and would provide annuities to survivors in the event of an early death, or to the worker and dependents in case of disability. They could be converted at any time into a private pension at the worker's request. Healthy competition between the government and private firms would foster the best and most efficient service to the American worker.

Those now paying into Social Security would receive the accumulated value of their past contributions in Retirement Bonds. Workers now retired would continue to receive their Social Security pensions, but the amounts of the pensions would grow each year at the same rate as the Bonds, in line with the Cost of Living Index.

Obviously, the full impact of such a plan would have to be thoroughly investigated, and I do not advocate it as the ideal solution, but I believe the proposal has merit. Such a plan would stimulate the economy, which now lags behind most other industrialized nations, in savings and capital needed to create jobs.

I also believe it is obvious that the American worker would be much better off if the present Social Security system could be improved by a plan of the type outlined. Hobbs and Powlesland concluded their proposal by noting that their suggestion "meets the coming fiscal crisis; *does not disrupt or diminish the benefits and investments of present Social Security beneficiaries and participants* (italics mine); and pro-

---

* An example of the greater efficiency of private services over government services can be found in a November 1975 General Accounting Office report. It cost the SSA almost twice as much to process each Medicare bill as it did three private insurance companies ($12.39 per bill for government; $7.81 for Travelers; $7.28 for Mutual; $3.55 for Maryland).

vides for a wider range of individual choice than the present ... system."

To accomplish this, free and informed debate is essential. It's to be hoped the manifest failures of so many of the "Great Society" programs of the 1960's and the recent collapse of fiscal integrity in New York City (which most hurt those least able to shoulder the burden) will teach us the folly of relying upon the government to do everything for us, without making certain the government is managing our money properly.

One final note—perhaps the most important one of all. You, the American public, will cast the deciding vote on whether or not the Social Security system will go the way of New York City.

In the final analysis, the Congress listens to no one but you. If your voice is loud enough, the system will be improved. Many Social Security reform proposals have been pending before the Congress for years, but the Congress has repeatedly ignored them.

It took the Congress just seven days to lift the "black-out" of professional football games—but reform of most Americans' national pension plan languishes while the system slowly destroys itself. Time is growing short.

EDUCATION AND THE ENVIRONMENT

BIOGRAPHY
of
The Honorable Robert E. Bauman
Maryland

Bob Bauman came to the House of Representatives from the First District of Maryland after winning a special election in August of 1973. Rep. Bauman had a great deal of experience in both national and State government while playing a fundamental role in national conservative political action.

Born April 4, 1937, Rep. Bauman attended high school in Easton, Maryland, and the Capitol Page School in Washington, D.C. He earned a B.S. Degree in International Affairs from the School of Foreign Service at Georgetown University in 1959, Washington, D.C., and continued at Georgetown's Law Center to achieve a Juris Doctor Degree in 1964. Representative Bauman served as State Senator for the Upper Shore from 1970 until his election to Congress.

Representative Bauman was a founder of the Young Americans for Freedom and its national chairman from 1962 to 1965. He also established and led the American Conservative Union.

In the House, Representative Bauman has been among the leaders in the fight to restore fiscal sanity and balanced budgets. He has made a reputation as a "fiscal watchdog" and has become known for his parliamentary skill in debate. In his first year of Congressional service he was chosen "Outstanding Freshman Legislator" by his Republican colleagues.

Representative Bauman is married to the former Carol Gene Dawson and they have four children. They live in Easton, Maryland, on Maryland's beautiful Eastern Shore.

FEEDING AT THE TROUGH:
A CASE STUDY OF FEDERAL GRANTS
by
Congressman Robert E. Bauman

Taxes may be thought of as a close second to death as a certainty in modern America, but that certainty gives little comfort to the average taxpayer. Every April each of us is reminded that well over a third of our annual income is taken in taxes to support government at all levels: local, state, and federal. This burden of taxation has constantly increased and if we have derived any benefit at all, it is in the awareness of individual taxpayers of the recklessness with which government bureaucrats spend our tax dollars.

No area of federal expenditures has produced more citizen complaints than the thousands of grants made annually by the National Science Foundation (NSF). Politicians and reporters make great copy out of publicizing individual grants with idiotic titles and questionable purposes, many of them running into the millions of dollars over the years.

A typical example came to light only recently when *Science* magazine (December 1975) published an extensive treatise written by an obscure professor at the University of Florida entitled, "Diversity and Adaptation in Rodent Copulatory Behavior." Charts, graphs, and illustrations detailed the frequency, manner, and methods of copulation of 32 species of rats and mice. The author, Dr. Donald A. Dewsbury, closed his scholarly article with a cheerful observation that after nine years he has only just begun.

Closer investigation has recently uncovered the fact that for almost a decade, continuing even now, NSF has shelled out nearly a quarter of a million tax dollars to finance this observation of copulating rodents; to be exact, $243,500 of your hard-earned tax dollars.

Scientific Knowledge

In attempting to justify this highly questionable research, NSF told me that such study is "increasing basic scientific knowledge of the life cycle of animals" and that already it had been shown that "the production of healthy offspring has been shown to relate directly to geographic conditions and environmental pressures affecting behavior." Imagine that!

NSF even suggested that such research could eventually result in controlling undesireable species; that is, in rat eradication, which would surely be beneficial to man.

No doubt it would. But after nine years Dr. Dewsbury has done little more than watch rats and mice perform sex acts and has apparently done nothing to suggest ways to prevent their procreation.

Surely such research has already been duplicated in numerous similar studies, public and private, over the years. As the scientist who called this to my attention suggested, "It's a pity we can't use the vulgar descriptive term that so aptly describes what is being done to the rats—and to the taxpayer. With funds short and vital medical research held back, this cannot be justified."

If this were an isolated instance of NSF grant behavior it might be dismissed as an aberration and not the rule. But the truth is that the entire NSF system lends itself to the making of often questionable awards to researchers whose credentials are not so important as who they know within the inbred NSF community. Meanwhile, worthy scientific research goes unfunded.

Why else would NSF make grants within a few months in 1975 such as $260,000 for a study of the origins and nature of passionate love, $41,700 for research into web building of three species of spiders, $34,400 to study the social behavior of prairie dogs, $84,000 for a study of why people fall in love, just to mention a few? Each day's list of recent NSF grants contains new enormities.

Members of Congress have denounced these senseless grants for years. As a newer Member of the House, when I read the irate comments of taxpayers in my mail, I became convinced that instead of just denouncing such spending Congress should accept its constitutional responsibility to oversee the public purse.

Congressional Review

On April 9, 1975, in the House of Representatives, I offered an amendment to the annual NSF authorization bill. The amendment would require NSF to submit all proposed grants to the appropriate committees of the Congress *before* they became effective rather than supplying us with a notice after the fact as is now done. If either House of Congress took no action within 30 days after submission of the list the grants would automatically take effect. Congress and its staff would review the lists and make additional inquiries concerning any NSF grant that appeared to be questionable. The amendment would also require that each grant contain a brief rationale for why it might be important to the national welfare.

After a short debate the amendment passed the House on a roll call vote of 212-199. To my surprise the other members of the House had been feeling pressure from home. This pressure, I am happy to say, translated itself into support for what came to be called, especially within the scientific community, the "Bauman Amendment."

Reaction to the House's adoption of the Bauman Amendment was not long in coming. Within 24 hours Senator Edward Kennedy (D, Massachusetts), chairman of the special subcommittee on NSF, issued a blast at the amendment and at the House for having the audacity to interfere in "scientific matters." Making it plain that he did not believe that the Congress had any ability to judge matters scientific, the Massachusetts liberal repeated the NSF denouncement of Congressional review of NSF grants as anti-intellectual and—wonder of wonders—potentially too expensive.

Clearly the entire point of my amendment and the ensuing debate was the refusal of Congress to accept true responsibility for money it appropriates to a federal agency such as NSF. This year NSF will have $751 million at its disposal for grants; a check written by the majority of Congress for the bureaucrats to dispense as they see fit. A check of the roll call on my amendment will show who is truly concerned about saving the taxpayers' money and who is not. (See vote 15 in Table I.)

Curriculum Reform

Is federal aid to the scientific community necessary or even desirable? Many people think so. Others are convinced that private research groups and firms could do a more economical and effective job of designing and carrying out experiments that will truly result in research "beneficial to mankind."

Of even more concern to many taxpayers is NSF's interference in the attitudes and morality to be taught in our local public schools. Under the guise of curriculum reforms some very nontraditional experiments have been carried out in the school rooms of our nation. The innocent subjects are not rats and mice. They are your children.

The year 1975 was probably one of the most controversial the National Science Foundation has seen. What began as a minor objection to a series of grants dealing with the Social studies curriculum has snowballed to the point that NSF may have to change some of its major policies—either voluntarily or by legislative decree of Congress. The curriculum that seems to have started the whole problem for the Foundation is *Man: A Course of Study* (MACOS), a fifth-grade social studies course that studies the culture of the Netsilik Eskimos in Canada. In the process of trying to understand how a course like MACOS could possibly have received federal funding, critics naturally began looking more and more closely at the internal workings of the Foundation. What has come to light is a pattern of a sloppy management policies that have allowed the entrenchment of a favored few career curriculum innovators. A highly secret grant review system, known as "peer review," approves all NSF grants. In this instance the system had been manipulated by individuals, so that their favorite idea in school curriculum development received funding. By implication, the same peer review system can open to abuse all of the research and support activities of the National Science Foundation. The proposals to change the peer review system, to force NSF to conduct needs assessments before it funds projects, to open the grant process to more competition, and to make NSF accept responsibility for what it funds are problems of broader interest to conservatives who are concerned with making bureaucracies both responsive and responsible.

NSF was established in 1950 by the National Science Foundation Act. In 1957 Congress first allowed the Foundation to supervise design of science curricula. Soon NSF had become actively involved in both developing and implementing science and social studies curricula as well. Although a specific congressional edict mandated development of school materials, there never has been any legislative basis for NSF's involvement in the actual promotion and marketing of these courses. During various congressional hearings over the years, many specific warnings were given, discouraging NSF involvement in promoting its own materials. Early in the history of the organization, Dr. Alan Waterman, the first NSF director, stated that the Foundation would assist only in the research portion of curriculum development, and would not attempt to extend its influence beyond that area.

Implementation

Implementation techniques of NSF have been a key issue, first with the controversial MACOS program and now in other curriculum projects as well, including "Exploring Human Nature," "Individualized Science Instructional System" (ISIS), and "People and Technology," to name a few. Parents continue to object to these courses for a broad range of reasons, and federal promotion of them is an added insult to the taxpayers.

In its course content, MACOS can be interpreted to condone brutality, cannibalism, and other violent practices.

But beyond the question of the merits or demerits of one particular course lie several questions of policy significance. First on that list is NSF's practice of funding the establishment of networks of educators across the country to disseminate the course materials to local school districts. Not only has the NSF been promoting an extremely questionable curriculum with federal funds, it has been attempting to influence the whole direction of social studies curriculum development across the nation, local school boards notwithstanding. According to an approved grant proposal submitted by the developer of MACOS to the NSF, the curricula are to be used as "wedges for systematic change," that will help in the "diminishing (of) traditional resistance to curricular change."[1]

The same grant also allowed the Educational Development Center (EDC), developers of MACOS, to sponsor an awareness conference for 40 local school district leaders. To be selected to attend, participants had to agree to set up awareness workshops in their own school districts upon their return. Another facet of implementation allowed EDC to prepare eight university/school district teams for leadership roles to interest local school personnel in using "Exploring Human Nature" (EHN), the tenth-grade sequel to MACOS. Each university center is told to involve "three to ten area classrooms in each curricula during the 1975-76 school year." (The curricula are MACOS, EHN, People and Technology, and others). These implementation techniques are openly being used for most of the NSF social studies curricula, as well as some of the regular science courses (ISIS); they are

---

[1] EDC NSF Proposal/Grant No. PES75-01635, January, 1975.

a basic and very serious violation of the strong tradition of local control of education.

It is clear that courses that received federal funding are competing unfairly with those developed by the private sector. But worst of all, continuation of these implementation practices allows the federal government's promotion of a particular set of highly controversial ideas and educational methodology according to the personal preferences of middle-level federal bureaucrats at NSF. Because of the closed peer review system, these bureaucrats have been subject to no real supervision.

Peer Review

A further word needs to be said about peer review. Peer reviewers are experts outside the National Science Foundation who read and review grant proposals submitted to NSF. They evaluate the proposals and recommend whether or not each should receive federal funds. The middle-level program managers choose who will write the reviews. When the reviews are received, verbatim copies, along with the names of the reviewers, are kept confidential. Summaries of the comments are available to the grantee, but names and actual statements are kept confidential. They have even been kept confidential from the House Committee on Science and Technology, the committee that is responsible for NSF oversight. Although the National Science Board had agreed to make the actual reviews available, it refused to release them with signatures attached.

Many of the manipulations of the system were revealed by my colleague Congressman John Conlan (R, Arizona). Months earlier Dr. John Tirrell of the American Association of Community and Junior Colleges testified: "The NSF peer review process has been described to me as: I approve B's, B approves C's, and C approves mine. This is fine if you are in the small fraternity of four-year peers—but very difficult to break if you are not in the selected fraternity."[2] Some of the worst manipulations of the process apparently took place when the Individualized Science Instructional System (ISIS) was being considered for a grant. A staff summary of reviewers' comments was submitted to the National Science Board containing a quotation from the review of Dr. Philip Morrison, professor at Massachusetts Institute of Technology.

---

[2]Testimony before the House Science and Technology Subcommittee considering NSF 1976 budget authorization, February 21, 1975.

Representative of the overall tone of the reviewers' comments is this excerpt from Dr. Morrison's review:

> The general scheme proposed—the system foreseen—has natural and conspicuous appeal. The flexibility and freedom of use are clear. . . .

The clear implication was that Dr. Morrison and all of the other reviewers gave their unqualified support for the ISIS proposal, and the National Science Board subsequently approved a two-year budget of $2.2 million for ISIS. But when Dr. Morrison was recently contacted by a member of Congressman Conlan's staff to ask if he had made those statements, he expressed surprise that the ISIS curriculum had received funding at all, stating that he and other reviewers had been critical of the proposal's design and of its underlying ideas.

Because of these and other complaints about NSF-sponsored curricula, the Foundation is now paying $60,000 to 70 paid consultants for an assessment of its curriculum program. No assessment of these programs has previously been done, nor was a survey of market demand made before development was funded.

Other irregularities in NSF supervision of contracts and the use of Foundation money have been revealed by a recent GAO report, "Administration of the Science Education Project 'Man: A Course of Study' (MACOS)." The report shows that illegal financial arrangements were made between the developer of the course, Education Development Center, and the publisher, Curriculum Development Associates. The EDC and the CDA worked out an "internal" professional services contract the NSF has admitted it did not supervise. The contract stated that the EDC would use the royalty money received from the CDA to help it with its information and teacher training activities—effectively allowing the reinvestment of money that should have gone to the federal treasury, to be used to further the project without NSF approval. The GAO report further revealed that the EDC used more than half of what the CDA paid it for purposes not directly related to MACOS. This was a cozy relationship by any standards, and all financed by the taxpayer.

Another discovery made by the GAO is even more serious. The CDA told the National Endowment for the Humanities that between October 1972 and December 1974 it wanted to make a $205,000 "gift" to another EDC project, a social studies curriculum for grades 5 to 7, called "People and Technology." The National Endowment for the Humanities agreed to make a matching grant and by June 30, 1975, the EDC received a total of $350,000. What was wrong? The "gift" the CDA told the National Endowment about was money it was already obligated to pay to EDC under the professional services contract. The money for the "gift" all came out of royalties CDA was earning under its publishing arrangement with EDC. The National Endowment did not look at the services agreement between CDA and EDC.

The GAO report went on to recommend that the National Science Foundation "should be particularly vigilant in monitoring publishing arrangements where low royalty rates and other non-routine arrangements are permitted." The report also suggested that the National Endowment for the Humanities find out whether the $175,000 it contributed can be recovered.

Accountability

A special report prepared by the Ad Hoc Science Curriculum Implementation Review Group, a citizens committee appointed by Olin Teague, chairman of the House Science and Technology Committee, made several recommendations. The first was:

> Recognition that the NSF and the Congress cannot avoid responsibility for both quality and content of curricula that are federally funded through NSF.

Although the Committee concentrated its effort on the school curriculum, the need to make the Foundation answerable to taxpayers obviously extends into the other project and grant areas as well, as I have shown.

In many ways, however, the citizens' committee report did not go far enough. It did not object to the continuation of blatantly unfair implementation policies of NSF, nor to NSF's continued funding of course development even though the Foundation has obviously been pushing particular radical educational theories. In the words of Mrs. Joanne McAuley, a commission member who wrote separate minority views:

There is no need for Federal Government intervention in the development and marketing of textbooks and other course curriculum.

*   *   *

Incentives for commercial firms to undertake such efforts will never be great so long as Federal Government insists on nursing the 'career curriculum innovation' centers. And the Nation will continue to suffer from multi-million dollar 'innovations' such as the New Math, the New Social Studies (MACOS), and other equally questionable courses concocted in Government-funded academic 'think-tanks.'[8]

Needless to say, it is expected that the authorization hearings which will be held in early 1976 for continued support of the National Science Foundation will be controversial. Although school curricula implementation funding was cut out of this year's appropriations bill for NSF, it is certain that attempts will again be made to incorporate it.

Several more permanent legislative proposals have been made. Senator Jesse Helms has introduced S. 2160. Although it does not completely cut off funds to be used for course development, it does force NSF to review and justify each of the courses it develops before it proceeds with dissemination activities. This amendment can be seen as a model that should be adjusted and applied to other government agencies that encourage similar activities. Another proposal, introduced by both Conlan and Helms is much more comprehensive. This proposal will:

- Open the peer review system to supervision by the NSF Board and Congress
- Establish better administrative oversight within the Foundation
- Ensure that an analysis of need for all science research is conducted before it receives funding
- Ensure that peer reviews are accessible to those who submit proposals.

[8]The Report of the Science Curriculum Implementation Review Group, the GAO report and an internal review of its own procedures by NSF are available from the House Committee on Science and Technology in a single bound volume called "National Science Foundation Curriculum Development and Implementation for Pre-College Science Education."

In addition I will offer a modified "Bauman Amendment" to the authorization legislation in an effort to curb NSF excesses.

The 1976 NSF battle will be a lively one, and there is great hope that at least some major changes will have to be made by the NSF as a result of the combined impact of so many well-documented criticisms. But unfortunately what has been revealed about the NSF applies, at the moment, not exclusively to that agency. The basic problems are far more widespread in government. Such remedial legislation fits into the category of "sunshine in government" because it would make NSF more accountable to Congress and to the taxpayer. And, as such, the proposal can have broad implications for other agencies that use similar procedures to approve grants.

The important principle in all this discussion is the role of the traditional parliamentary power of the purse that legislative bodies in the past have guarded jealously. Along with the power to tax, the government must accept the obligation of proper and thorough congressional review of such programs. Too often Congress has tried to solve a problem or promote a program by the simple expedient of throwing great quantities of money—your money—at it, hoping for the best. In the case of NSF, and too many other agencies, the results have been not just poor, but actually detrimental to the best interests of the taxpayers who are compelled to pay the bill.

Some members of the House and Senate are trying to right this critical situation. To achieve our common goals we need your support and the support of all Americans who value their freedoms.

BIOGRAPHY
of
The Honorable Thomas M. Hagedorn
Minnesota

Thomas M. Hagedorn, a farmer from a farmer's state, was elected to the 94th Congress from the Second District of Minnesota.

Mr. Hagedorn was born in Blue Earth, Minnesota, on November 27, 1943, and graduated from Blue Earth High School in 1961. After service in the Navy, Tom Hagedorn began working a 160 acre grain and livestock farm in Martin where he, his wife, the former Kathleen Mittlestadt, and their three children live.

Mr. Hagedorn was a recipient of the 1972 Truman Jaycees' Distinguished Service Award and is active in many local organizations such as the Watonwan County Farm Bureau, the Truman Development Corporation, the Minnesota Crop Improvement Association, and the Truman and Minnesota Jaycees. He also received the 1975 "Man of the Year" award from the Minnesota Young Americans for Freedom.

Prior to his election to Congress, Cong. Hagedorn served two terms (1970-74) in the Minnesota State Legislature. He was also a delegate to the Republican state and county conventions in 1968 and 1972, and has worked for Republican Presidential candidates since 1964.

Cong. Hagedorn is a member of the House Agriculture Committee and the House Public Works and Transportation Committee.

AN ENVIRONMENT FOR PEOPLE
by
Congressman Thomas M. Hagedorn

In the late 1960s and early 1970s concern about the environment developed into major proportions that sometimes reached panic. This unusual public involvement provided a fertile climate for the adoption of hastily conceived and overly restrictive controls. Offered as the cure for environmental ills, these restrictive measures easily passed Congress. Because of their "emergency" status they were not as well considered as they should have been.

Attention on these environmental measures was restricted to the *physical* environment—air, water, and land. The premise was that "clean" air and water coupled with unscarred land would provide the ideal environment for humans. This approach called for prohibiting various forms of pollution altogether. The strategy was a crash program of stringent and intrusive laws and regulations. The consequences to the social and economic environment were not considered.

But reality is finally calling our attention to these impacts. Public enthusiasm for federal environmental controls is abating. Unless there is a reorientation of the environmental effort, the expected result will be further loss of public support. But apathy on the people's part would be inappropriate. A healthy environment demands stable government policies, not continuing reaction to crisis. This requires public understanding and support. Public support can be recruited *if* the public can be convinced that environmental control decisions directly and indirectly affect our food supplies, employment, and financial stability as well as health, safety, housing, recreation, and transportation.

As an example, pesticides, improperly used, could indeed harm animals and humans. Properly used they are indispensable to farmers seeking increased productivity, and to consumers seeking stable food prices. We have seen that authorities administering pesticide and fungicide regulations failed to balance agricultural and other concerns, with strictly environmental ones. Late in 1975 the Congress had an opportunity to return some stability to the pesticide controversy, but it failed to act positively. Congressman Richard Kelly (R-Florida) offered an amendment to the Federal Insecticide,

Fungicide, and Rodenticide Act (H.R. 8841) which required that before the administrator of the EPA could permanently cancel the use of any pesticide the Secretary of Agriculture would have to concur with that decision. This attempt to give the farmer a voice in this decision-making process was defeated by a vote of 164-233 (see vote 16 in Table I).

The public must learn that the environment to be controlled is the human environment. To do that, the environment has to be considered as an entity and in its totality.

The environmental issue must be reevaluated in terms of both ecology and economics. Both have the same Greek root, eco-, for family or household. Ecology is the science of the interrelationships of members of a household in supplying the needs of its members. Both must be appraised simultaneously. Our present troubles result in large measure because one has been allowed to control, often with no attention given to the other.

Ecological analysis must go beyond the simple demand for clean air, pure water, and an unscarred landscape. The hardcore environmentalists, if taken literally, would nearly eliminate population in order to eliminate "pollution." We must require clear definition of terms as well as factual determination of the quality of air, land and water necessary for protection of users. Failure to do so is an indictment of those who espouse ecology but in reality misuse it.

When enthusiasm and concern over saving the environment reaches fever pitch, ecology loses its full meaning; economic considerations are limited to the reporting of estimated construction costs for pollution control facilities. Ecology is construed erroneously to mean protection of nonhuman animal and plant life—in theory, protect them and man would be protected as a result. Human health was relegated to the protection of the nonhuman. For example, programs that established controls to protect some aquatic animals had an impact on people that was inadequately evaluated.

Similarly, economics has not been fully considered in terms of commitments of energy, funding, and resources that are for particular pollution control programs and that are thus unavailable for other environmental improvement needs, these needs could have been defined if the ecological analysis had been adequate. Priorities have not been assigned.

Many specific examples can be shown of instances where we have departed from sensible principles while attempting to regulate the environment. I would like to comment on some of the more important departures.

Cost Increases

Since its creation in 1969 the Environmental Protection Agency (EPA) has been a single-purpose agency by definition. It serves a very special clientele and looks almost solely to it for support. Its "missionary" role has attracted personnel who have internalized the values of the environmentalist community it serves. As the experience with pesticide controls demonstrates, EPA is not equipped to make trade-off decisions between environmental and other objectives. As a result many EPA decisions have been based on data that is not scientifically accurate or conclusive. To reach these decisions officials distort data to fit a previously desired conclusion of environmental extremists. This type of bureaucratic regulation has taken its economic toll on each of us.

The Environmental Protection Act of 1969 requires that federal agencies with licensing powers over public works file "environmental impact" statements concerning the effect of such proposals upon the earth, its atmosphere and waterways. The concept has spread to other provinces of government with findings of adverse "environmental impact" stalling projects that include nuclear power plants, improvement of electrical facilities, and construction of refineries. These controls have had drastic counterproductive results and have adversely affected our economy in numerous crucial areas.

When regulations are not based on sound scientific and economic data they frequently add greatly to the consumer cost of energy. Further, they contribute to the energy shortage. Just look for a moment at the rapid rise in utility rates. When a power company, harassed by incomprehensible environmental regulations, must battle a federal agency in order to construct a generating plant, somebody has to pay the bill. You guessed it; the consumer pays the bill.

Increased costs of environmental regulations to consumers are not confined to direct energy costs alone. They are reflected in higher costs for practically all goods and services. It has been estimated that when all such goods and services are taken into consideration, the average American family pays approximately $1,000 a year in higher prices. To right this situation we must begin to assess economic impact on equal basis with environmental impact.

Land Use Planning

A related and equally dangerous trend has been specifically hailed by its proponents as "a fundamental change in the American way of life." It is the Federal Land Use Planning legislation that constitutes an assault on traditional concepts of private property. In 1974 the legislation (H.R. 10294) was defeated in the full House of Representatives. In 1975 it was defeated in the House Interior Committee. Undaunted, Congressman Morris Udall (D-Arizona) once again introduced his bill (H.R. 8932) after this defeat.

Legislation of this type is more than a sparring match between environmental and development economics. It is a massive yet subtle assault on private property rights and the free enterprise system. By encouraging and possibly forcing states to expand their police powers of zoning, it opens the door to property confiscation without compensation.

The genesis of the land use legislation lies in part with a 1972 report from the Council on Environmental Quality, "The Quiet Revolution in Land Use Control." The report in part states: "This is the onset of a transformation in the concept of land to a national resource in which all citizens have rightful interest." The task force that developed the report recommended:

—The right to own property should not include the right to develop it.

—Tough restrictions should be placed on private land and the landowners should bear the restrictions without compensation by government.

—Growth should be regulated by government rather than by the market system.

—Courts should be encouraged in a new approach to the "taking clause" of the Fifth Amendment of the United States Constitution.

I know of no place on earth where comprehensive legislated planning has been successful. It is destructive to human rights and to the fabric of society. Yet we are asked to commit the entire land resources of this nation to government planners. As society grows more complex, government grows increasingly unable to make wise economic decisions.

Individuals may not necessarily make wiser decisions than government. But individual mistakes have consequences that are never so catastrophic as those made by government fiat. Private property rights have converted a hostile land into the freest, most productive nation in our history. I am convinced that government planning could not have improved upon that.

The question is not whether we should have land use planning. We already have it. We have it in the form of local zoning ordinances and we have it in the market system. The issue is whether these decisions should be transferred from owners of property to political proxies of the Secretary of Interior.

To lure states into cooperating voluntarily with the land use planning program, the Udall bill authorized financial aid of more than $500 million over six years for participating states. With the narcotic of federal money in the air, will any State be able to resist? And when the dust settles, how painful will be the lessons they have learned—that federal money means federal controls, and that today's federal suggestions and guidance are tomorrow's requirements and dictates.

Proponents of land use bills tell us that they are intended only to encourage the states to do their own planning and develop their own policies and procedures. Land use bills, they say, are designed to create conditions under which environmental, social, economic, and other requirements of present and future generations can be met. Surely these causes are difficult goals for politicians to quarrel with.

We have seen "voluntary participation" in price control lead to the legislated disasters of shortened supply and unemployment. Once these bills are passed the actual implementation will necessarily be determined by regulations, agencies, and the courts. "Voluntary" participation will be a dream of the past.

Land Use and Property Rights

The issue of property rights is central to a discussion of this legislative approach. As my colleague Congressman Sam Steiger (R, Arizona) stated in his minority views on the 1974 version of the Udall Land Use Bill:

H.R. 10294 (it) is keyed to the exercise of the police powers of the various States to implement the provisions of the State land-use planning process. Traditionally, diminution of use of private property occasioned by a State's exercise of its police powers for the general welfare—as in the case of zoning—has been treated by the courts as not giving rise to a right to compensation on

159

the part of the landowner. Although one use may be prohibited, the owner can utilize the land in another manner so as to attempt to justify his investment.

The land use bills currently under consideration carry two important, interlocked provisions. One is the definition of "areas of critical State concern." The other is the requirement that the State have authority to regulate (originally read: "to prohibit") the use of land in such areas, as well as in other areas if the proposed use is inconsistent with the land use plan. The wording of the bill makes it clear that the "areas of critical State concern" carries the connotation that no use might be allowed in such areas. Moreover, the definition of these critical areas is so open-ended that any type land area could arbitrarily be designated critical to suit someone's purpose.

Further, the proposal does not require the state that prohibits certain use of land to utilize its powers of eminent domain thereby compensating the owners. With powers granted by the bill it is conceivable that a state lacking adequate funds for compensation might proceed to implement these provisions of the bill. Partial or total denial of use for the land owner might be administered under the police powers of the state—the power of zoning. This tactic effectively circumvents the issue of compensation since zoning is not normally a compensable land use control mechanism. It places upon the property owner the burden of instituting an inverse condemnation proceeding in order to gain a judgment against the state—to prove that the state's action was an invalid exercise of its police powers and that just compensation is required.

Property rights and the value of property ownership consist mainly of the right to develop it. Without that provision property rights are meaningless. Thus Federal land use planning affects the traditional meaning of private property beyond abstract arguments over the use, nonuse, and misuse of land. The true ramifications of this measure go against the essence of our free enterprise system. Historically, the marketplace has dictated the best use of land. Federal land use planning would substitute noneconomic judgments in defining the uses of large amounts of land; thus would these provisions render the marketplace irrelevant. When the use of land is tightly restricted, its productivity is impaired. A federal land use bill will stimulate regulation of private property.

160

With the potential for litigation evident throughout this legislation and with the addition of two more layers of bureaucracy, delays will be inevitable. Real constraints would be placed upon growth, and environmental protection programs would be instituted at the expense of human needs.

Another critical environmental issue currently being considered by the Congress is the amendments to the Clean Air Act of 1970. This Act is just one more example of "good sounding" legislation that is resulting in overkill—a fact with which even the EPA must now find it difficult to disagree. This Act also marks one of the first attempts by the Congress to legislate scientific knowledge and technological innovation simply by establishing arbitrary (but firm) dates for required action.

While the Congressional establishment of these firm deadlines may have served to demonstrate the urgency of compliance to some extent, necessary response did not magically occur simply because a law had been passed. Many of the ill-conceived regulations, based on inadequate information, had to be promulgated hastily and without inadequate consideration to the best interests of the whole country. But these tightly mandated deadlines, backed up with liberal citizen-suit provisions, provided little or no flexibility. They have resulted in some of the most controversial and questionable concepts associated with the 1970 Act. These undefined concepts include significant deterioration, indirect source controls, air quality maintenance areas, and transportation controls. Many Members of Congress have now recognized that certain of these court-legislated measures are both publicly unsupportable and politically unpalatable, and it is to be hoped that the large-scale imposition of mandatory action on short deadlines will be minimized in the amendments that the Congress is now considering.

The nondegradation or *significant deterioration* issue is one of the most important and controversial issues to be decided by this Congress. I believe that everyone in labor and in the business community must understand the far-reaching impact of the implementation of a national policy of nondegradation.

Nondegradation began to form as a legislative issue when the Supreme Court in 1973 upheld on a tie vote a lower court decision. That decision interpreted Congressional intent as establishing a policy where the air quality in undeveloped areas of the country should not be allowed to be "degraded" even though that air may already be far cleaner than present national standards.

Early in 1975, EPA regulations designated as Class II all undeveloped areas of the country that already met health and welfare ambient air quality standards. In Class II areas development would be allowed until stated increments were reached. These very small increments approximate the emissions from a 150-megawatt power plant—one so small that none is ever built. In addition, a buffer zone of 60 to 100 miles would be created around all areas designated Class I areas (pristine undeveloped areas).

Under these regulations a state would, at its discretion, designate as Class I areas of aesthetic, scenic, or historic value; no development would be allowed. Other areas could be renamed by the state as Class III. Development could occur in Class III areas as long as secondary (welfare) standards are met.

The 94th Congress when it began its hearings on the Clean Air Act was expected either to 1) endorse the Ford Administration's proposal to clarify Congressional intent as *not* establishing a policy of significant deterioration or 2) to incorporate the present EPA regulations into the statute, since the regulations are under litigation from parties on both sides of the issue.

But it now appears that what Congress may come up with is a policy much tougher than even the EPA regulations. What may result is a policy of federal land use control on the basis of a single criterion—clean air. The 1970 Clean Air Act was aimed at protecting public health in developed, urban areas of the country; the present attempt to establish a tough nondegradation policy would expand the Act to protect "aesthetics" in rural, undeveloped areas. Combined with the 1975 EPA regulations against any new construction that will violate "applicable portions of the control strategy or will result in a violation of a national standard," this decision would leave developers and major industries almost no place to build in this country. This is a counterproductive policy at anytime; more clearly so when the construction industry is at its lowest level of activity since World War II. It is unconscionable when chronic unemployment persists year after year.

It is important to note that EPA's own studies show that readings in many rural and "pristine" areas already exceed allowable emission levels. Natural emissions are causing these

162

high readings. Allowable increments designed to allow for a minimum amount of industry development in these areas, is already accounted for by nature since the maximum range of these emissions vary from their natural average more than the allowable increment.

The result is that most of these areas will be shut off from development. Since most new major development will not be permitted in developed, "dirty air" areas, future development in all major industrial areas will be seriously crippled by EPA regulations.

Energy Controls

Again this year the Congress will be considering a comprehensive federal surface mining control bill. Fortunately, the House sustained President Ford's veto of this legislation in 1975 (see vote 17 in Table I), but the proponents are continuing to push for its eventual enactment.

Any bill that Congress considers will permanently affect our ability to produce coal in the United States. As with so many other pieces of legislation that Congress considers, the basic aim of the legislation sounds good.

In this case, the bill's sponsors tell us the aim is to protect the environment, and it's difficult to quarrel with that. Moreover, no one wants to see land permanently destroyed by mining.

On the other hand, it must be understood that future energy production will be seriously curtailed if outside constraints prevent environmentally sound production of coal. Yet this is just what will happen if the current surface mining legislation is passed. The Department of the Interior and the Federal Energy Administration estimated that the bill, H.R. 25 (sponsored by Reps. Udall and Mink) vetoed by President Ford would have reduced production by 62-162 million tons (8 to 22 percent) in the first full year of its application. These estimates did not include delays from litigation or stringent interpretation of ambiguous provisions of the bill. In addition, the Administration estimated that the bill had the *potential to prevent* mining up to 72 billion tons of coal that represents up to 53 percent of the total 137 billion tons of coal in the nation's demonstrated reserve base that are potentially mineable by surface methods. It goes without saying that this will contribute to our undesirable dependency on foreign sources of oil for our energy production requirements.

Federal regulation of surface mining is based on the premise that the states are incapable of controlling effectively the environmental problems associated with surface mining of coal. A few years ago that premise probably would have been correct, but it is now of doubtful validity.

Thirty-two states now have laws dealing with regulation of surface mining operations and reclamation of the land. Many of these state laws have been on the books for many years, but twenty-five of the existing laws have been enacted or updated since 1970.

Each of these state laws deals with the problems particular to that state, varying according to climatic, geologic, geographic, and chemical and other conditions peculiar to that state. These state laws can and do work.

One of the problems Congress always forces in attempting to enact national legislation is assuring that the legislation is broad enough to take state differences into account yet specific enough to solve the problem at hand. This nation is so diverse in its climate, its geography, its geology, and in its chemical and physical properties that it is exceedingly difficult to enact one law for all states.

The current bill does not adequately take this diversity into account. Rather, it attempts to enact a uniform standard to cover any and all of the states. Then it tells the states they must meet these standards or face a federal takeover. It is doubtful that a single federal standard would appropriately cover all of the federal lands in the United States that contain coal deposits, much less all the state lands.

The states that have enacted surface mining laws have done so in recognition of the fact that surface mining activities must be controlled, and in recognition of the particular and peculiar circumstances present in each state. I doubt very seriously that a single federal law can adequately recognize these particular and peculiar circumstances with the same degree of precision that the state laws do. A *federal* surface mining bill, along with its federal mandates, is not needed.

Until the Congress begins to view the quality of life in the specifics of human needs, and to view these needs in terms of the total environment, proposals for enhancing the environment cannot be adequately appraised. De-emotionalizing the issues and developing an adequate data base is essential. The Congress must begin providing the forum for exploring ways to accelerate that understanding.

BIOGRAPHY
of
The Honorable Trent Lott
Mississippi

Trent Lott is a second term Congressman from the Fifth District of Mississippi.

Born on October 9, 1941, in Grenada, Mississippi, Trent Lott went to elementary schools in Grenada and Duck Hill before attending and graduating from Pascagoula High school in 1959. He earned a Bachelor's Degree in public administration in 1963 and a Juris Doctor Degree in 1967 from the University of Mississippi.

Mr. Lott practiced with the Pascagoula firm of Bryan and Gordon (1967-8) and then came to Washington as the Administrative Assistant to Rep. William M. Colmer from 1968 to 1972. In 1972, Mr. Lott succeeded Rep. Colmer. He served on the Merchant Marine and Fisheries Committee and the Judiciary Committee during his first term. He was re-elected by 73 percent of the vote to a second term in 1974. He now serves on the critically important House Rules Committee and the Post Office and Civil Service Committee.

Mr. Lott is a member of the American Bar and of the Mississippi and Jackson County Bar Associations. He belongs to the National Forest Reservation Commission and has been presented with the Watchdog of the Treasury Award. Mr. Lott is a Mason; Scottish Rite.

Trent Lott and his wife, the former Patricia E. Thompson, have two children.

PROTECT CITIZENS: PUNISH CRIMINALS
by
Congressman Trent Lott

The United States is one of the most crime-ridden countries in the world. We are all too familiar with the statistics: For the year 1974 the FBI states that there were over 10 million reported crimes, or almost 5,000 per 100,000 inhabitants. In 1974 there was a murder every 26 minutes, forcible rape every 10 minutes, a robbery every 71 seconds, burglary every 10 seconds, and assault with intent to kill every 70 seconds. The figures are appalling; they highlight the constricting effect the crime picture has on the quality and character of our national life. Shocking as these figures are, we should remember that they reflect only a *portion* of actual crime committed. Attorney General Levi estimates that fully one-third of all violent crimes go unreported.

Urban areas bear a large portion of this burden but the suburban areas also have come to suffer from a rapidly increasing rate of crime. And although crime is lowest in the rural areas, even there crime is on the increase. For all areas as a whole, violent crimes have increased 11 percent from 1973 to 1974, and crimes against property increased by 17 percent. From 1960 to 1974 murder has increased about 125 percent, assault with intent to kill approximately 200 percent, forcible rape roughly 224 percent, and robbery over 300 percent. These figures are based on reported crime only.

Available figures indicate that much of the increase can be attributed to juvenile crime. According to the Uniform Crime Reports of the FBI, juvenile arrests in the city for 1974 rose 9 percent over those for 1973 compared to a rise of less than 1 percent in the arrest of adults. In the suburban areas the arrests of juveniles increased more than 10 percent over 1973 compared to a 3.3 percent increase in the arrest of adults for the same period. Only in the rural areas does the picture change. Arrests of juveniles increased by 4.3 percent while the arrest of those over 18 increased by 4.7 percent.

Last year 45 percent of all serious crimes committed in the United States were committed by persons under 18. This includes such crimes as robbery, murder, assault with intent to kill, and burglary—it does *not* include such juvenile-related offenses as pot smoking, vandalism, and the like. Fifteen appears to be the peak age for commission of violent crimes by juveniles. Of those arrested for serious crime (excluding murder), 45 percent are under the age of 18 and a full 75 percent are under 25.

Crime May Not Pay, But It Costs!

It is clear that the ever-increasing rate of crime adversely affects our society in a variety of ways, and one of the most accessible measures is economic. The total crime expense works out to over $400 for each adult and child in the United States. The "hidden tax" paid by consumers for the $5.6 billion of merchandise shoplifted each year, according to the Department of Commerce, amounts to about $100 per family. Estimates regarding the overall cost of crime have ranged from about $75 billion to close to $90 billion. According to one report, the cost of crime has risen 73.4 percent in the four years from 1970 to 1974.

Other costs of crime can be measured in dollars and cents: The costs to the taxpayer of the federal, state, and local police; the penal system; and the court system. A study conducted by the Law Enforcement Assistance Administration several years ago noted that the combined cost of the criminal justice system was approximately $15 billion.

Organized crime and business and property losses account for two-thirds of the entire national crime bill. Illegal gambling takes at least $37 billion out of the American pocket. Crimes against business and property account for losses of over $21 billion, up from $13 billion in 1970. Although the tragedy of homicide can never be measured in terms of human suffering and grief, it has been estimated that homicides and assaults account for about $3 billion of the total crime bill. Drunken driving accounts for about $6.5 billion, including lost wages, property damage, and medical costs.

Another cost of crime is the amount businesses and private individuals spend for security provisions they feel law enforcement cannot provide. Such costs were about $6.6 billion in 1974, compared to $5.5 billion in 1970.

For drug-related crime a conservative estimate for annual property loss is $6.3 billion. Add to that about $620 million for the cost to the criminal justice system for perpetrators of drug-related crime who are caught. Additional social costs in terms of unproductive lives can never be measured.

It appears that in many cases crime *does* pay, and this fact is indicative of the abject failure of our present system of crime control. An effective system of criminal justice must emphasize deterrence. How effective are the controls? Let's look at the statistics. For every 100 serious crimes just over 20 result in arrests, and only 5 lead to convictions. It is safe to say that even fewer result in actual prison sentences.

Recidivism is another disturbing aspect of the crime picture. According to the Uniform Crime Reports about 70 percent of all those who have been through the criminal justice system return to prison. Additionally, it has been stated that there are fewer persons in state and federal prisons today than there were 15 years ago.

The causes for the failure of our system of crime control are many, and few would agree on all of them. We can point to lack of recognition of authority and the trend toward "permissiveness" in our culture. We can see that the excess workload for our police, prosecution, and court systems makes it virtually impossible to respond swiftly to provide the immediate and sure impact that would provide the desired deterrent effect.

What can be done to improve this depressing picture? I believe that the situation must be approached from many different but cohesive angles. Certainly the police and the courts cannot be expected to resolve all of our society's failings.

First, we must recognize that the major function of prison is punishment and separation from the rest of society. Well-meaning individuals have urged that prison should be primarily a place of rehabilitation and reeducation to prepare the prisoner to take a useful place in society, but this well-intentioned approach is not based upon reality. Reformers say it does no good to place an offender behind bars for a number of months or years but they err, for while the criminal is out of circulation he is not robbing, stealing, raping, or killing. We should continue to attempt to rehabilitate the 10 or 20 percent or so who, according to an article by James J. Kilpatrick which appeared in the April 1975 issue of *Business Week* magazine, may in fact be amenable to change. However we should cease to think chiefly in terms of correction and instead view imprisonment as it should be intended: for punishment of offenders and protection of the rest of society.

Second, greater use should be made of consecutive sentences and far less of concurrent sentences. With concurrent sentences, a criminal may just as well rob ten establishments instead of one, or steal from twenty homes instead of five, for his sentences will run all at the same time instead of consecutively. This is not to advocate that judges should be permitted no discretion in this area, but I believe the current practices must be reevaluated.

A third aspect that should be reevaluated is plea bargaining. This aspect of our criminal justice system may be efficient in terms of time and expense saved, but it seriously weakens the effect of crime control. Plea bargaining is the process whereby a defendant is permitted to plead guilty to a lesser offense than he is charged with. The advantage of this to our overworked court system is that it obviates the need for trial. But plea bargaining often permits the defendant to avoid the consequences of conviction of the more serious offense. In addition, it has an adverse effect on the public's attitude toward the courts, as it does not even give the appearance of justice to the average citizen.

A fourth factor concerns juvenile crime. One step that should be taken is the review of the Youth Correction Act. A defendant aged 22 or under may elect to be sentenced under this Act which provides for an indeterminate sentence not to exceed a specific number of years. The sophistication of many of today's juvenile criminals has led a number of jurisdictions to consider lowering the age of adults for prosecution purposes from 18 to 16 years. I believe that change or elimination of the Youth Correction Act, together with a reduction in the age at which juveniles are treated as adults for prosecution purposes to 16, would provide a partial answer to the problem of juvenile crime.

Mandatory sentences are another effective and firm approach in dealing with those convicted of the more serious crimes. Mandatory sentences have been subject to attack in some quarters because they leave the judge with no discretion. I believe, however, that a sentence that is mandatory with no allowance for suspension, probation, or parole will greatly assist in providing a sure deterrent to criminals who otherwise may receive a light or suspended sentence for serious crimes. Mandatory sentencing is particularly appropriate in cases where the defendant is a repeat offender.

In addition, provisions that call for an additional amount of time in prison in instances where a firearm was used in the commission of a crime should be made mandatory as well. Where such laws are on the books today, they appear to be relatively little used. To make the additional sentence mandatory would assure that it would be imposed in each instance where a firearm was used in the commission of a crime. Its effect as a deterrent would be enhanced. Imposition of such sentence would be certain, and not sporadically imposed. The mandatory provision ought to apply whether or not the firearm used is loaded or even in working order. It should apply in every instance where a toy weapon or broken one is used that appears to the victim to be a firearm. The threatening effect on the victim is the same.

Two bills have been introduced in the House which provide for mandatory penalties when a firearm has been used in the commission of a crime. H. R. 524, proposed by Congresswoman Holt of Maryland, provides a 5- to 10-year prison sentence and for second offenders 10 years to life. Similar legislation, H. R. 6056, has been offered by Congressman Beard of Tennessee.

An aspect of the effects of crime that has been largely overlooked is the harm and disruption caused the victims and their families, not only monetarily but also in many instances emotionally. The disruption and the emotional harm to innocent victims and their families can never be adequately rectified, but I believe that our society should give much greater attention than it has so far to the issue of restitution to the victim. In some states today the innocent victim is permitted to apply for recovery of expenses such as medical expenses and other losses, not to exceed a certain amount.

I believe this program ought to be expanded. In addition, the concept should be broadened to make the perpetrator share this responsibility with the state. The responsibility of the criminal is direct: That of the state is indirect for failing to protect the innocent victim from the criminal. One approach might be to require the criminal to pay the victim or the victim's estate 50 percent of the amount the criminal can earn while in prison or while participating in a "work-release" program.

Swift and Sure Punishment

Quite frankly, while our society has suffered from an increase in all types of crime, it has exacted an ever-diminishing price from those who commit crime. Not only those who are direct victims of crime suffer from the results of this spiral; society as a whole suffers, too. It is a natural result of our many years of permissiveness in dealing with criminals at ev-

171

ery step of the criminal justice system. Increased attention to the rights of the criminal, coupled with an apparent neglect of the rights of the innocent citizen, are indicative of this unfortunate trend.

As an example, figures published as late as September 1974 show that the conviction rate for burglary is less than half the rate of 15 years ago. For auto theft, the conviction rate is less than one-third of the 1960 rate. It has been estimated that an adult burglar risks about 24 chances in 10,000 of being imprisoned for any offense. A juvenile can expect imprisonment at a rate as little as half that.

Some economists have begun to advance the theory that because the overall chance of apprehension, conviction, and imprisonment are so appallingly low many criminals have determined that crime *does* pay. They maintain that most criminals are not confused, irrational persons victimized by an unjust society, but rather decision-makers who arrive at their choice of crime by weighing the risks and alternatives. It follows that toughening up on crime after so many years of permissiveness will have a salutary effect. I believe that such a reversal in attitude is long overdue.

At least two measures that have been introduced in the House do toughen up on crime. Congressman Steiger of Arizona has proposed in H. R. 5628 an alternative to the exclusionary rule in federal criminal proceedings. The exclusionary rule provides that evidence obtained in violation of the Fourth Amendment cannot be included in a criminal trial. H. R. 5628 would repeal this rule and at the same time would make the United States liable for any damages caused by violation of the Fourth Amendment.

Another measure that cracks down on crime is a provision of H. R. 6056, a bill introduced by Congressman Robin Beard of Tennessee. This bill would increase certain penalties for gun control offenses and allows the United States to obtain appellate review of suspended or probationary sentences given in the case of a first offender who uses a firearm. (See proposal I in Table II.)

Stricter measures such as those mentioned here may involve additional expense to the taxpayer. The costs of crime prevention, however, have advantages to society that far outweigh the cost of crime itself, both in monetary terms and in an enhanced quality of life. It is fair to say that swift and sure punishment may alter the picture of risks and alternatives not viewed by the criminal and the potential criminal.

Some of the tougher methods require new legislation; some simply require redirection of resources and new attitudes by those involved in making the decisions regarding our criminal justice system. In many cases pressure by the public on its officials and representatives could have a salutary effect in changing entrenched attitudes. Unless a conscious and concerted effort is made by the average law-abiding citizen to change the existing entrenched attitudes regarding crime and the criminal, I fear that the majority of legislators, criminologists, and all those involved in our criminal justice system will continue to reinforce the attitude that criminals, and not their innocent victims, are the real "victims" of society.

Rights Of The Criminal

Provisions of the Parole Reorganization Act of 1975 will serve as a closing example typifying the current attitude that the rights of the criminal must be expanded. This Act has been passed by both houses and is now waiting for conference between the House and Senate. One of the provisions included in the Act would shift the burden of acceptability for parole from the convicted inmate to the Parole Commission. This is a dangerous shift; it has the effect of fostering the impression that parole is a right rather than a privilege. Many citizens believe that our criminal justice system is far too lenient on the convicted criminal and that too many are released prematurely—to the detriment of the rest of society. Legislation of this type cannot but encourage further lawlessness, something our society cannot tolerate without further straining the precepts of our founding fathers that ours is a government of laws, and not men. (See vote 18 in Table I.)

Of course, this particular aspect of the Parole Reorganization Act must be defeated, as must similar laws reflecting the same attitude already on the books. I agree with my colleague, Congressman L. A. (Skip) Bafalis of Florida, when he states that it is high time for us all to change our attitudes toward criminals. Our permissiveness has gone too far. Our subscription to the theory of collective guilt rather than individual guilt and responsibility has caused untold damage to the fabric of our society. I close this article by quoting from Congressman Bafalis' comments on the Criminal Justice Reform Act:

"The only difference between life in a jungle and life in a

civilized society is that civilization has rules to protect everyone. Those who break the rules must be punished, swiftly and surely. Otherwise, the rules stand for naught.

There are those among us who interpret any sign of weakness in the enforcement of the law as an invitation to break the law. All that keeps them from returning to the law of the jungle is the knowledge that punishment may be in the offing.

Take away the certainty of punishment—as the liberals on the courts and in the Congress have done—and we move closer to a return to the old concept of 'survival of the fittest.' "

BIOGRAPHY
of
The Honorable Steven D. Symms
Idaho

Steve Symms describes his political affiliation as "Individualist Republican", and the emphasis, one may surmise, falls on "Individualist."

Mr. Symms represents the First District of Idaho, and was first elected to Congress in 1972. Despite his short incumbency, Mr. Symms has already gained the respect and admiration of his colleagues, as well as a strong national following, for his spirited defense of the individual and his freedom against the collectivism and the coercion of big government. A man of principle, he understands what makes freedom work, and defends freedom and free enterprise on principle. He brings an excellent understanding of economics to the Congress, a sparkling sense of humor and a grasp of the meaning of personal freedom unexcelled on Capitol Hill.

Steve Symms was born on April 23, 1938, in Nampa, Idaho, and attended public schools in Canyon County. After graduating from the University of Idaho in 1960 with a degree in agriculture and economics, he served with the U.S. Marine Corps for three years. From his nearly ten years as production manager for the Symms Fruit Ranch, he gained an appreciation for the free enterprise system and a desire to help in preserving a healthy environment for it. This background contributed to his selection by the House Republican Leadership to serve on two major legislative committees: the Committee on Agriculture and the Committee on Interior and Insular Affairs.

FEDERAL REGIMENTATION OF SCHOOLS
by
Congressman Steven D. Symms

Americans have always accepted the assumption that the way to a better world lies through education. Since John Dewey and the progressives, schools have been regarded as the best place to attempt a cure for the ills that plague society. Schooling not only makes individuals happier, smarter, and eventually wealthier, but in the process can change society by forming better citizens. With so many hopes lodged in education, it was almost inevitable that the federal government would undertake and continue funding education, despite the fears of many that local control would be lost. And it is funding it in a big way. The most recent appropriation came to $7.9 billion.

But recently many members of Congress who are still supporting ever increasing allocations for education seem to be out of step with a very noticeable change of attitude toward schooling. The public has lost faith in the system as it is now being run. More and more school bond issues are being rejected nationwide where they were never rejected before. As *The New York Times* writer Edward Hoffman puts it, "we are witnessing today the beginning of a long-predicted collapse of the schooling balloon." The public, he points out, has begun to realize that education is not a panacea for the world's ills. In fact, on the practical level, a college education no longer even guarantees the graduate a job.

Here in Washington, a survey of public attitudes toward schools was recently conducted by the Bureau of Social Science Research. There were three categories: very good and good; fair and poor; and undecided. In 1973 28 percent of those surveyed thought schools in the District of Columbia were very good or good; in 1975 only 18 percent thought so. In 1973 57 percent thought the schools were fair or poor and in 1975 the figure had gone up to 65 percent. For the entire metropolitan area 53 percent thought the schools were very good or good in 1973. In 1975 only 43 percent thought so. Those who dislike the public schools in the area rose from 29 percent in 1973 to 34 percent in 1975. Similar changes were also evident for surrounding areas in Maryland and Virginia.*

This disaffection with public education exists not only in the District of Columbia, but nationwide. In many areas, groups of activist parents working outside of the more established channels are descending on their local legislators and school boards. They are demanding changes in curricula, teaching methods, disciplinary action, and other formerly sacrosanct areas of administrator/teacher concern. Responding to the requests of several such concerned parent groups in Maryland, the Hon. J. Hugh Nichols has introduced a resolution in the House of Delegates allowing greater parental participation in the textbook selection process. Late in 1975 activist groups from around the country met in Dallas, Texas, to form a new national coalition, the National Congress for Educational Excellence. The primary goals of the group are "to support parental and family rights; to insure local autonomy of public schools; and to emphasize the teaching of traditional basic skills."

The cause of these parents' concern is their discovery that the schools are no longer teaching children the fundamental skills needed to function in society even on the most rudimentary level. A four-year study recently conducted by the University of Texas at Austin and supported by more than $1 million from the U.S. Office of Education showed that about one-fifth of the nation's adult population is "functionally incompetent," lacking the basic educational skills needed to get along as workers, citizens, and parents. Approximately 23 million persons, according to the study, are unable to make change from a $20 bill or fill out a personal bank check. The same number did not know that every state in the union has two senators in the U.S. Congress.

Black psychologist Kenneth Clark recently accused the Washington, D.C., schools of becoming "instruments for producing illiterates," and although it is easy to dismiss his statement as applying only to the schools in one city, studies conducted nationwide show a constant decline in academic achievement.

With some exceptions such as my home state of Idaho, test scores on the College Entrance Examination Board's Scholastic Aptitude Test have fallen steadily for the last thirteen

---

* All Washington, D.C. school statistics are from articles in *The Washington Post* and *The Washington Star*.

years. In 1962-63 the average verbal score was 478. The average for 1974-75 was 434. The average math score has similarly fallen from 502 in 1962-63 to 472 in 1974-75. Between 1974 and 1975, the number of students scoring between 700 and 800 decreased by 20 percent. In the fall of 1975 the Board released a report showing that the average SAT scores among 1975 high school graduates had declined ten points on the verbal part and eight points on the math, the largest drop in any single year since the decline first began in 1962. The board has further announced that it has set up an advisory panel to study the recent decline in the scores and the reason for this decline. Sidney Marland, president of the board, stated that "research efforts to date convince us there is nothing basically wrong with the test."

Achievement scores have similarly been declining in the primary and secondary grades. In Iowa a study of math skills was conducted in 1973 for grades six and eight. A test which had been given in 1936, 1951-55, and 1965 was given to students in 1973. The results were discouraging. The 1973 students scored lower than all students from all previous periods.

These results are not surprising when recent curricular innovations designed to make learning "relevant" at the expense of real content are considered. In Michigan, it has been suggested that slum children be given credit in school for "street skills." Many mathematics teachers have been allowing the use of hand calculators in class, not only for checking basic problems, but also for finding the solutions. The National Council of Teachers of Mathematics and the National Association of Secondary School Principals are on record as encouraging the use of calculators to make math learning "more thorough and more fun." To most people it would be fairly obvious that such devices undercut the child's ability to make basic calculations on his own. But to the Office of Education the effects of their use are worthy of a $35,000 federally-funded experiment under Title III of the Elementary and Secondary Education Act (ESEA) to learn whether children can add, subtract, multiply, and divide better with or without the machines.

Both directly and indirectly the federal government has been giving its support to curricular change and to making those changes acceptable to a justifiably skeptical public. The recent controversy over "Man: A Course of Study" and "Exploring Human Nature" brought to public attention the fact that some government agencies use taxpayers' money to develop and widely disseminate materials which, although supposedly based on highly reputable educational theories, are repugnant to most parents and children alike. Several doctors have testified that they believe these two courses to be psychologically harmful to children who take them. Besides assisting the dissemination of actual curricular materials, government funds also support the circulation of allegedly innovative ideas among educators. In 1969 the Hawaii Master Plan for Public Education was developed with ESEA Title V funds; it was intended to identify broad-scale changes that should occur in the system and to set forth the appropriate steps to bring about such changes. Among other things the plan advocated was the use of drugs to enhance learning. These drugs are highly experimental and in some cases dangerous to children. The plan recommended methods for educators to overcome parental opposition to their use in public schools.

The above two cases may appear somewhat extreme at first, but they represent typical programs that receive federal funding. As many current laws are written they set up programs to encourage innovative ideas in education, such as behavior modification and value clarification projects, even at a time when clearly there has been too much innovation and not enough evaluation of methods. As a recent study published by the Hudson Institute points out:

> Even the federal government's education specialists may not be aware of the extent of the problem, primarily because they apparently do not collect achievement data. Billions of federal dollars, much for primary and secondary education, are dispensed without requiring any evidence of the resulting output.

Clearly, although it is not now doing so, the National Institute of Education (NIE) or some similar education research institute should be collecting achievement data on a state-by-state basis from schools receiving federal funds. Such data would make it easier to identify programs that are not working and eliminate them, and to improve those that are working.

Furthermore, the recently proposed Conlan amendment to H.R. 4723, forcing the National Science Foundation to submit to Congress summary reviews and justifications for courses it would like to disseminate before any funds are given for that purpose, should be made a prototype for all government agencies that currently fund curriculum activities. (See vote 19 in Table I.)

Ideally, we should put an end to all federal funding for both development and implementation of such courses. Such funding creates tax-subsidized competition with private publishers and jeopardizes local control of schools. But since it is almost impossible to reverse the already existing federal involvement in education, the effort to make agencies submit such summaries would at least slow down reckless experimentation and make for greater accountability to the taxpayer.

Nevertheless, the initiative for changing public education belongs on the local level, and it is there that the movement for "basic alternative" schools has been gaining momentum. The Council for Basic Education in Washington, D.C., reports that there are at least a dozen such schools in existence nationwide, and many more proposed. A basic alternative school is one that is set aside within a school district for the specific purpose of teaching the basics through traditional discipline procedures, curricula, and teaching methods. The initiative for the establishment of these schools has come from local school boards and groups of parents. Many of the schools have long waiting lists for the limited places available.

Besides the weakening of curricula and the resulting decline in achievement scores, a further reason for public disillusionment is that costs to support schooling at all levels are rising at a phenomenal rate. It has been a common assumption until recently that increased spending to modernize school facilities and to develop new teacher-training methods and new curricula would result in better education. Because of this assumption and also because of increased teacher-union pressure for higher wages, smaller classes, and shorter days, spending on public education has increased nearly tenfold since 1950 while student enrollment has not even doubled (28.6 million to 49.7 million). Expenditures by local, state, and federal agencies rose from $6.7 billion in 1950 to about $61.6 billion in 1974. As a percentage of the gross national product, costs rose from 3.4 percent in 1950 to over 7.4 percent in 1974. On a per-pupil basis, Market Data Retrieval reports that the average cost of educating a student in the nation's schools rose from $553.95 during 1967-68 to $1,168.22 during the 1974-75 school year.

The federal share of these expenses has increased dramatically since 1958, when the National Defense Education Act was passed, and with it has come increased federal control of education down to the local level. In 1958 the federal government spent approximately $900 million on all education programs. By 1965 it was spending about $3.4 billion, including allotments for ESEA. Total federal outlays for education in 1975 amounted to $15.6 billion. For fiscal year 1976 Congress is heading toward record education spending, over the objections of the Ford Administration.

Beyond the fact that the Congress is spending huge amounts of money for education at a time when the economy can ill afford the strain, many of the major programs that are being funded have not been evaluated, and in some cases where the negative results are in, the Congress has continued funding the same questionable projects. For fiscal year 1976 ESEA Title I has been allocated $150 million more than last year's $1.9 billion. Title I allows funds to be distributed to almost every school district in the country for compensatory education programs for the disadvantaged. The Title I allocation accounts for the largest single block of funds in the above 1976 appropriations bill.

Although providing compensatory education can be viewed as a laudable goal, no convincing proof of the program's effectiveness has been forthcoming since it was first begun eight years ago. In fact, there is considerable evidence to the *contrary*. A 1970 survey found that 65 to 95 percent of the students participating in noninstructional Title I programs were judged by their teachers to have no critical need for the health, food, counseling, and other services being provided. Another study found that six times as many students were participating in health programs as needed assistance and that nearly two-thirds of those participating in cultural enrichment programs were similarly without need. As it now operates, program funds are so widely distributed as to provide less than one hour per week of remedial instruction for each participating student. Furthermore, a March 1972 study by American Institutes for Research concluded that:

Participants [in federal educational programs] gained less during the period of instruction than nonparticipants and consequently fell further behind their nonparticipating peers and national norms.

The study showed that participants in special reading programs for disadvantaged pupils under Title I actually lost ground in reading skills while nonparticipants gained.*

Another part of Title I funds goes toward buying school equipment to improve the general school environment. In 1971 HEW investigators stated that considerable amounts of equipment had been purchased through Title I with "no evidence" that it contributed to meeting the needs of Title I children. As educator Christopher Jencks has pointed out, "giving children better schools is not going to eliminate inequality in cognitive skills. . . ." The Coleman Report similarly showed that variations in school resources have far less to do with achievement disparities than social class and family influences do.

Despite this evidence, there has been a continuing push both on the state and on the federal level for school finance equalization. Much of the justification for this movement is based on the 1971 California Supreme Court decision *Serrano v. Priest,* in which it was decided that the state's finance system, based on local property taxes, discriminated against children living in poorer districts. Not only did the decision set a dangerous precedent toward centralizing control of public schools, but it denied that scores could be used to measure the quality of education being received. Quality education in California must be determined by "input," including funding for school facilities, not by "output," meaning achievement scores.

The Serrano decision was followed by similar rulings in Texas, Minnesota, and New Jersey. In 1972 and 1973 amendments were introduced in seven different states to eliminate reliance on local property taxes for school funding. The proposals differed significantly from state to state, but everywhere there was one common element. Because the proposals invariably required greater state assumption of costs and control of the redistribution of funds, they were uniformly opposed and eventually defeated primarily on the grounds of the loss of local control of education. It is interesting to note that even John E. McDermott, chief attorney for the plaintiffs in *Serrano v. Priest,* admits that the power of the purse is the power to control virtually all aspects of education.

Control over the method of raising and spending revenues—the power of the purse, as it were—is often con-

* See the *Congressional Record,* October 3, 1973, p. H 8530.

gruent with control over the program, and is frequently utilized to promote educational policy objectives. Federal categorical aid programs to local school districts are a conspicuous example.

On the federal level, many proposals to increase direct federal funding of all public education and to encourage states to increase their financial control over local education have been made since 1972. The most recent proposal has been made by Congressman Carl Perkins (D-Kentucky) in H.R. 10145. The bill would provide one-third federal funding of public schools and would cost an estimated $14.5 billion.

Between proposals such as the above and the increasing number of court decisions relating to finance, discipline, and desegregation, it is clear that there are heavy clouds on the horizon for local control of public schools. Nor are conservatives the first to perceive this to be the case. William Hazard, writing for *Phi Delta Kappan,* said recently:

Myths die hard in education. But the myth of local control is in a terminal state, because the courts, along with state and federal governments, have taken over.

Many of the changes that are now eroding local control came as a result of well-meaning but misguided attempts to eliminate discrimination which have set into motion a whole sequence of ominous precedents. The Department of Health, Education and Welfare recently informed 29 colleges that their funds would be cut off because of unacceptable hiring and promotion policies unless they agreed to sign a model affirmative action plan. HEW has taken this stand even though no conclusive evidence is available to show whether there are enough *qualified* minority professors to achieve quotas. Furthermore, because these regulations will increase fiscal pressures on colleges it becomes more likely that the federal government will have to provide more and more aid, thereby increasing government control over all institutions of higher education that accept funding.

An even broader threat is now being posed against private schools by the Internal Revenue Service. In February 1975 it published a proposed set of regulations forcing schools to comply with expensive quota-fulfillment procedures or lose their tax exemption. The proposal would make private schools undertake large-scale advertising campaigns to draw in minority students, as well as comply with a host of other guidelines, even down to recordkeeping.

Worse by far than either of these attacks on freedom is the continuation of forced busing, despite the facts that most Americans are opposed to it and it has not accomplished its objectives. A Gallup opinion poll conducted in May 1975 showed that among whites, 15 percent favor busing and 75 percent oppose it. Among nonwhites, 40 percent favor busing while 47 percent are against it. Besides the overwhelming popular sentiment against busing, study after study has shown that even voluntary busing programs *fail* to improve minority achievement and *don't help* improve cross-racial understanding. In fact, the study which the courts used as their primary justification for compulsory busing, the Coleman Report, has been renounced by its author. Recently a change of sentiment became obvious in the Senate when some formerly pro-busing northern senators, led by Senator Joseph Biden (D, Delaware), completely reversed themselves on the issue. As Senator James Allen (D. Alabama) recently pointed out, "Senators can vote against forced busing and not lose their civil rights credentials." The issue is no longer civil rights, but the necessary elimination of what Senator Biden calls "a bankrupt concept." With the Brown decision the judiciary made an aggressive foray into the area of public policymaking, a movement that will be very difficult to reverse and that has severely weakened local control of public schools.

Unfortunately, as recently as November 19, 1975, the House Democratic Caucus, the policymaking body of the Democratic members of the House of Representatives, did not seem to understand the major opposition to forced busing found throughout the country. By a vote of 172-96, the Caucus turned aside an attempt to urge the House Judiciary Committee to report out a Constitutional amendment aimed at prohibiting forced busing. (See vote 20 in Table I.)

Several weeks after the vote of the Democratic Caucus, on December 4, 1975, the House voted on a motion by Congressman Robert Bauman (R, Maryland) urging concurrence with Senator Byrd's amendment to the Labor-HEW appropriation bill H.R. 8069. That amendment prohibited funds appropriated in H.R. 8069 to be used for forced busing. This time the vote was more reflective of the sentiments of the American people at large, for the motion carried by a vote of 260-146. (See vote 21 in Table I.)

Unlike the Democrats, the Republican Party has responded to the wishes of the majority of the American people on this issue. It went on Record as early as 1972 as "irrevocably opposed to busing for racial balance." In its platform, the Republican Party stated:

> Such busing fails its stated objective—improved learning opportunities—while it achieves results no one wants—division within communities and hostility between classes and races. We regard it as unnecessary, counter-productive and wrong. . . . We favor the neighborhood school concept. . . . If it is necessary . . . we would favor consideration of an appropriate amendment to the Constitution.

By contrast to the action of the House Democratic Caucus, its Republican counterpart, the Republican Policy Committee, called on the House Judiciary Committee to hold prompt hearings on measures to curb federally-forced busing and to report such a measure to the Floor for action. Unfortunately, Republican efforts to stop forced busing have not been successful in the Democratic-controlled Congress. Outnumbered two to one by the Democrats, the Republicans simply do not have the numbers to bring this issue to the Floor of the House. It will require the concurrence and support of the Democratic majority and leadership.

At this point the only real cure for compulsory busing is a constitutional amendment prohibiting it. The House Judiciary Committee has so far adamantly refused to allow bills of this type out of committee. The only alternative is to continue introducing amendments whenever possible to restrain busing orders. School districts receiving emergency school aid funds should be encouraged to use money they might otherwise spend on busing to promote their academic programs.

For education in general there is no easy brake to the momentum that has been increasing since 1958 toward federal involvement in all aspects of education, both public and private, even down to the most mundane record-keeping. Over the years federal policies have had a growing impact on local schools as a result of ever-expanding programs and ever-increasing funding, but they have never seriously been reexamined. ESEA, for instance, has been extended through June 30, 1978, and the Omnibus Education Amendments of 1974 carry a potential authorization of $28 billion through 1978. Although Title VI of those amendments consolidates certain federal programs, it perpetuates the growing tendency toward categorical aid by authorizing certain special projects such as metric, consumer, art, and women's equity education. To quote McDermott again:

> Obviously, if federal aid to education moves in the direction of general aid, the role of the federal government in educational policy-making will diminish, and with it the scope of federal judicial power over school financing. . . .

By limiting or ending categorical aid programs, federal educational policy would become basically a nonpolicy. Although the ideal, of course, is the return of all educational initiative to state and local governments and individuals, if concerned legislators can at the very least undercut the federal control of curricula, teaching methods, and other matters of internal concern to the schools by eliminating as many categorical programs as possible, some of the worst abuses of the current system may be eliminated.

Aside from changing the structure of the educational law, a great deal more should be done to protect the rights of parents and children, who after all are supposed to be the final beneficiaries of these programs. The Buckley amendment, "Family Educational Right and Privacy Act of 1974," was a step toward protecting the privacy of school records, which were being increasingly used by government agencies without parental permission.

Probably the most needed reform to protect the rights of individuals is lowering the age at which students can leave school. Elimination of compulsory school attendance laws would prevent government interference with family life, enhance individual preferences, and keep the schools from becoming custodial institutions.

The National Commission of the Reform of Secondary Education, a nationally prominent group of educators, has taken these problems into account and recommends that the compulsory age be lowered so that high schools will not become adolescent day-care centers. Unfortunately, most people simply assume that compulsory education is good for all children, and for this reason unless some initiative is taken to counter this assumption, the laws will be very difficult to change. On the federal level, studies of the results of forcing children to attend school should be done and amendments should be attached to relevant legislation giving states incentives to lower the minimum age at which children can leave school. The idea, of course, is to set momentum going so that states will continue to reexamine the whole idea of compulsory education.

These are only a few suggestions in a field that is begging for reform. Education is a particularly vital area because it touches the lives of everyone both directly and indirectly. For this reason parents want the power to control an institution that is charged with the very important responsibility of educating their children during the most formative years of their lives. And the only way to make those institutions responsive to the wishes of the community is to make them answer directly to that community. The assumption behind so many of the proposals to increase federal aid is that huge government agencies are somehow more qualified to direct the lives of children than their parents and the local elected school boards are. Government has no place in the substitute parent business, but if current trends in that direction are not soon reversed, local control will indeed become a memory.

NATIONAL SECURITY

BIOGRAPHY
of
The Honorable David C. Treen
Louisiana

A lawyer with a long career of service to his profession and his community, David C. Treen, who represents the Third District of Louisiana, was born on July 16, 1928, in Baton Rouge. He attended schools in East Baton Rouge, Jefferson, and Orleans Parishes before he graduated from Fortier High School in 1945. He received a B.A. in political science and history from Tulane University in 1948 and a law degree with honors from the same institution in 1950.

Commissioned to the Air Force in 1950, First Lieutenant Treen was counsel in court martial trials in the United States and overseas during his tour of active duty from 1951 to 1952. After his release from military service, Mr. Treen became vice-president and legal counsel for Simplex Manufacturing Corporation. In 1957, Mr. Treen joined the firm of Beard, Blue, and Schmitt which eventually became Beard, Blue, Schmitt, and Treen. From this position, Mr. Treen came to Congress in 1972 as the first Republican elected to this body from Louisiana since Reconstruction.

Always active in State politics, Mr. Treen is a member of the State Central Committee. He chaired the executive committee of Jefferson Parish (1963-1967) and the Louisiana Delegation at the 1968 and 1972 Republican National Conventions. He was also the National Committeeman from Louisiana from 1972 to 1974.

A distinguished member of the Armed Services Committee, Congressman Treen is most concerned with the deteriorating state of the nation's defense.

The Louisiana Congressman also serves on the Merchant Marine and Fisheries Committee and the Select Committee on Intelligence.

Married to the former Dolores Brisbi, David Treen has three children.

OUR FOREIGN POLICY:
A TIME FOR REEVALUATION
by
Congressman David C. Treen

In whatever region of the globe we examine—from Southeast Asia, where the United States in 1974 suffered its worst defeat, to Africa, where recent events indicate that a major Soviet triumph is in the offing in Angola; to Europe, where the military balance grows steadily more favorable to the Soviet bloc—the position of the West appears to be deteriorating, and that of our adversaries to be gaining.

At first glance it might seem surprising that the United States has fared so poorly in the struggle with the Communist enterprise, particularly in the struggle of ideas. Since the founding of the Republic a solid consensus of Americans has believed not only that American values are relevant to other peoples and other nations everywhere but also that, over the long run at least, political systems embodying those values were destined to appear in all parts of the globe. Moreover, since early in our nation's history it has been the assumption of many of our most prominent statesmen that American power and influence—in ways often unspecified—would play a major role in ensuring that the political evolution of the world developed in the proper direction.

In some important respects, however, it was precisely this kind of thinking about the world and the United States role in it that has proved to be our undoing. Beginning with American involvement in World War I, our statesmen have tended to assume that this nation possesses sufficient power and wisdom to direct the political fortunes of all nations, solve all pressing international problems, and deal effectively with all threats to international peace and stability. This attitude has led to a lengthy series of treaties and commitments binding the United States to 40 or more nations and to our involvement in most international crises of the postwar period, most unhappily of course in Vietnam.

The Challenge

Robert Strausz-Hupe, the noted scholar who for many years was Director of the Foreign Policy Research Institute at the University of Pennsylvania, and who now serves as United States Ambassador to Sweden, has written:

> The greatness of a nation lies neither in the abundance of its possessions nor in the strength of its arms. A people rather finds greatness in its response to the historical challenge—in its success in harnessing its own power and strivings to the aspirations and ideas of the age.

Dr. Strausz-Hupe was in fact writing about the present as well as the past: The challenge to the western world at this juncture in history is at the level of ideas. The totalitarian political movement centered in Moscow and Peking, which in our time competes with the West for world political supremacy, is only the third in a series of such movements that have dominated the world scene since 1900. Twice the West has risen to the challenge and, gathering military, economic, and moral force, has defeated the aggressor and made good its claim to represent the best aspirations of humanity. But bold is the man who predicts with confidence that the outcome of the present struggle will be as fortuitous. A hard look at historical fact reveals that since 1945 a steady rise has been seen in communist power and influence with a concomitant decline in the powers and influence of the West. This fact suggests that unless there is a radical reversal of recent trends in world politics, the West may follow into oblivion the great civilizations of the past.

This book is not the place to comment on either the wisdom of that involvement or the manner in which the United States pursued its role in Vietnam, except to observe that had we handled the latter with greater skill, few individuals would today be questioning the former. We will simply observe that Americans have been left confused and demoralized by 30 years involvement in world politics, at enormous cost in national resources and in human lives that has shown little progress toward the kind of world which our people have been led to believe would be the direct result of this involvement. Weariness with world politics has led to a loss of confidence in the relevance of American ideals, to a rampant neo-isolationism that denies the importance of a strong and active American foreign policy, and to an uncritical belief that something called "detente" with the Soviet Union will solve America's most pressing international problems. At the most fundamental of levels, then, the United States is losing the battle of ideas: the dominant concepts held by many Americans about the proper role for the United States in the contemporary world have little to do with reality. And it is no comfort to say that the reason for this is the equal irrelevance of many of the ideas that preceded them.

A Course for the Future

What, then, is the proper course for the United States under current international conditions? How should we attempt to define American interests in the contemporary world? What should be the nature of America's world role? A good beginning at answering these questions was made six years ago when a Republican Administration attempted to grapple with the effects of the Vietnam War upon American political life. In fact, well before 1969, both President Nixon and Dr. Kissinger had come to believe that popular discontent with Vietnam had undermined the consensus concerning the U.S. global role—consensus that had sustained American foreign policy throughout the postwar period. Both Nixon and Kissinger, believed, with good reason, that virtually all the factors shaping world politics were in the process of profound transformation.

The principal changes were held by President Nixon and his foreign affairs advisors. First, Japan and the nations of Western Europe, the latter gradually drawing closer together economically and politically, had recovered from the ravages of World War II and were capable once again of assuming major roles in the world political system. Second, most of the new nations of Africa and Asia had substantially matured since the early period following independence and many appeared able to resist external aggression and hold their own in relations with bigger powers. Third, the one-time communist monolith had been shattered, replaced by a loosely organized bloc whose members quarreled as often as they cooperated. Fourth, U.S. military preeminence had given way to a condition of strategic parity between the U.S.S.R. and the United States, reducing American freedom of maneuver in crisis situations but simultaneously creating new possibilities for detente based on the stability of a "balance of terror." Fifth, the old "isms"—the once-vibrant ideologies that for 20 years animated the foreign policies of the great powers—had lost their vitality, and more traditional national goals such as security and economic progress had become the primary concerns both of the United States and the Soviet Union. Finally, our own foreign policy was inhibited by serious internal constraints, one of the several aftermaths of the Vietnam War. Our citizens' psychological resources had been exhausted, their moral strength has been undermined, and the nation's ability to play a major role in world politics was therefore considerably diminished.

President Nixon's world view thus combined both pessimism and optimism. Although the power of the United States is in decline, especially relative to that of the Soviet Union, other changes that are occurring in the world are more favorable to American interests, especially if the latter are more restrictively defined than in the past. President Nixon believed that a substantially reduced role for America in maintaining world security was both desirable and possible; moreover, for the first time since the end of World War II the opportunity existed to create a "new structure of relations" with our traditional adversaries and thereby achieve a "durable peace" that will survive at least until the end of this century. Particularly if the economies of the U.S. and the U.S.S.R. could be bound together through a series of interlocking agreements, the Soviets would have a vested interest in continually improving relations with the West. Somewhat later, as events in the Middle East and the massive Soviet military buildup following the first Strategic Arms Limitation Talks (SALT I) aroused doubts about the assumed Soviet desire for a constructive relationship with the United States, Administration spokesmen began to stress the necessity of avoiding nuclear war as the primary rationale for the policy of detente.

Regardless of the considerable merits of the basic views on the U.S. role in the world which undergirded what came to be known as the Nixon Doctrine, it is clear that the rosy hopes for a new era of detente have gone largely unfulfilled.

There have been no serious concessions by the Soviets in any of the several ongoing negotiations with the western powers on political and military issues. The talks on mutual force reductions in Europe are deadlocked, apparently awaiting the next American accommodations. The Salt talks contain as many pitfalls for the United States as they do hopes for progress toward arms control. As for other areas of conflict between the two superpowers, the record speaks for itself. Not only were the Soviets intimately involved in the preparations for the Middle East War, but they urged radical Arab states to maintain the oil embargo in force virtually to the day the embargo was lifted. There is no evidence to indicate that they have supported Kissinger's efforts to move the opposing parties toward a mutually satisfactory settlement since the embargo ended. Breshnev himself has repeatedly stated during the period since SALT I that the ideological and political struggle between the two powers will go on. At a conference of Eastern European party leaders in mid-1973 Breshnev explained that the precise purpose of the Soviet policy of detente with the Western powers was to buy time for the Soviets to acquire total strategic superiority over the West; at that point, he said, the U.S.S.R. would set about to achieve the reorganization of world politics on its terms, which has always been the ultimate objective of Soviet foreign policy.

There is, in short, little evidence so far that true detente now exists between the U.S. and the U.S.S.R.

Steps Toward a Credible Foreign Policy

If there are few signs that true detente now exists between the United States and the Soviet Union, on what basis should the United States attempt to conduct relations with the world's other superpower? Should the purpose of our foreign policy in the 1970s be victory over communism, as Senator Barry Goldwater (R, Arizona) advocated a decade ago? Or is the mere containment of the Soviet Union enough? Alternatively, should we drastically reduce American involvement with the outside world, as the "limitationists" advise, or perhaps even attempt a withdrawl to a Fortress America, relying upon our strategic nuclear forces to ensure our survival? To raise these questions is merely to ask what are the national interests of the United States, and how can they be best protected under contemporary conditions?

In the present instance, both principle and self-interest point clearly to a firm United States policy stand toward the Soviet Union. At the level of principle, it is difficult to maintain that the Soviet regime is morally superior to the American. Whatever may be the thrust of the changes that have occurred in the U.S.S.R. since Stalin, the Soviet regime remains a tightly controlled one-party dictatorship. All political dissent in the Soviet Union is carefully circumscribed and respect for basic human freedom and dignity is virtually nonexistent. The United States, by way of contrast—and, more broadly speaking, the civilization of the West in general—embodies principles of politics that are eminently defensible on

195

ethical grounds, however imperfectly some of those principles may be realized in practice. Thus the Western nations have both the right and the obligation to defend their values and principles as well as the political systems based upon them, and indeed to extend their influence where it is possible and prudent to do so.

At the level of self-interest, it is clear that the threat to American interests abroad and to our security and survival is increasing rather than diminishing. What is therefore required in response is a policy toward the U.S.S.R. based on a clear apprehension of current realities rather than on desires and dreams. In the words of former Secretary of Defense James Schlesinger, "unless we are to plan only by intuition, we must continue to build our peace structure on the hard facts of the international environment rather than on gossamer hopes for the eminent perfectability of mankind."

We can recognize that in the current circumstances a realistic policy toward the U.S.S.R. cannot advocate a crusade to roll back the Iron Curtain or to bring down the Soviet regime by force. Edmund Burke long ago taught us that prudence is the central virtue of politics; in the nuclear age such a crusade could result only in disaster. It is equally obvious that the time has long since passed when we could attempt an international quarantine of the U.S.S.R. or even refuse to negotiate with the Soviets on the whole range of East-West issues. In any event, few objections can be raised against the concept of detente properly defined, or against a policy of detente properly pursued. And, indeed I have supported such a realistic policy. What the United States requires now is consistent firmness and realism in assessing Soviet intentions and policies and in devising responses to them.

Future arms control agreements, for example, must be based on true equivalence at a minimum, and must not proceed from the baseless assumption that one-sided agreements are satisfactory if only because they contribute to the momentum of detente. Trade agreements likewise must contain equal economic advantages for both powers, and under no circumstances should strategic materials or military-related technology be transferred to the U.S.S.R. Finally, even arms control and economic agreements limited by these principles must be offered to the U.S.S.R. at a price. That price must be a demonstrated moderation in Soviet behavior, at home and abroad—on tactics involving Europe and in the Middle East as well as on the issues of submarine deployments in Cuba and emigration from the Soviet Union. Pressure on the U.S.S.R. on the emigration issue has already led to some modification of Soviet policies. If the Soviets are seriously interested in obtaining access to American technology, a consistent U.S. hard line on the emigration issue—which will serve to demonstrate to others our continuing moral commitment—might well lead to further changes in Soviet behavior. If not, nothing of consequence will have been lost and a great knowledge of Soviet intentions and flexibility will have been gained.

The same approach points the way to new directions for American policy elsewhere in the world. Clearly our alliance systems are in a state of disrepair. A foreign policy rooted in a clear understanding of current political realities would make the revitalization of NATO and the Japanese alliance a first order of business. The European nations and Japan must be persuaded that we have no intention of separating American security interests from theirs. Beyond that, the firm United States position in Southeast Asia, particularly in cooperation with our own allies in Korea and Taiwan, must be sustained, and efforts should be set in motion to create—under the inspiration of one of the more cogent aspects of the Nixon Doctrine—a NATO-style mutual defense arrangement among the noncommunist nations of the region, through which they can assist one another in dealing with local insurgencies and other threats.

I have been encouraged this past year in the Congress by at least a few hopeful signs that the majority of Members are coming to realize the importance of a realistic foreign policy which places the just interests of the United States and of our reliable allies first. A majority of the Members of the House of Representatives has assured the Republic of China in a series of resolutions (see positive proposal M in Table II) that our close ties will continue; that they will not be compromised by our thawed relations with the People's Republic of China. Nationalist China has long been a close political and economic friend of the United States; one which our country cannot afford to lose. These House resolutions should avert this possibility.

Congressman Gene Snyder, Republican of Kentucky, introduced an important amendment to the State Department Appropriation Bill (H.R. 8121) which would have prohibited the State Department from using any such funds for negotiations relinquishing any U.S. rights in the Panama Canal Zone. This amendment was adopted, 246-164. (See vote 22 in Table I.) I only regret that 164 members of Congress were willing to countenance a weakening of American control over this vital waterway. We have a treaty with Panama which provides for American sovereignty over the Zone; the Panamanians receive fair, indeed, generous material benefits as a result of the American presence in the Zone and many Latin Americans are happy to know that this installation so important to their own security is safely guarded by American forces. I might add that I and many other members hope that our good friends in Latin America will receive greater consideration and attention from the United States than they have received in recent years.

My good friend and colleague, Congressman John Rousselot, Republican of California, introduced a very illuminating amendment to the South Vietnamese Assistance Bill (H.R. 6096) which condemned the flagrant violations of the Paris Peace Accords by the North Vietnamese who at that time were invading in large force the Republic of Vietnam. Although this amendment was adopted overwhelmingly (329-72), it saddens me that there were 72 Members of Congress who, for various reasons, could not bring themselves to acknowledge this obvious fact of life. (See vote 23 in Table I.)

Another blow for American interests was struck in the U.S. Congress when the House defeated H.R. 1287 to amend the United Nations Participation Act of 1945 in order to align the United States with the U.N.-sponsored boycott of Rhodesian Chrome. This bill, which would have forced the U.S. to rely upon more expensive Soviet chrome (a much-needed defense item) was turned down by a vote of 187 to 209. (See vote 24 in Table I.)

These are, as I said, hopeful signs. Still, much remains to be done if American foreign policy is to become what it once was, "the Shield of the Republic." I would hope that all of my colleagues would read carefully a perceptive editorial which appeared recently in a leading British newspaper, *The Daily Telegraph*. This editorial, obviously written by a sincere friend of the United States, states some truths which badly need to be heard:

It is time America's friends spoke out, with some nasty questions to the so-called liberal East Coast establishment. By that we mean sections of the press, sections of Congress, television commentators and comedians, university pundits and a lot of other people who may think there is a dollar to be made out of denigrating their country's institutions and leaders. We all know about the trauma of Vietnam and Watergate, but it's getting a bit boring. How long has the rest of the free world got to put up with these tender-minded people recovering from their trauma indefinitely? America is accustomed to, and has merited, a good deal of deference from her allies. But deference can be a disservice. The United States should know that her European cousins and allies are appalled and disgusted by the present open disarray of her public life. The self-criticism and self-destructive tendencies are running mad, with no countervailing force in sight.

She has no foreign policy any more, because Congress will not allow it. Her intelligence arm, the CIA, is being gutted and rendered inoperative. The names of its staff being published so that they can be murdered. Her President and Secretary of State are being hounded, not for what they do but simply because they are people here, to be pulled down for the fun of it. . . . Please, America, for God's sake pull yourself together.

From my experience on the House Select Committee on Intelligence, I can only say, "Amen."

It has obviously not been possible within the scope of this essay to specify in detail the kind of foreign policy which we believe necessary for the United States. Enough has been said, we hope, to indicate the nature of the approach. More than a decade ago, in one of his most illustrious books, a well-known professor of international relations wrote cogently of the relationship between power, principle, and world order:

Whenever peace—conceived as the avoidance of war—has been the primary objective of a power or a group of powers, the international system has been at the mercy of the most ruthless member of the international community. Whenever the international order has acknowledged that certain principles could not be compromised even for the sake of peace, stability based on an equilibrium of forces was at least conceivable.

The Professor was Henry A. Kissinger. The hour is now late. But there is still time for the United States to heed this warning, to make the difficult decisions and sacrifices dictated by principled realism, and more toward *realistic* detente.

BIOGRAPHY
of
The Honorable Floyd Spence
South Carolina

Floyd Sepnce was elected to the 92nd Congress in 1970 to represent the 2nd District of South Carolina.

Born in Columbia, South Carolina, on April 9, 1928, Congressman Spence was educated in West Columbia and Lexington where he was president of his high school student body. He was also president of the student body at the University of South Carolina, from which he was graduated in 1952 with a B.A. in English. After getting his law degree, Mr. Spence served six years in the State House of Representatives as a Democrat member.

In 1966, after a few years of private law practice with the firm of Callison and Spence, the Congressman entered the State Senate in 1966 as a Republican member and served as the Minority Leader during his entire time in the Senate (1966-1970). He was also chairman of the Joint Senate-House Internal Security Committee.

Among his civic affiliations are the State and National American Legion, the Veterans of Foreign Wars, the Farm Bureau, and the American Bar Association.

As a third term Congressman, Mr. Spence sits on the Armed Services Committee and on the Standards of Official Conduct Committee. His long-standing interest in all areas of international relations makes him an ideal author for a chapter on the nation's foreign policy.

Floyd Spence and his wife, the former Lula Hancock Drake reside in Lexington, South Carolina, with their four sons.

IN DEFENSE OF FREEDOM
by
Congressman Floyd D. Spence,

Despite the fact that our fleet was devastated after the surprise attack at Pearl Harbor in 1941, we were able to regroup and fight back. Unfortunately, the dimensions of an all-out nuclear attack on our country today would be such that no amount of American ingenuity and perserverance could save us, should we again be caught unprepared. We would be left with the unpleasant alternatives of unconditional surrender to our enemies, or total destruction. This is why there should be no higher priority in Congress than maintaining a defense posture that is sufficient to keep us out of such a dilemma.

The problem, of course, is determining what level of strength is sufficient for that purpose. How much is necessary? With severe budget deficits plaguing the economy, we must ensure that no federal agency, including the Department of Defense, is allowed to waste tax money. But the question of "how much is enough" in the area of national defense is especially critical, because the price of miscalculation is one that none of us would be willing to bear.

How much is enough?

What is the overall level of strategic and conventional military strength that is sufficient to ensure the survival of the United States and protect our interests abroad? It is a difficult question, and the answer has never been apparent. Complicating factors include the need to determine which types of weapons systems are necessary to meet all potential threats, how many personnel under arms would be required in the event of attack, and where those troops should be deployed.

The problem has been accentuated by the uncertainties of the nuclear age. Today the deterrence of war is as important a function of military strength as the capacity to fight wars and win them. Thus, the most highly visible components of a nation's military strength may never be used, and may thus come ultimately to be taken for granted.

The difficulties involved in shaping a sensible military posture for the United States are further complicated by the dilemmas inherent in allocating relatively scarce natural resources among competing public policy areas. The enormous cost of high-technology weaponry is a significant aspect to this competition for limited resources. Also, the impact of detente on the thinking of many Americans about national security problems, as well as the lingering effects of Vietnam on the public attitude toward defense, pose additional problems for military planners.

The fact is, no area of public policy deserves more attention than defense. U.S. military strength remains the ultimate guarantee of the American system of government, not to mention the security of countless other nations throughout the world. Maintenance of an adequate level of military strength is therefore the most important single responsibility of our federal government.

For these reasons I find the current trends in world military balance to be extremely disturbing. The question of how much is enough can only be answered in relative terms—by considering the strength of our primary enemy, which is now formidable indeed.

The Strategic Balance

Ten years ago the Soviet Union possessed fewer than 300 ICBM launchers, most of them containing early-generation missiles of doubtful reliability and low accuracy. By contrast, the United States had deployed more than 850 and was rapidly building toward a peak level of more than 1,000.

We were ahead not only in numbers but in quality. The missiles in our arsenal were technologically superior in every way to those of the Russians. Under development was the jewel in America's technological crown—the multiple independently-targeted reentry vehicle (MIRV). This weapons system was deployed in 1970 on submarine-launched missiles that were vastly superior in numbers to those of the U.S.S.R.

By the time the first phase of the Strategic Arms Limitation Talks (SALT I) was completed seven years later the picture had changed radically. The Soviets had now substantially pulled ahead of the United States in the number of ICBMs and were moving rapidly ahead with a submarine missile program of massive proportions. They had also deployed nearly 300 heavy modern ICBMs with the capacity to carry a 25-megaton warhead. In return for a Russian pledge to halt construction of both new ICBM and SLBM launchers, the United States agreed in SALT I to permit the Soviets a 1,618 to 1,054 disparity in land-based intercontinental missiles. We also agreed to give them an advantage of 740 to 656 in submarine-launched ballistic missiles. The United States also gave up the right to further deployment of its highly-promising ABM system in return for a similar Russian pledge concerning their technologically-inadequate "Galosh" ABT1 complex.

The Administration clearly hoped that the SALT I agreement would stabilize the military relationship between the superpowers on the basis of the "rough parity" then thought to exist. It was thought that our technological advantages would offset Soviet superiority in the numbers of missile launchers and also in the size of their missiles. But it soon became clear that the Soviets had no intention of remaining satisfied with the advantages provided them by the SALT I agreement.

Three and a half years have elapsed since the Nixon-Brezhnev accord in 1972, and the Soviets have set in motion a strategic arms buildup called by former Secretary of Defense James Schlesinger "unprecedented in its breadth and depth." Another high Department of Defense official characterized it as "staggering."

Why? Since 1972, the Soviets have tested five new types of long-range strategic missiles. At least three and possibly four of these have been tested with multiple independently-targeted warheads. All have new bus-type warhead dispensing systems and reentry vehicles streamlined for greater accuracy. The new sea-launched missile, the SS-N-8, has a range of 4,300 miles, which makes it equal to the United States Trident I missile. Our Trident will not be ready to enter service before 1978.

New ballistic missile submarines continue to be supplied to the Soviet navy at a frequent rate. Ten or more additional strategic missile systems are reportedly under development. The swing-wing Backfire bomber is now in service production, with at least 50 already in service. A new supersonic heavy bomber is expected to be next.

Up to now, moreover, there is no indication that the proposed SALT II agreement will inhibit ongoing and planned Soviet strategic deployments. Although the proposed SALT II is an improvement over the 1972 accord in that it permits both sides to deploy an equal number of strategic delivery vehicles, it will also allow each side to deploy 1,320 MIRVed launchers. Since Soviet missiles—especially the new SS-18 and SS-19—are substantially larger than their American counterparts, and have a much greater throw-weight, the Russians will be able to deploy more and larger warheads on their land-based missiles than will we.

Not only will the Soviets thus have pulled ahead of us in one of our last remaining areas of technological superiority, but they may well possess a significant counterforce capability, able to threaten the United States Minuteman force by the early 1980s. Perhaps more important, they will have achieved superiority on yet another index of strategic power and thereby increased their ability to coerce the United States and our allies, or the third-world nations, in moments of international crisis.

The Conventional Balance

The general picture relative to conventional balance is also disquieting. The Soviets maintain a large, well-trained, well-equipped, and highly diversified military capability. They are increasingly able to project that military power into the far corners of the globe—whether it be Cuba, Angola, Southeast Asia, or the Indian Ocean.

Categorical comparisons are especially depressing, as the Soviets outnumber us better than two to one in total armed forces, four to one in tanks, seven to one in interceptor aircraft, and nearly two to one in artillery pieces. On the Central Front in Europe, long considered the key potential battle-front between the East and West, the Soviets possess substantial advantages in manpower and equipment. Tanks offer a dramatic example, with the Warsaw Pact outnumbering NATO 19,000 to 7,000 on the Central Front.

In naval forces as well the Soviets have made enormous progress in recent years. While the United States remains generally superior to Russia in overall maritime strength, they have surpassed us in many respects. For example, Soviet ships designed for short-duration offensive strikes against Western naval forces are armed to the teeth with the most modern weapons—especially cruise missiles. Moreover, the U.S.S.R. is now for the first time deploying aircraft carriers, which will substantially increase her capacity to support interventionist activities abroad.

It is worth noting that in the conventional—as well as in the strategic-areas the Soviets have overcome many of the traditional advantages in technology formerly enjoyed by the United States. Aircrafts such as the Russian SU-19 Fencer, the Mig-23 Flogger, and the Mig-25 Foxbat are highly efficient war machines. These fighters are equalled or exceeded on our side only by the F-14 Tomcat and the F-15 Eagle, and procurement of both of these aircrafts has been slowed or reduced due to the high costs involved.

The latest Soviet main battle tank, the M-1970 (T-64), appears to be equal to anything in the Western arsenal.

The Defense Expenditure Balance

The unprecedented buildup in Russian military strength compared to the United States is easy to understand when relative expenditures are taken into consideration. The U.S.S.R. is now devoting substantially more of its resources to most of the significant categories of defense than is the United States. In terms of American prices, Russia now outstrips the United States by 20 percent in overall research and development, by 25 percent in procurement, and by 60 percent in strategic nuclear offensive forces.

Yet, in the face of figures such as these, some Americans seem to agree with one prominent Democrat senator who said recently, "The United States defense budget is swollen beyond all reason, and must be cut and cut drastically."

Let us take a look at our "swollen" defense budget. Defense spending as a percentage of our gross national product has declined from 9.4 percent in fiscal 1968 to 5.8 percent in 1976. We now have 1.4 million fewer men under arms than we did in 1968.

Those who believe that we are spending too much on defense usually discuss budget trends in terms of current dollars. They point to the 1955 appropriation, which was $38 billion, and compare it to this year's $92 billion budget.

They fail to note, however, that the same inflation that plagues every family in this country also seriously affects the buying power of our defense establishment. A far more accurate reflection of military spending is provided by constant dollars, which are adjusted for inflation. Using that $38 billion budget in 1955 as a base, the $92 billion budget this year is worth only $35 billion in purchasing power. *In other words, in real terms the defense budget is now the lowest it has been in 30 years.*

Another point often forgotten or ignored is that nearly 60 percent of the defense budget is now consumed by personnel costs, as compared with slightly more than 30 percent a decade ago. It has been estimated that the funds that are actually devoted to those areas most Americans think of as defense expenditures—research and development, new weapons systems, and the like—amount to only about 8 percent of the total budget of the U.S. government.

Rather than imposing massive and arbitrary cuts in the defense budget, Congress should be carefully examining our military posture to determine those areas in which *increases* in expenditures will be required to protect American security at home and our interests abroad in the late 1970s and early 1980s.

In the face of these facts, what do we do next? How do we respond to these disturbing trends and statistics?

Irrespective of the foregoing figures, the United States does not now stand naked before its enemies. Neither are these trends irreversible. What is required for the future is nothing more or less than a critical examination of all aspects of American national security policy, in order to assess areas of weakness, real and potential threats, and alternative courses of action.

Strategic Forces

It is clear that the United States cannot afford to fall farther behind the U.S.S.R. in the principal indicators of strategic strength. The SALT II accord may afford us the opportunity to draw even once again with the Russians in some areas. For example, top priority should be accorded the deployment of additional SLBMs of the Trident type, and the procurement of B-1 bombers to replace our aging B-52s.

It is also essential, in view of the growing counterforce capability of the U.S.S.R., that the United States develop a comparable capability. This would serve two purposes: It would prevent any misconceptions from arising—either among our friends or our enemies—concerning the relative strategic strength of the superpowers. Equally important, it would give the United States strategic options. We would be able to pursue effective courses other than the equally wretched alternative of all-out holocaust and total submission to Soviet demands.

Thus, programs recently begun to improve the size and accuracy of ICBM and SLBM missiles and warheads, such as those associated with the ABRES, LABRV, and MARV programs, must receive continued funding.

Conventional Forces

The streamlining and modernization of our military forces, which were begun during the tenure of Secretary Schlesinger, must be continued and accelerated. The "teeth-to-tail" ratio in the United States Army must continue to be improved by reducing numbers of support personnel and filling their places in the ranks with combat men. Development and procurement of new high-technology weapons must continue and in some cases be stepped up in order to provide more firepower with fewer pieces of equipment.

The modernization of our nuclear forces abroad is necessary so that large-yield weapons of uncertain reliability can be replaced with new systems that promise reduced damage to civilians if used. Not only does this enhance deterrence through improved credibility, but also it would add to the combat effectiveness of our forces, especially in Europe, should war occur.

Wherever possible when selecting new weapons primarily for deployment in Europe, joint procurement programs with our NATO allies should be arranged, with an eye both to reducing costs and standardizing weapons in the Alliance. One possible area for such a program would be the new main battle tank for the Army. Finally, aircraft and ship construction programs must continue at least at present levels, until reliance on "hi-lo" mixes, such as the F-15/F-16 mix of tactical aircraft for the Air Force, is increased.

Clearly, this strategy allows for no sharp decrease in military expenditures in the near future. On the contrary, it means at least some increases, if for no other reason than to keep pace with inflation. In view of the continuing threat to Western interests posed by the growth of Soviet military power, however, no other course is adequate to ensure what John Adams called "the first task of government"—the security of the American people.

I have been somewhat encouraged this past year to see that an increasing number of our Representatives are coming around to the conclusion that the provision of a strong defense is indeed our first duty to the American people.

In May, 1975, for instance, Congresswoman Patricia Schroeder (D, Colorado) introduced an amendment to the fiscal 1976 research, development and procurement bill (H.R. 6674). This amendment which would have cut off funds for three airborne warning and control system aircraft (AWACS) was decisively defeated by a vote of 136 in favor and 260 against. (See Vote 25 in Table 1) These radar-equipped aircraft will be able to scout enemy airplanes

209

and direct allied air defense operations. Another amendment to cut back on the Trident submarine program was turned back by a voice vote.

On the same day, another amendment to the same bill was introduced by Congressman Les Aspin (D, Wisconsin) which would have delayed the production of the B-1 bomber, which is badly needed to replace our aging B-52s. My friend and colleague, Congressman Steven Symms (R, Idaho), pointed out that the projected cost of the new B-1 bombers would be no more than the original cost of the B-52s, after a necessary allowance is made for inflation. The vote on this amendment was 164 for and 227 against (see vote 26 in Table I), so the new bomber will move ahead on schedule. I only regret to say that two-thirds of the freshmen Members went against the general trend of their more experienced colleagues and voted to delay the bomber.

Perhaps the most significant vote that reflects the view of a Congress becoming more responsible on defense matters was the response to the amendment offered by Congressman Ronald Dellums (D, California) to withdraw 70,000 of our troops from their overseas posts by 1976 (including the vital areas of NATO and South Korea). This proposed cutback was resoundingly defeated by a vote of 95 in favor and 311 against. (See vote 27 in Table I.) The recent events in Southeast Asia apparently had an effect on many Members since a similar amendment the year before failed by a closer vote of 163 to 240. A key factor in this switch was the changed position of Majority Leader Thomas P. ("Tip") O'Neill, (D, Massachusetts), who told the House that in view of the trouble spots around the world—Korea, the Middle East, Portugal—the Dellums amendment "comes at the wrong time." My colleague, Congressman G. William Whitehurst (R, Virginia), summed up the debate very well when he told us, "What we need to do this afternoon is to defeat this amendment ... [in order to] send an emphatic message to friend and foe alike that this country has not abdicated its responsibilities."

These recent trends are certainly encouraging but we must be constantly on our guard against any weakening of our defenses or of our resolve to defend freedom. History shows that wars occur because of weakness. When expansionist nations perceive weakness or lack of resolve among other peoples or nations, they are encouraged to take advantage of what they think is an auspicious opportunity to further their expansionist goals. Thus, we must learn the lessons of history and remain so strong that no potential enemy will be misled into taking an adventuresome course.

If the key Members of Congress continue to ignore these lessons, and turn away from the facts available to us, one must wonder how much longer our nation can remain both free and at peace.

TABLE I—VOTES

1. HR 2559—Cost-of-Living Pay Increases
This bill provides automatic annual cost-of-living pay increases for Members of Congress and top officials of the Executive and Judicial branches (more than 23,000 persons). This will allow the Members of Congress to receive pay raises without having to publicly vote on them. A "yes" vote is in favor of the pay increase. Passed the House on July 30, 1975 (214-213). *See Introduction and Chapter 7, pp. 4, 85.*

2. HR 7575—Consumer Protection Act
This bill sets up a super advocacy agency to intervene in all federal agencies' decisions which "substantially affect consumer interests." Instead of reforming existing agencies that already have been established to aid the consumer, this bill seeks to correct problems that may exist by adding still another layer of federal bureaucracy. A "yes" vote indicates support for establishing this agency. Passed the House on November 6, 1975 (208-199). *See Introduction and Chapter 4, pp. 4, 52.*

3. HR 5900—Common Situs Picketing
This bill would amend the Taft-Hartley Act to allow a single striking subcontractor to picket an entire construction site, thereby completely closing down the site. This would cause higher prices and greater unemployment in the construction industry. A "yes" vote is in favor of this picketing bill. Passed the House on December 11, 1975 (229-189). *See Introduction, p. 4.*

4. HR 10481—Federal Loans for New York City
This bill provides a federal loan of $2.3 billion to New York City, allowing that city to go even further into debt at the expense of taxpayers throughout the country. A "yes" vote is in favor of this loan. Passed the House on December 2, 1975 (213-203). *See Introduction, p. 5.*

5. HR 10647—Supplemental Appropriation Bill—(Michel motion to recommit)
This was a motion by Congressman Michel to recommit

the supplemental appropriations bill with instructions to reduce the amount of the new federal loan to New York City from $2.3 billion to $1.3 billion. A "yes" vote is in favor of recommitting the bill with instructions to reduce the amount of the loan to New York City. Failed in the House on December 15, 1975 (187-219). *See Introduction, p. 6.*

6. *S.622—Energy Policy Conservation Act*—(Vote on Conference Report)
This bill sets up a complex price regulation structure, by the federal government, for domestic crude oil. It calls for a roll back in the average market price of domestic crude oil to a level which affords little or no economic motivation to producers. Many experts have warned that this bill will result in lower domestic oil production, increased dependence on higher priced foreign oil, and cause a heavy loss of jobs for American workers. A "yes" vote is in favor of setting up this federal control structure and regulation of domestic crude oil. Passed the House on December 15, 1975 (236-160). *See Introduction and Chapter 1, pp. 5, 13.*

7. *HR 10585—Debt Ceiling Increase*
By this vote the Congress increased the debt ceiling to $595 billion, a full $100 billion higher than the ceiling was at the beginning of 1975. A "yes" vote was in favor of raising the ceiling on the federal debt. Passed the House on November 13, 1975 (213-198). *See Chapter 2, p. 31.*

8. *H. Con. Res. 366—Second Concurrent Resolution on the Budget (FY 1976)*
This resolution indicates that the Congress believes that a debt limit for the quarter beginning July 1, 1976 of $641 billion would be "appropriate"; that represents an expected increase in the national debt of an *additional* $46 billion after only six months of overspending. A "yes" vote approved this resolution. Passed the House on Dcember 12, 1975 (189-187). *See Chapter 2, p. 31.*

9. *Substitute to H. Con. Res. 466*—(Rousselot Balanced Budget Resolution)
This Rousselot substitute would require essentially a bal-

213

anced federal budget, assuring that the federal government would not live beyond its means. A "yes" vote favored the balanced budget substitute. The measure failed in the House on November 12, 1975 (127-283). *See Chapter 2, p. 33.*

10. *HR 5559—Tax Reduction Extension* (Vote to override Presidential veto)
This bill would have extended the tax reduction without correspondingly reducing federal expenditures. It thus ignored the long term harmful consequences resulting in further deficit spending, and in further borrowing to cover the deficit. A "no" vote is a vote to sustain the President's veto of this fiscally unsound and potentially inflationary measure. Thus, a "no" vote is the fiscally responsible position. The attempt to override the President's veto failed in the House on December 18, 1975 (265-157). *See Chapter 3, p. 43.*

11. *HR 8069—Labor–HEW Appropriations—*(Findley Amendment)
This amendment exempts employers of twenty-five or fewer from first instance penalties for OSHA violations. This is to encourage small businessmen to seek out and correct violations without fear of penalty while trying to determine how to comply with OSHA. A "yes" vote is in favor of the Findley Amendment. This amendment failed the House on June 25, 1975 (186-231). *See Chapter 5, p. 65.*

12. *HR 8617—Federal Employee's Political Activities*
This bill "de-Hatched" civil servants and allowed them to participate actively in partisan politics. A "yes" vote is in favor of political participation by civil servants. Passed the House on October 21, 1975 (288-119). *See Chapters 7, 8, pp. 84, 90.*

13. *HR 5546—Health Manpower Act—*(Broyhill Amendment)
This amendment deletes provisions in the Act which would have established a new bureaucracy to determine first year medical residencies throughout the nation not only by number but also by specialty, deciding which

hospitals would have them. A "yes" vote is in favor of the Broyhill amendment opposing the establishment of this new bureaucracy. The amendment passed the House July 11, 1975 (207-146). *See Chapter 9, p. 96.*

14. *HR 10647—Supplemental Appropriations Bill—*(Findley Amendment)

This amendment would have limited food stamp eligibility to those with incomes at or below the officially-defined government poverty index (currently, $5050 for a family of four; updated annually in accord with cost-of-living). Presently, the food stamp program has no gross income ceiling. A "yes" vote in favor of the Findley amendment indicates support for real food stamp reform. Failed in the House on November 13, 1975 (159-230). *See Chapter 11, p. 127.*

15. *HR 4723—National Science Foundation (NSF)—*(Bauman Amendment)

The Bauman Amendment requires the NSF to submit proposed NSF grants to Congress and allows either House of Congress to disapprove those proposed grants which Congress feels to be of questionable value. A "yes" vote is in favor of the Bauman Amendment. Passed the House April 9, 1975 (219-199). *See Chapter 13, p. 145.*

16. *HR 8841—Federal Insecticide, Fungicide, and Rodenticide Act—*(Kelly Amendment)

This amendment would have required that before the Administrator of EPA could permanently cancel the use of any pesticide the Secretary of Agriculture would have to concur in that decision. A "yes" vote is in favor of the Kelly Amendment. Failed in the House on October 9, 1975 (164-233). *See Chapter 14, p. 156.*

17. *HR 25—Surface Mining Control & Reclamation Act—* (Vote to Override Veto)

This bill would have established unreasonably rigid federal regulations and controls over the mining of coal. The Ford Administration estimated that this bill would cause a reduction in coal production of eight to twenty-two percent (8-22%) in its first year of application, result in the loss of thousands of jobs, and add an additional eight to fifteen percent (8-15%) to consumers utility bills. A "yes" vote is to override the veto. Attempt to override failed in the House (a two-thirds vote is required to override) on June 10, 1975 (278-143). *See Chapter 14, p. 163.*

18. *HR 5727—Parole Reorganization Act*
This bill establishes a regional U.S. Parole Commission as an independent agency within the Justice Department, and makes changes in parole procedures including shifting the burden of acceptability for parole from the inmate to the Commission, leaving the impression that parole is a right rather than a privilege. A "yes" vote is in favor of this Act. Passed the House on May 21, 1975 (260-137). *See Chapter 15, p. 173.*

19. *HR 4723—National Science Foundation (NSF)—(Conlan Amendment)*
This would have required specific Congressional approval before any curriculum program, course or materials could be implemented or marketed by the NSF. This would assert tight Congressional review over expenditures of taxpayer funds for the controversial "MACOS" program. A "yes" vote favors the Conlan Amendment. This amendment failed to pass the House on April 9, 1975 (196-215). *See Chapter 16, p. 181.*

20. *House Democrat Caucus Busing Vote*
The Democrat Caucus (all Democrat Members of the House) voted in a meeting of the causus to table a motion that would have requested the House Judiciary Committee to report out a Constitutional amendment to prohibit forced busing. The caucus, by tabling the motion, defeated this attempt to bring this important issue to the House floor for a vote by all the Members of Congress. A "yes" vote is in favor of tabling the attempt to bring this Constitutional amendment to the House floor. The tabling motion passed in the caucus on November 19, 1975 (172-96). *See Chapter 16, p. 185.*

21. *HR 8069—Labor–HEW Appropriations—(Bauman Motion)*

This motion urged House concurrence with a Senate amendment which would prohibit funds appropriated in HR 8069 to be used for forced busing. A "yes" vote is in favor of the anti-busing amendment. Passed the House December 4, 1975 (260-146). *See Chapter 16, p. 185.*

22. *HR 8121—State Department Appropriation Bill—*
   (Snyder Amendment)
   This amendment prohibits the State Department from using appropriated funds to negotiate the relinquishment of any U.S. rights in the Panama Canal Zone. A "yes" vote is in favor of the Snyder Amendment. Passed the House on June 26, 1975 (246-164). *See Chapter 17, p. 198.*

23. *HR 6096—Vietnam Humanitarian Assistance & Evacuation Act—*(Rousselot Amendment)
   This amendment condemned flagrant violations of Paris Peace accords by North Vietnam which was then invading The Republic of Vietnam. A "yes" vote is in favor of the Rousselot Amendment. Passed the House on April 23, 1975 (329-72). *See Chapter 17, p. 198.*

24. *HR 1287—Rhodesian Chrome Act*
   This bill would have aligned the United States with the United Nations-sponsored boycott of Rhodesian chrome (and forced the United States to rely upon more expensive Soviet chrome for this important defense resource). A "yes" vote accepts this boycott and prohibits the importation of Rhodesian chrome. Failed in the House on September 25, 1975 (187-209). *See Chapter 17, p. 198.*

25. *HR 6674—Military Procurement Authorization Bill—*
   (Schroeder Amendment)
   This Schroeder Amendment would have had the effect of cutting off $260.3 million for three airborne warning and control system aircraft (AWACS) which will be able to scout enemy airplanes and direct allied air defense operations. A "yes" vote is in favor of the Schroeder Amendment. Failed in the House May 19, 1975 (136-260). *See Chapter 18, p. 209.*

26. *HR 6674—Military Procurement Authorization Bill—* (Aspin Amendment)

This Aspin Amendment would have deleted $108 million for procurement of "long lead-time items" needed to produce the B-1 bomber (planned replacement for the aging B-52s). This would have had the effect of delaying eventual production of the B-1. A "yes" vote is in favor of the Aspin Amendment. Failed in the House on May 20, 1975 (104-227). *See Chapter 18, p. 210.*

27. *HR 6674—Military Procurement Authorization Bill—* (Dellums Amendment)

This Dellums Amendment would have had the effect of withdrawing 70,000 of our troops from their stations overseas thus weakening our defenses and undermining our credibility with both friends and foes. A "yes" vote is in favor of the Dellums Amendment. Failed in the House on May 20, 1975 (95-311). *See Chapter 18, p. 210.*

TABLE 1—VOTES

	1	2	3	4	5	6	7	8	9	10	11	12	13	14	15	16	17	18	19	20	21	22	23	24	25	26	27
ALABAMA																											
Bevill, 4	Y	N	Y	Y	N	Y	Y	Y	Y	Y	Y	Y	Y	Y	Y	Y	N	Y	Y	N	Y	Y	Y	N	N	—	N
Buchanan, 6	N	N	Y	Y	Y	N	N	N	N	N	N	N	Y	—	Y	Y	N	Y	Y	N	Y	Y	Y	N	N	N	N
Dickinson, 2	Y	N	Y	Y	Y	N	N	N	Y	N	Y	Y	Y	Y	Y	Y	N	N	N	—	Y	Y	Y	Y	N	N	N
Edwards, 1	Y	N	Y	Y	Y	N	N	N	Y	N	Y	Y	—	—	—	—	N	N	N	—	Y	Y	Y	—	—	N	Y
Flowers, 7	Y	N	Y	Y	N	N	Y	N	N	Y	Y	N	Y	Y	Y	Y	N	N	Y	Y	Y	Y	Y	N	Y	—	N
Jones, 5	Y	N	Y	Y	Y	N	N	N	Y	N	Y	Y	N	Y	N	N	N	N	Y	—	Y	Y	Y	N	N	N	N
Nichols, 3	N	N	Y	Y	N	Y	N	N	Y	Y	Y	—	Y	Y	Y	Y	N	N	N	N	Y	Y	Y	N	N	—	N
ALASKA																											
Young	Y	—	N	N	Y	N	—	N	Y	N	Y	—	Y	Y	Y	Y	N	—	Y	—	Y	Y	Y	N	N	—	N
ARIZONA																											
Conlan, 4	Y	N	Y	N	N	N	—	Y	N	Y	Y	Y	N	N	N	N	N	N	N	Y	N	N	Y	Y	N	N	N
Rhodes, 1	N	N	Y	N	Y	N	N	N	Y	Y	Y	N	N	Y	Y	Y	N	N	N	—	Y	Y	Y	N	N	N	N
Steiger, 3	N	N	Y	N	N	N	N	N	Y	Y	Y	N	Y	N	N	N	N	N	Y	—	Y	N	Y	N	N	N	N
Udall, 2	—	N	N	—	Y	Y	N	Y	N	Y	N	—	Y	Y	Y	Y	Y	—	—	Y	N	—	—	—	—	—	Y
ARKANSAS																											
Alexander, 1	Y	N	Y	Y	Y	N	N	N	Y	Y	Y	—	—	—	—	—	Y	N	—	Y	Y	N	Y	Y	Y	Y	N
Hammerschmidt, 3	N	Y	N	Y	Y	N	N	N	N	Y	N	N	Y	Y	Y	Y	N	N	N	—	Y	Y	Y	N	N	N	N
Mills, 2	Y	N	Y	N	Y	Y	N	N	Y	Y	N	N	—	Y	N	N	Y	N	N	—	Y	N	Y	N	N	Y	N
Thornton, 4	N	Y	Y	Y	Y	Y	Y	N	Y	N	N	Y	Y	N	Y	Y	N	N	Y	—	Y	N	Y	—	—	N	N
CALIFORNIA																											
Anderson, 32	Y	N	Y	N	N	N	—	N	Y	Y	Y	—	Y	—	Y	Y	N	—	—	N	Y	Y	Y	N	N	N	Y
Bell, 27	N	N	Y	Y	N	N	N	N	N	Y	Y	N	—	Y	Y	Y	N	N	Y	—	Y	Y	Y	N	N	—	N
Brown, 36	Y	Y	N	N	Y	N	—	N	Y	Y	Y	Y	Y	Y	Y	Y	N	Y	Y	—	Y	Y	Y	N	N	—	—

CALIFORNIA (Continued)

	1	2	3	4	5	6	7	8	9	10	11	12	13	14	15	16	17	18	19	20	21	22	23	24	25	26	27
Burgener, 43	Y	Y	Y	Y	N	Y	Y	Y	N	Y	N	Y	N	Y	N		Y	Y	N	Y		N	N	Y	Y	Y	Y
Burke, 28	Y	Y	Y	Y	N	N	Y	N	N	Y	N	Y	N	N	Y		Y	Y	N			N	N	N	N	N	N
Burton, J., 5	N	Y	Y	Y	N	Y	Y	N	N	Y	Y	Y	N	Y	N	N	Y	Y	N		Y	Y	Y	Y	N	Y	N
Burton, P., 6	N	N	Y	Y	N	Y	N	N	N	Y	Y	Y	N	Y	N	N	Y	Y	N		N	N	N	Y	N	Y	N
Clausen, 2	Y	Y	Y	Y	Y	Y	Y	Y	N	Y	Y	Y	Y	Y	Y	Y	Y	Y	Y	N	N	N	Y	Y	Y	Y	Y
Clawson, 33	Y	Y	N	N	N	Y	Y	Y	Y	Y	N	N	N	Y	N	N	Y	Y	N	Y	N	N	N	N	Y	Y	Y
Corman, 21	N	N	Y	Y	N	Y	N	N	N	Y	N	Y	N	Y	N	N	Y	Y	N		N	N	N	N	N	N	N
Danielson, 30	Y	Y	Y	Y	Y	Y	N	N	N	Y	Y	Y	N	Y	N	N	Y	Y	N	Y	N	N	N	N	N	Y	Y
Dellums, 8	N	N	N	N	N	N	N	N	N	N	N	Y	N	N	N	N	Y	N	N		N	N	N	N	N	N	N
Edwards, 10	Y	N	Y	Y	N	Y	N	N	N	Y	N	Y	N	Y	N	N	Y	Y	N		Y	N	N	Y	N	Y	Y
Goldwater, 20	Y	Y	Y	Y	N	Y	Y	Y	Y	Y	N	Y	N	Y	Y	Y	Y	Y	Y		Y	Y	Y	Y	Y	Y	Y
Hannaford, 34	Y	Y	Y	Y	Y	Y	N	N	N	Y	N	Y	N	Y	N	N	Y	Y	N	N	N	N	N	N	N	N	N
Hawkins, 29	N	N	N	N	N	N	N	N	N	N	N	Y	N	N	N	N	Y	N	N		N	N	N	Y	N	N	N
Hinshaw, 40	Y	Y	Y	N	N	Y	Y	N	N	Y	N	Y	N	Y	N	N	N	Y	N		N	N	N	N	N	N	N
Johnson, 1		Y	Y	Y	Y	Y	N	N	N	Y	Y	Y	N	Y	N	N	Y	Y	N		N	Y	N	N	Y	N	N
Ketchum, 18	N	N	N	N	N	N	Y	N	Y	Y	N	Y	N	N	N	N	Y	N	N			N	N	N	N	N	N
Krebs, 17	Y	Y	Y	Y	N	Y	N	N	N	Y	N	Y	N	Y	N	N	Y	Y	N		Y	N	Y	Y	N	Y	Y
Lagomarsino, 19	Y	N	Y	Y	Y	Y	Y	Y	Y	Y	N	N	Y	Y	N	N	Y	Y	N	N	N	N	N	N	N	Y	Y
Leggett, 4	Y	Y	Y	Y	N	N	N	N	N	Y	N	Y	N	Y	N	N	Y	Y	N	Y	Y	Y	N	Y	Y	Y	N
Lloyd, 35	Y	N	Y	Y	N	N	N	N	N	Y	N	Y	N	Y	N	N	Y	N	N		N	N	N	N	N	N	N
McCloskey, 12	N	N	Y	N	N	N	N	N	N	N	N	Y	N	Y	N	N	Y	Y	N		Y	N	N	Y	N	Y	N
McFall, 14	Y	Y	Y	Y	Y	Y	Y	N	N	Y	N	Y	N	Y	N	N	Y	N	N	N	N	Y	N	N	N	N	N
Mineta, 13	Y	Y	Y	Y	N	Y	N	N	N	Y	Y	Y	N	Y	N	N	Y	N	N	N	Y	Y	N	Y	N	Y	Y
Miller, 7	N	N	Y	Y	N	Y	N	N	N	N	N	Y	N	Y	N	N	Y	N	N		N	N	N	N	N	N	N
Moorhead, 22	Y	Y	Y	Y	Y	Y	Y	Y	Y	Y	N	Y	Y	Y	Y	Y	Y	N	Y		Y	Y	Y	Y	N	N	Y
Moss, 3	Y	Y	Y	Y	N	N	N	N	N	Y	N	Y	N	Y	N	N	Y	N	N	N	N	N	N	N	N	N	N
Patterson, 38	Y	Y	N	Y	Y	Y	Y	Y	Y	Y	N	Y	N	Y	N	N	Y	N	N	N	N	N	N	N	N	N	N
*Pettis, 37																											
Rees, 23	Y	Y	Y	N	Y	N	N	N	N	Y	N	Y	N	Y	N	N	Y	Y	N	Y	Y	Y	N	Y	Y	Y	Y
Rousselot, 26	Y	Y	Y	Y	N	Y	N		Y	Y	Y	N	N	Y	N	N	N		N		N	N	N	N			Y
Roybal, 25	Y	N	Y	Y	N	Y	N	N	N	Y	N	Y	N	Y	N	N	Y	Y	N		Y	Y	Y	Y	N	Y	N
Ryan, 11	Y	Y	Y	Y	Y	Y	Y	N	N	Y	N	Y	Y	Y	N	N	Y		N		Y	Y	N		N	N	Y
Sisk, 15	Y	Y	Y	N	N	Y	N	N	N	Y	Y	Y	N	Y	N	N	Y	N	N		N	Y	N	Y			Y
Stark, 9	N	Y	Y	N	Y	Y	Y	N	Y	N	Y	N	N	Y	Y	N	N	N	N		Y	Y	N	N	N	Y	N

	1	2	3	4	5	6	7	8	9	10	11	12	13	14	15	16	17	18	19	20	21	22	23	24	25	26	27
CALIFORNIA (Continued)																											
Talcott, 16.	Y	Y	Y	N	N	Y	Y	N	N	Y	N	Y	N	N	N	N	Y	Y	N	Y	N	Y	Y	Y	Y	Y	N
Van Deerlin, 42	N	Y	Y	Y	Y	Y	Y	Y	Y	Y	Y	Y	Y	Y	Y	Y	Y	Y	Y	N	Y	Y	Y	Y	N	Y	Y
Waxman, 24	N	Y	Y	Y	Y	Y	Y	Y	Y	Y	Y	Y	N	Y	Y	N	Y	Y	Y		Y	Y	Y	N	Y	Y	Y
Wiggins, 39	Y	Y	Y	Y	Y	Y	N	Y	Y	Y	Y	N	Y	Y	N	Y	Y	Y	Y	N	Y	Y	Y	N	Y	N	N
Wilson, 31	N	Y	Y	Y	N	N	N	N	Y	Y	Y	Y	Y	Y	Y	Y	Y	Y	Y	N	Y	Y	N	N	Y	N	Y
Wilson, Bob, 41	Y	Y	Y	Y	Y		Y	Y	Y	Y	Y	Y	Y	N	Y		Y	Y	Y		Y	Y	Y	Y	Y	N	Y
COLORADO																											
Armstrong, 5	Y	N	Y	Y	Y	N	N	N	N	Y	N	Y	N	N	Y	N	Y	Y	N	Y	Y	N	N	Y	N	N	N
Evans, 3	Y	Y	Y	Y	Y	Y	Y	Y	Y	Y	Y	Y	Y	Y	N	Y	Y	Y	Y		Y	Y	Y	Y	Y	Y	Y
Johnson, 4	N	Y	N	Y	Y	Y	N	N	Y	Y	Y	Y	N	N	Y	N	Y	Y	N	Y	N	N	N	N	Y	N	N
Schroeder, 1	N	Y	Y	Y	Y	Y	Y	Y	Y	Y	N	Y	N	Y	Y	Y	Y	Y	Y		Y	Y	Y	N	Y	Y	Y
Wirth, 2	N		N	Y	Y	Y	Y	Y	Y	Y	Y	N	N	N	N	N	Y	Y	Y		N	Y	Y	Y	Y	Y	Y
CONNECTICUT																											
Cotter, 1	N	Y	Y	Y	Y	Y	N	Y	Y	Y	Y	Y	Y	N	N	N	Y	Y	N		Y	N	N	Y	N	N	Y
Dodd, 2	N	N	Y	Y	Y	N	N	Y	Y	Y	Y	Y	N	Y	Y	Y	Y	Y	Y	Y	Y	N	Y	N	Y	Y	Y
Giaimo, 3	Y	Y	Y	Y	N	Y	Y	Y	Y	Y	N	Y	Y	Y	N	Y	Y	Y	Y	Y	N	N	Y	Y	Y	Y	Y
McKinney, 4	Y	N	N	Y	Y	Y	Y	Y	Y	Y	N	Y	Y	N	N	N	Y	Y	N	N	Y	N	N	Y	N	Y	Y
Moffett, 6	Y	Y	Y	Y	Y	N	Y	Y	N	Y	N	Y	Y	Y	Y	Y	Y	Y	Y	Y	N	N	Y	Y	Y	Y	Y
Sarasin, 5	Y	Y	N	Y	Y	N	Y	N	N	Y	N	N		Y	Y	N	N		N		N	N	Y	Y	Y	Y	Y
DELAWARE																											
du Pont	Y	Y	N	N	Y	N	N	N	N	N	N	Y	Y	Y	Y	N	Y		N		Y	N	Y	Y	Y	Y	N
FLORIDA																											
Bafalis, 10	N	Y	Y	Y	N	N	N	N	N	Y	N	Y	Y	N	Y	Y	Y	Y	Y	Y	Y	Y	Y	Y	N	N	Y
Bennett, 3	N	N	Y	Y	N	Y	Y	Y	Y	Y	N	Y	N	N	Y	Y	N	Y	Y		Y	N	N	Y	Y	Y	N
Burke, 12	N	N	N	N	Y	Y	Y	N	Y	Y	Y	N	Y	Y	N	Y	Y	Y	Y	Y	Y	Y	Y	N	N	Y	N
Chappell, 4	N	N	Y	Y	Y	N	N	N	Y	Y	Y	N	Y	N	Y	N	Y	Y	N		Y	Y	Y	N	Y	Y	N
Fascell, 15	N	Y	Y	Y	N	N	Y	Y	N	Y	Y	Y	Y	Y	N	N	Y	Y	Y		N	Y	N	N	Y	Y	N
Frey, 9	Y	N	Y	N	Y	Y	Y	N	Y	Y	Y	Y		N	Y	Y	Y	N	N		Y	Y	Y	Y	Y	Y	N
Fuqua, 2	N	N	Y	Y	N	Y	Y	Y	Y	Y	Y	N	Y	N	Y	N	Y		Y		Y	N	N	N	Y	Y	N
Gibbons, 7	Y	Y	Y	Y	N	Y	Y	Y	N	Y	Y	N	N	Y	N	N	Y	Y	Y		N	Y	Y	Y	Y	Y	N
Haley, 8	Y	N	N	N	N	Y	Y	N	Y	Y	Y	Y	N	N	N	N	Y	N	Y	Y	N	Y	N	Y	Y	Y	N
Kelly, 5	N	N	N	N	Y	N	Y	Y	Y	Y	N	Y		N	Y	N	Y		N		Y	Y	Y		N	Y	N
Lehman, 13	Y	Y	Y	Y	Y	N	N	Y	Y	Y	Y	Y	Y	Y	N	N	Y	Y	Y	Y	N	N	Y	Y	N	Y	N
Pepper, 14	Y		Y	Y	Y	Y	Y	Y	Y	Y	Y	Y		N	N	N	Y	Y	Y		Y	Y	Y	Y	Y	Y	N

221

	1	2	3	4	5	6	7	8	9	10	11	12	13	14	15	16	17	18	19	20	21	22	23	24	25	26	27
FLORIDA (Continued)																											
Rogers, 11	N	N	N	N	Y	Y	N	N	Y	N	Y	N	N	N	N	N	Y	Y	N	N	N	N	N	N	N	N	N
Sikes, 1	N	N	N	N	Y	Y	N	Y	Y	Y	Y	N	N	Y	N	N	N	N	N	N	N	N	N	N	N	N	N
Young, 6	N	Y	N	N	Y	N	N	N	N	Y	Y	Y	Y	Y	Y	Y	Y	Y	N	N	N	Y	Y	N	N	N	N
GEORGIA																											
Brinkley, 3	Y	Y	Y	Y	Y	Y	Y	N	Y	Y	N	Y	Y	Y	Y	Y	Y	Y	N	N	Y	Y	Y	Y	Y	Y	Y
Flynt, 6	N	Y	N	Y	N	Y	N	Y	N	N	Y	N	Y	Y	Y	Y	N	N	N	N	Y	Y	Y	Y	Y	Y	Y
Ginn, 1	N	N	N	N	Y	Y	N	N	Y	Y	Y	N	N	N	N	N	Y	Y	Y	N	Y	Y	Y	N	N	N	N
Landrum, 9	N	N	N	N	Y	Y	N	Y	Y	Y	Y	Y	Y	Y	Y	Y	Y	N	N	N	Y	Y	Y	N	Y	Y	Y
Levitas, 4	N	N	N	N	Y	N	Y	N	N	Y	Y	Y	Y	Y	Y	Y	N	Y	N	N	Y	Y	Y	N	Y	Y	Y
Mathis, 2	N	N	N	Y	Y	Y	N	N	Y	N	Y	Y	Y	Y	Y	Y	Y	N	N	N	Y	N	Y	Y	Y	Y	Y
McDonald, 7	N	N	N	N	Y	N	N	N	Y	N	Y	N	Y	Y	Y	Y	Y	Y	N	Y	Y	Y	Y	N	N	N	N
Stephens, 10	N	N	N	N	Y	N	Y	N	N	Y	N	Y	Y	Y	Y	Y	Y	Y	N	N	Y	Y	Y	N	Y	Y	Y
Stuckey, 8	N	N	N	N	Y	N	N	N	Y	Y	N	Y	Y	Y	N	Y	Y	Y	Y	N	Y	N	Y	N	Y	N	N
Young, 5	Y	Y	Y	Y	Y	Y	N	N	Y	Y	Y	Y	Y	Y	Y	Y	N	N	N	N	Y	Y	Y	N	N	N	N
HAWAII																											
Matsunaga,	N	N	N	N	Y	Y	N	N	Y	N	Y	Y	Y	Y	Y	Y	Y	Y	N	N	N	Y	Y	N	N	N	N
Mink, 2	N	N	N	N	Y	Y	N	Y	Y	Y	Y	N	N	N	N	Y	N	N	N	N	N	Y	Y	Y	N	N	N
IDAHO																											
Hansen, 2	N	N	N	N	N	N	N	N	Y	N	Y	Y	Y	Y	Y	Y	Y	Y	Y	Y	Y	Y	Y	Y	Y	Y	Y
Symms, 1	N	N	N	N	N	N	N	N	Y	N	Y	Y	Y	Y	Y	Y	Y	N	N	N	N	N	Y	Y	N	N	N
ILLINOIS																											
Anderson, 16	Y	Y	Y	Y	N	N	N	N	Y	Y	N	Y	Y	Y	N	Y	Y	Y	Y	N	N	N	Y	N	N	N	N
Annunzio, 11	Y	Y	Y	Y	N	N	N	Y	N	Y	N	Y	Y	Y	N	N	Y	N	N	N	Y	Y	Y	N	N	Y	N
Collins, 7	N	N	N	Y	N	Y	Y	Y	Y	N	N	Y	Y	N	Y	Y	Y	Y	Y	N	Y	Y	Y	Y	Y	N	N
Crane, 12	Y	Y	N	N	Y	N	N	N	Y	N	N	Y	Y	N	N	Y	Y	Y	Y	N	Y	N	Y	N	N	Y	Y
Derwinski, 4	Y	Y	N	Y	N	Y	Y	Y	Y	Y	N	N	Y	Y	Y	N	Y	Y	N	N	Y	Y	Y	N	N	Y	Y
Erlenborn, 14	N	N	N	Y	Y	N	Y	N	N	N	Y	Y	Y	Y	Y	Y	Y	N	Y	N	Y	Y	Y	Y	N	Y	N
**Fary, 5	Y	Y	Y	Y	N	N	N	N	Y	Y	N	N	N	N	N	N	N	N	N	N	N	Y	Y	Y	Y	Y	Y
Findley, 20	Y	N	N	Y	Y	N	N	N	Y	Y	N	N	N	N	N	Y	N	N	N	N	Y	N	Y	N	N	N	N
Hall, 15	Y	Y	Y	Y	Y	N	N	N	Y	Y	N	N	N	N	N	N	N	N	N	N	Y	Y	Y	N	Y	Y	Y
Hyde, 6	N	N	N	N	Y	Y	N	N	Y	N	N	Y	Y	Y	Y	Y	Y	N	N	N	Y	Y	Y	N	N	N	N
Madigan, 21	Y	N	N	N	Y	N	N	Y	Y	N	Y	N	N	Y	N	N	Y	Y	N	N	Y	Y	Y	N	Y	N	N
McClory, 13	Y	Y	Y	Y	Y	N	N	N	Y	Y	Y	Y	Y	Y	Y	Y	Y	N	N	N	Y	Y	Y	N	N	N	N
Metcalfe, 1	N	N	N	N	Y	N	N	N	Y	Y	Y	N	Y	Y	Y	Y	N	N	N	N	Y	Y	Y	N	N	N	N

222

	1	2	3	4	5	6	7	8	9	10	11	12	13	14	15	16	17	18	19	20	21	22	23	24	25	26	27
Michel, 18	N	N	N|	N	Y	N	N	N|	N	N	Y	N	Y	Y	Y	N	Y			N			Y	Y			N	N			N
Mikva, 10	Y	Y	Y	Y	N	Y	Y	Y	Y	Y	N	N	Y	Y	Y	Y	N	Y	N	Y	N	Y	N	Y	N	Y	Y
Murphy, 2	N	N	Y	N	Y	Y	Y	N	N	N	Y	N	N	Y	Y	Y	Y	Y	N	<	N	Y	Y	N	Y	Y	N
O'Brien, 17	Y	Y	Y		Y	Y	Y	Y	Y	Y	N	N	Y		Y	N		Y	Y	Y	Y	N			Y	Y	Y	Y	Y	Y	N
Price, 23	Y	Y	<	Y	Y	Y	Y	Y	Y	N	Y	Y	N	N	Y	Y	Y	Y	Y	Y|	N	N	Y	N	N	Y	Y
Railsback, 19	N	Y	<	N	Y	N	N	Y	N	Y	Y	Y	N	N	Y	N	Y	Y	Y	<	<	N	Y	Y	N	N	N
Rostenkowski, 8	Y	N	N	Y	N	Y	Y	N	Y	Y	Y	Y	Y	Y	Y	Y	Y	Y	N			Y	Y	Y	Y	Y	Y	Y
Russo, 3	N	N	Y	N	Y	Y	Y	Y	N	Y	N	Y	N	N	Y	Y	Y	Y	Y	<	Y	Y	Y	N	Y	N	N
Shipley, 22	N	Y	N	Y	N	N	Y	Y	N	Y	N	N	N	Y	N	N	N	N	Y	N	N	Y	N	N	N	Y	N
Simon, 24	Y	N	Y	N	Y	N	N	Y	N	Y	N	N	Y	Y	Y	Y	N	Y	Y	<	Y	N	Y	Y	Y	Y	N
Yates, 9	Y	Y	<	Y	Y	N	N	Y	Y	Y	N	Y	N	Y	Y	Y	Y	Y	Y	N	Y	Y	Y	Y	Y	Y	Y

INDIANA

	1	2	3	4	5	6	7	8	9	10	11	12	13	14	15	16	17	18	19	20	21	22	23	24	25	26	27
Brademas, 3	Y	Y	<	N	N	Y	Y	Y	N	Y	Y	Y	N	Y	Y	Y	Y	Y	Y	<	Y	Y	Y	Y	Y	Y	Y
Evans, 6	N	Y	N	Y	N	Y	N	Y	N	N	N	N	N	N	N	N	Y	Y	N	<	N	N	Y	Y	N	Y	Y
Fithian, 2	N	N	N	N	N	N	N	Y	Y	Y	N	<	N	Y	N	N	Y	Y	N			N	N	N	N	N	Y	N
Hamilton, 9	Y	Y	<	Y	<	Y	Y	Y	N	Y	Y	Y	Y	Y	Y	Y	Y	Y	Y			<	N	<	N	N	Y	Y
Hayes, 8	Y	Y	N	N	N	Y	Y	Y	Y	Y	N	Y	N	Y	Y	N	Y	Y	Y	<	<	N	Y	N	N	Y	N
Hillis, 5	Y	Y	Y	Y	N	Y	Y	Y	Y	Y	N	Y	N	N	Y	Y	Y	Y	Y			Y	N	Y	Y	Y	N	Y
Jacobs, 11	N	Y	N|	N	N	Y	N	Y	N	N|	N	Y	N	N	N	N	Y	N	Y	Y|	N	Y	Y	N	Y	Y	Y
Madden, 1	Y	N			Y	Y	N	Y			N	<	Y	Y	Y	N	Y	N	Y	Y			N	N	N	N	Y	N	<	N
Myers, 7	N	Y			N	N	N	N			N	<	Y	Y	Y	N	Y	N	Y	Y			<	Y	N	Y	Y	N	N	N
Roush, 4	Y	Y	N|	Y	Y	Y	Y	<	N	<	Y	<	N	N	Y	Y	Y	Y	Y	<	Y	N	N	Y	N	Y	Y
Sharp, 10	Y	N	Y	N	N	Y	N	Y	N	Y	Y			N	Y	N	N	Y	N	N	N	Y	Y	Y	Y	Y	N	N

IOWA

	1	2	3	4	5	6	7	8	9	10	11	12	13	14	15	16	17	18	19	20	21	22	23	24	25	26	27
Bedell, 6	Y	Y	<	Y	N	Y	Y	Y	N	Y	N	Y	N	N	Y	Y	Y			N	<	N	N	N	Y	N	Y	N
Blouin, 2	Y	N	Y	Y	Y	Y	Y	Y	N	Y	Y	Y	N	Y	Y	Y	Y	Y	Y	<	Y	Y	N	Y	Y	Y	Y
Grassley, 3	N	N	N|	N	Y	Y	Y	Y	Y	Y	N	Y	N	Y	Y	Y	Y	Y	Y			N|	N	Y	Y	N	Y	Y
Harkin, 5	Y	N	Y	Y	Y	Y	Y	Y	Y	Y	Y	Y	<	N	Y	Y	N	<	Y	<	Y	Y	Y	Y	N	Y	Y
Mezvinsky, 1	Y	Y	<	N	Y	Y	Y	Y	Y	Y	N	N	N	N	Y	Y	Y	N	Y	<	N	Y	Y	N	Y	N	N
Smith, 4	N	N	N	N	N	N	Y	N	N	N	N	N	N	Y	Y	N	N	N	N	N	N	N	N	Y	N	Y	N

KANSAS

	1	2	3	4	5	6	7	8	9	10	11	12	13	14	15	16	17	18	19	20	21	22	23	24	25	26	27
Keys, 2	Y	Y	Y	Y	N	Y	Y	Y	N	Y	Y	Y	N	Y	Y	Y	Y	Y	Y	Y	N	Y	<	N	N	<	N
Sebelius, 1	N	Y	Y	N	N	N	N	N	Y	Y	Y	Y	N	Y	Y	Y	N	Y	Y			<	Y	Y	N					Y
Shriver, 4	N	N	N	N	Y	Y	Y	Y	N	N	Y	Y	Y	N	Y	Y	N	Y	N	<	Y	Y	N	Y	N	Y	Y

	1	2	3	4	5	6	7	8	9	10	11	12	13	14	15	16	17	18	19	20	21	22	23	24	25	26	27
KANSAS (Continued)																											
Skubitz, 5	N	Y	N	N	Y	Y	N	Y	N	N	N	N	Y	N	N	N	Y	Y	N	N	Y	Y	Y	Y	N	Y	N
Winn, 3	Y	Y	Y	Y	Y	Y	Y	Y	Y	Y	Y	Y	Y	Y	Y	Y	Y	Y	N	Y	Y	Y	Y	Y	N	Y	N
KENTUCKY																											
Breckinridge, 6	N	N	N	N	Y	Y	N	N	Y	Y	N	Y	N	Y	Y	Y	Y	Y	Y	N	N	N	N	N	Y	N	N
Carter, 5	Y	Y	Y	Y	Y	Y	Y	Y	Y	Y	Y	Y	Y	Y	Y	Y	Y	Y	Y	N	Y	Y	Y	Y	Y	Y	Y
Hubbard, 1	Y	Y	Y	Y	Y	Y	Y	Y	Y	Y	Y	Y	Y	Y	Y	Y	Y	N	Y	N	Y	Y	Y	Y	Y	Y	Y
Mazzoli, 3	N	N	N	N	Y	N	N	N	Y	Y	Y	Y	Y	Y	Y	Y	Y	N	Y	N	N	Y	N	N	Y	N	N
Natcher, 2	N	N	N	N	Y	Y	N	Y	Y	Y	Y	N	N	Y	Y	Y	Y	Y	N	N	Y	Y	Y	N	Y	N	N
Perkins, 7	N	N	N	N	Y	N	N	N	N	N	Y	N	N	N	N	N	Y	Y	Y	N	N	N	Y	N	N	N	N
Snyder, 4	N	N	N	N	Y	Y	N	Y	N	N	N	N	Y	N	N	N	Y	Y	N	N	Y	Y	Y	Y	N	Y	N
LOUISIANA																											
Boggs, 2	N	N	N	N	Y	Y	N	N	Y	Y	Y	Y	Y	Y	Y	Y	Y	Y	Y	N	Y	Y	Y	Y	Y	N	N
Breaux, 7	Y	Y	Y	Y	Y	Y	Y	Y	Y	Y	Y	N	N	Y	Y	Y	Y	Y	Y	N	Y	Y	Y	Y	N	N	N
Hebert, 1	Y	Y	Y	Y	Y	Y	Y	Y	Y	Y	Y	N	N	Y	Y	Y	Y	Y	Y	N	N	Y	Y	Y	N	N	N
Long, 8	N	N	N	N	Y	Y	Y	Y	N	N	Y	N	Y	Y	Y	N	N	Y	Y	N	Y	N	Y	N	N	N	N
Moore, 6	Y	N	Y	N	Y	N	Y	Y	Y	Y	Y	Y	Y	N	Y	Y	Y	Y	Y	N	Y	N	N	N	N	N	N
Passman, 5	N	Y	N	N	Y	Y	N	N	Y	Y	Y	N	N	Y	Y	N	Y	N	Y	N	N	Y	Y	Y	N	N	N
Treen, 3	Y	Y	Y	Y	Y	Y	Y	Y	Y	Y	Y	N	Y	Y	Y	Y	Y	N	Y	N	Y	Y	Y	N	N	N	N
Waggonner, 4	N	N	N	N	Y	N	N	N	Y	Y	N				Y	N	N	Y	Y		N	Y	Y	N	N	Y	Y
MAINE																											
Cohen, 2	N	N	N	N	Y		N	N	Y	Y	Y	N	Y	N	N	N	Y	Y	Y	N	N	Y	Y	Y	N	Y	N
Emery, 1	N	Y	N	N	Y	Y	N	Y	N	Y	N	N		N	Y	N	Y	N	Y		N	N	N	Y	N	Y	N
MARYLAND																											
Bauman, 1	N	N	N	N	Y	Y	N	N	Y	Y	N	N	N	N	N	N	Y	N	Y	N	N	N	N	N	N	Y	N
Byron, 6	N	N	N	N	Y	Y	N	N	Y	Y	Y		Y	Y	Y	Y	Y	Y	Y		N	Y	N	N	Y	N	N
Gude, 8	N	N	N	N	Y	Y	N	Y	Y	Y	Y	N	Y	Y	Y	N	Y	Y	Y		N	Y	Y	Y	N	N	N
Holt, 4	Y	Y	Y	Y	Y	N	Y	Y	Y	Y	Y	Y	Y	Y	Y	Y	Y	Y	Y	N	Y	Y	Y	Y	N	N	N
Long, 2	N	N	N	N	Y	Y	N	N	Y	Y	Y	N	Y	Y	Y	N	N	N	Y		Y	Y	Y	Y	N	Y	N
Mitchell, 7	N	Y	N	N	Y	N	N	N	N	N	N	N	Y	N	N	N	Y	Y	Y	N	Y	N	Y	N	N	N	N
Sarbanes, 3	N	N	N	N	Y	N	N	N	Y	Y	Y	N	Y	N	N	N	Y	Y	Y		Y	Y	Y	Y	N	N	N
Spellman, 5	N	N	N	N	Y	N	N	N	Y	Y	Y	N	Y	N	N	N	N	Y	Y		Y	Y	Y	Y	N	N	N
MASSACHUSETTS																											
Boland, 2	N	Y	N	N	Y	Y	N	Y	Y	Y	Y	Y	Y	Y	Y	N	Y	N	Y	N	Y	Y	Y	Y	N	Y	N
Burke, 11	Y	Y	Y	Y	Y	Y	Y	Y	Y	Y	Y	N	Y	Y	Y	Y	Y	Y	Y	N	N	N	Y	N	N	N	N

224

	1	2	3	4	5	6	7	8	9	10	11	12	13	14	15	16	17	18	19	20	21	22	23	24	25	26	27
MASSACHUSETTS (Continued)																											
Conte, 1	Y	Y	Y	Y	N	N	N	Y	N	Y	N	N	Y	Y	N	N	Y	Y	N		N	N	Y	Y	N	Y	Y
Drinan, 4	Y	Y	Y	Y	N	Y	Y	N	N	N	Y	Y	N	Y	N	N	Y	Y	N	Y	Y	N	N	N	N	Y	Y
Early, 3	Y	Y	Y	Y	N	N	Y	N	N	N	N	Y	N	N	N	N	Y	Y	Y	N	N	N	Y	Y	Y	Y	Y
Harrington, 6	Y	Y	Y	Y		N	Y	N	N	Y	N	N	N	N	N	N	Y		Y		N	N	N	N	N	Y	N
Heckler, 10	Y	Y	Y	Y	N	Y	N	Y	N	N	N	N	N	Y	N	N	Y	Y	N	Y	N	Y	N	Y	N	N	N
Macdonald, 7	Y	N	Y	Y			N	N	N	N	N		N	N	N	N	Y	Y	Y		N	N	N	Y	Y	Y	N
Moakley, 9	Y	Y	Y	Y	N	Y	Y	N	N	N	N	N	N	N	N	N	Y	Y	Y	N	N	N	Y	N	N	Y	N
O'Neill, 8	Y	Y	Y	Y	N	N	N	Y	N	N	N	Y	Y	N	Y	Y	Y	Y	N	N	N	N	N	Y	N	Y	N
Studds, 12	N	Y	Y	Y	Y	Y	Y	N	N	N	N	Y	Y	Y	N	N	Y	Y	N	N	N	N	N	N	Y	N	N
Tsongas, 5	N	Y	Y	Y		Y	Y	N	N	Y	N	Y	Y	N	N	N	Y	Y	N	N	N	N	N	Y	N	N	N
MICHIGAN																											
Blanchard, 18		N	Y	Y	N	Y	N	Y	Y	N	N	N	Y	N	N	N	Y		N	Y	N	N	N	Y	Y	Y	Y
Brodhead, 17		Y	Y	Y	N	N	Y	N	Y	Y	N	Y	N	N	Y	Y	N		Y	N	N	N	N	Y	Y	Y	N
Broomfield, 19	N	Y	N	Y	N	Y	N	Y	N	N	Y	N	Y	N	Y	N	N	Y	N	Y	Y	Y	N	Y	Y	Y	N
Brown, 3	N	Y	Y	Y	Y	N	Y	N	N	N	Y	N	Y	Y	Y	Y	N	Y	N	N	Y	N	Y	N	Y	Y	N
Carr, 6	Y	Y	Y	Y		Y	Y	Y	N	Y	N	Y	Y	N	N	N	Y	Y	Y		Y	N	Y	N	Y	N	Y
Cederberg, 10	Y	Y	Y	Y	N	N	N	Y	N	N	N	N	Y	N	Y	N	N	Y	N	N	Y	Y	N	Y	N	Y	Y
Conyers, 1	N	Y	N	Y				N	N	N	Y			Y	N	N	Y	N	N	N	N	N	N	N	N	N	N
Diggs, 13	Y	Y	Y	N	Y	N	N	N	N	Y	N	Y	N	N	N	N	Y	Y	Y		N	N	N	N	N	N	Y
Dingell, 16	N	Y	Y	Y	Y	N	Y	Y	N	N	N	Y	N	Y	Y	Y	Y	Y	N	N	Y	Y	Y	N	N	Y	N
Esch, 2	Y	Y	Y	Y	N	N	N	N	N	N	Y	N	N	N	N	N	Y	Y	N	Y	N	N	N	N	N	N	N
Ford, 15	N	Y	Y	Y				N	N	Y	N	N	Y	N	N	N	Y	Y			Y	Y	Y	Y	Y	Y	Y
Hutchinson, 4	Y	Y	Y	Y	Y	Y	Y	Y	N	N	N	Y	Y	N	N	Y	Y	Y	N		Y	N	N	N	N	N	N
Nedzi, 14	N	Y	Y	Y	Y	N	Y	N	N	N	N	Y	N	N	N	N	Y	Y	N		Y	Y	Y	N	N	Y	N
O'Hara, 12	N	Y	N	Y	N	Y	N	N	N	N	N	Y	Y	Y	N	N	Y	Y	N	N	Y	N	N	Y	Y	Y	N
Riegle, 7	Y	Y	Y	Y			Y		N	Y		N	N	N	Y	Y	Y	Y	N	N	Y	Y	N	N	N	N	Y
Ruppe, 11	Y	Y	Y	Y	N	Y	N	Y	N	N	N	N	N	N	Y	N	Y	Y	N	N	Y	Y	Y	Y	Y	N	Y
Traxler, 8	N	Y	N	Y			Y		N	N	N	Y	N	Y	Y	Y	Y	Y	Y		N	N	N	N	Y	Y	N
Vander Jagt, 9	Y	Y	Y	Y	N	N	N	Y	N	Y	N	Y	Y	N	N	N	N	Y	N		Y	Y	Y		N	N	Y
Vander Veen, 5	Y	Y	Y	Y	N	N	Y		Y	N	N	N	Y	Y	Y	N	Y	Y	N	N	N	N	Y	N	N	Y	N
MINNESOTA																											
Bergland, 7	Y	Y	Y	Y	N	N	N	Y	N	Y	Y	Y	Y	N	N	N	Y	Y	N	N	N	N	Y	Y	Y	Y	Y
Fraser, 5	Y	Y	Y	Y	N	Y	N	Y	N	Y	N	Y	N	N	N	N	Y	Y	N	N	N	N	N	Y	N	Y	N
Frenzel, 3	Y	Y	N	Y	N	Y	Y	Y	N	Y	N	N	N	N	N	N	Y	Y	N	N	N	N	Y	Y	Y	Y	Y

225

	1	2	3	4	5	6	7	8	9	10	11	12	13	14	15	16	17	18	19	20	21	22	23	24	25	26	27
Hagedorn, 2	N	N	Y	N	Y	N	N	Y	N	Y	Y	Y	N	N	Y	Y	Y	N	N	N|	Y	Y	Y	Y	Y	Y	N
Karth, 4	N	N	Y	N	Y	N	N	Y	Y	Y	Y	Y	N	N	Y	Y	N	Y	N	Y	N	N	N	Y	Y	Y	Y
Nolan, 6	N	Y	Y	Y	Y	Y	Y	N	Y	N	Y	Y	N	N	Y	Y	Y	Y	Y	N|	Y	Y	Y	N	N	N	N
Oberstar, 8	Y	Y	Y	Y	Y	Y	Y	Y	N	Y	Y	Y	Y	Y	Y	Y	Y	Y	Y	Y	Y	Y	Y	N	N	N	N
Quie, 1	N	N	N	N	N	N	N	N	Y	N	N	Y	N	N	N	N	N	N	N	N|	Y	Y	Y	Y	Y	N	N
MISSISSIPPI																											
Bowen, 2	N	N	Y	N	N	N	N	N	Y	N	N	Y	N	N	Y	N	Y	Y	Y		Y	Y	Y	N	N	N	N
Cochran, 4	N	N	N	N	Y	N	N	N	N	N	N	Y	N	N	Y	Y	Y	N	Y		Y	Y	Y	Y	Y	Y	Y
Lott, 5	N	N	Y	N	Y	N	N	N	N	N	N	Y	Y|	N	Y	Y	Y	N	Y	N	N	N	Y	Y	Y	Y	N
Montgomery, 3	N	N	N	N	Y	N	N	N	N	N	N	Y	N	N	Y	Y	Y	N	Y		Y	Y	Y	Y	Y	Y	N
Whitten, 1	N	N	N	N	Y	N	N	N	N	N	N	N	N	N	Y	Y	N	N	N		Y	Y	Y	Y	Y	N	N
MISSOURI																											
Bolling, 5	Y	Y	Y	N	Y	Y	Y	Y	Y	Y	Y	Y	N	Y	Y	Y	Y	Y	Y	N|	N	N	Y	N	N	N	N
Burlison, 10	Y	N	Y	N	Y	Y	Y	Y	Y	Y	Y	Y	Y|	Y	Y	Y	Y	Y	Y	N|	Y	N	Y	N	N	N	N
Clay, 1	Y	Y	Y	Y	Y	Y	Y	Y	Y	Y	Y	Y	N|	Y	Y	Y	Y	Y	Y	N|	Y	N	Y	N	N	N	N
Hungate, 9	N	N	Y	N	Y	N	Y	Y	N	Y	Y	Y	N	Y	Y	Y	Y	Y	Y	N|	Y	N	Y	N	N	N	N
Ichord, 8	N	N	Y	N	Y	N	Y	Y	Y	Y	N	Y	N|	Y	Y	Y	N	Y	Y	N|	Y	Y	Y	Y	Y	Y	N
Litton, 6	N	N	Y	N	N	N	Y	Y	N	N	N	Y	N|	Y	Y	Y	N	Y	Y	N|	Y	Y	Y	Y	Y	Y	N
Randall, 4	N	N	Y	N	Y	N	Y	Y	N	Y	Y	Y	N|	Y	Y	Y	N	Y	Y	N|	Y	Y	Y	Y	Y	Y	N
Sullivan, 3	Y	N	Y	Y	N	N	Y	Y	N	Y	Y	Y	N	Y	Y	Y	Y	Y	Y	N|	Y	N	Y	N	N	N	N
Symington, 2	N	N	Y	N	Y	N	N	Y	N	N	Y	Y		Y	Y	Y	Y	Y	Y	N	Y	N	Y	N	N	Y	N
Taylor, 7	N	N	N		Y	N	N	N	N	N	N	N	N|	N	Y	Y	Y	N	Y		Y	Y	Y	Y	Y	Y	N
MONTANA																											
Baucus, 1	N	N	Y	N	Y	N	N	N	Y	N	Y	Y	N|	N	Y	Y	N	Y	Y	N	N	N	N	Y	Y	Y	Y
Melcher, 2	Y	N	Y	N	Y	N	N	N	Y	N	N	Y	Y|	Y	Y	Y	N	N	Y	Y	Y	Y	Y	N	N	N	N
NEBRASKA																											
McCollister, 2	N	N	N		Y	N	N	Y	Y	N	Y	Y	Y|	Y	Y	Y	N	Y	Y		N	N	N	Y	Y	Y	N
Smith, 3	N	N	N		Y	N	N	Y	Y	N	Y	Y	Y|	N	Y	Y	N	N	Y		Y			Y	N|	N	N
Thone, 1	N	N	N		Y	N	N	Y	Y	N	Y	Y		N	Y	Y	N	N	Y		Y	Y	Y	N|	N|	N	N
NEVADA																											
Santini	Y	N	Y	N	N	N	N	Y	N	Y	Y	Y	N|	N	Y	Y	Y	Y	Y	N|	Y	Y	Y	N	N	N	N
NEW HAMPSHIRE																											
Cleveland, 2	N	Y	N	N	Y	N	N	Y	Y	N	Y	Y	Y|	Y	Y	Y	N	Y	N	N|	N	N	Y	Y	Y	Y	N
D'Amours, 1	N	Y	N	N	Y	N	Y	Y	Y	N	Y	Y	N	N	Y	Y	Y	N	Y		Y	Y	Y	N	N	N	N

226

	1	2	3	4	5	6	7	8	9	10	11	12	13	14	15	16	17	18	19	20	21	22	23	24	25	26	27
NEW JERSEY																											
Daniels, 14	Y	Y	Y	Y	N	Y	Y	Y	N	Y	N	N	N	N	Y	N	Y	Y	N	Y	Y	Y	Y	Y	Y	Y	Y
Fenwick, 5	N	Y	N	Y	N	Y	Y	Y	N	Y	N	Y	N	N	N	N	Y	Y	N	Y	N	N	N	Y	N	N	N
Florio, 1	Y	Y	Y	Y	N	Y	Y	N	N	Y	N	Y	Y	N	Y	N	Y	Y	Y	N	Y	Y	Y	Y	Y	Y	Y
Forsythe, 6	Y	Y	Y	Y	N	Y	Y	N	N	Y	N	Y	N	N	Y	N	Y	Y	N	Y	Y	Y	N	Y	Y	Y	Y
Helstoski, 9	Y	Y	Y	Y	N	Y	Y	Y	N	Y	N	Y	N	N	Y	N	Y	Y	Y	Y	Y	Y	Y	Y	Y	Y	N
Howard, 3	Y	Y	Y	Y	N	Y	Y	Y	N	Y	N	Y	N	N	Y	N	Y	Y	Y	Y	Y	Y	Y	Y	N	Y	N
Hughes, 2	Y	Y	Y	Y	N	N	Y	N	N	Y	N	Y	Y	N	Y	N	Y	Y	Y	N	Y	Y	Y	Y	Y	Y	Y
Maguire, 7	Y	Y	Y	Y	N	Y	Y	Y	N	Y	N	Y	N	N	Y	N	Y	Y	Y	Y	N	Y	Y	Y	Y	Y	N
Meyner, 13	Y	Y	Y	Y	N	N	Y	N	N	Y	N	N	N	N	Y	N	Y	Y	N	N	Y	Y	Y	N	Y	Y	Y
Minish, 11	Y	Y	Y	Y	N	Y	Y	N	N	Y	N	Y	Y	N	N	N	Y	Y	Y	N	Y	Y	Y	Y	Y	Y	Y
Patten, 15	Y	Y	Y	Y	N	Y	Y	N	N	Y	N	N	N	N	Y	N	Y	Y	Y	N	Y	Y	N	Y	Y	Y	Y
Rinaldo, 12	Y	Y	N	Y	N	Y	Y	Y	N	Y	N	N	N	N	Y	N	Y	Y	N	Y	N	Y	Y	Y	Y	Y	Y
Rodino, 10	Y	Y	Y	Y	N	Y	Y	Y	N	Y	N	Y	N	N	Y	N	Y	Y	Y	N	Y	Y	Y	Y	Y	Y	Y
Roe, 8	Y	Y	Y	Y	N	Y	Y	N	N	Y	N	N	Y	N	Y	N	Y	Y	Y	Y	Y	N	Y	Y	Y	Y	Y
Thompson, 4	Y	Y	Y	Y	N	Y	Y	N	N	Y	N	Y	N	N	Y	N	Y	Y	Y	Y	Y	Y	Y	Y	Y	Y	Y
NEW MEXICO																											
Lujan, 1	N	N	N	N	Y	N	—	N	Y	Y	Y	Y	—	—	Y	Y	N	N	Y	N	Y	Y	Y	Y	Y	Y	Y
Runnels, 2	N	N	N	N	—	N	—	N	Y	Y	Y	Y	—	—	Y	N	—	N	Y	—	Y	Y	Y	Y	N	N	N
NEW YORK																											
Abzug, 20	Y	Y	Y	Y	N	Y	Y	N	N	Y	N	N	N	N	Y	N	Y	N	Y	—	Y	Y	Y	Y	N	N	Y
Addabbo, 7	Y	Y	Y	Y	N	Y	Y	Y	N	Y	N	N	N	N	Y	N	Y	Y	Y	Y	Y	Y	Y	Y	Y	Y	Y
Ambro, 3	Y	Y	Y	Y	N	Y	Y	N	N	Y	N	N	N	N	Y	N	Y	Y	Y	—	Y	N	N	Y	Y	N	N
Badillo, 21	Y	Y	Y	Y	N	Y	Y	N	N	Y	N	N	N	N	Y	N	Y	Y	Y	N	Y	Y	Y	Y	Y	Y	Y
Biaggi, 10	Y	Y	Y	Y	N	Y	N	Y	N	Y	N	Y	Y	N	Y	N	Y	Y	N	N	Y	Y	N	Y	Y	Y	Y
Bingham, 22	Y	Y	Y	Y	N	Y	Y	N	N	Y	N	N	N	N	Y	N	Y	Y	Y	N	Y	Y	Y	Y	Y	Y	Y
Chisholm, 12	Y	Y	Y	Y	N	Y	Y	N	N	Y	N	N	N	N	Y	N	Y	Y	Y	N	Y	Y	Y	Y	Y	Y	N
Conable, 35	N	Y	N	N	N	Y	Y	Y	N	Y	Y	N	N	N	Y	N	N	N	N	N	N	N	N	Y	Y	Y	Y
Delaney, 9	Y	Y	Y	Y	N	Y	Y	N	N	Y	N	Y	N	N	Y	N	Y	Y	Y	Y	Y	Y	Y	Y	N	N	Y
Downey, 2	N	Y	Y	Y	N	Y	Y	N	N	Y	N	N	N	N	Y	N	Y	Y	Y	—	N	Y	Y	Y	N	N	N
Fish, 25	Y	Y	Y	Y	N	Y	Y	Y	N	Y	N	Y	N	N	N	N	Y	Y	Y	—	N	N	N	Y	Y	Y	Y
Gilman, 26	N	Y	Y	Y	N	Y	Y	N	N	Y	Y	N	Y	N	Y	N	N	N	Y	Y	Y	Y	Y	Y	N	N	N
Hanley, 32	Y	Y	Y	Y	N	Y	Y	Y	N	Y	N	N	N	N	N	N	Y	Y	Y	Y	Y	Y	Y	N	Y	Y	Y
Hastings, 39	N	Y	Y	Y	N	Y	N	Y	N	Y	Y	Y	N	N	Y	N	Y	Y	N	Y	N	N	N	Y	N	N	N
Holtzman, 16	Y	Y	Y	Y	N	Y	Y	Y	N	N	N	N	N	N	Y	N	Y	Y	Y	Y	Y	Y	Y	N	N	N	N

	1	2	3	4	5	6	7	8	9	10	11	12	13	14	15	16	17	18	19	20	21	22	23	24	25	26	27
Horton, 34	Y	Y	N	N	Y	Y	Y	N	Y	Y	N	Y	N	Y	N	Y	Y	N	Y	N	Y	Y	Y	N	N	N	N
Kemp, 38	Y	Y	N	N	Y	Y	N	N	Y	Y	Y	Y	Y	N	Y	Y	Y	N	Y	N	Y	Y	Y	N	Y	Y	N
Koch, 18	N	Y	N	N	N	N	N	N	Y	Y	Y	Y	Y	N	Y	N	Y	N	Y	N	Y	Y	Y	N	N	Y	N
LaFalce, 36	N	Y	N	N	N	N	N	N	Y	Y	Y	N		N	Y	Y	Y	N	Y	Z	Y	Y	Y	N	N	Y	N
Lent, 4	N	Y	N	N	N	N	N	N	Y	Y	Y	Y		Y	Y	Y	Y	N	Y	Z	Y	Y	Y	N	Y	Y	N
McEwen, 30	N	Y	N	N	Y	N	Y	N	N	N	Y	Y		N	Y	Y	Y	N	Y	Z	Y	Y	Y	Y	N	Y	N
McHugh, 27	N	Y	N	N	N	N	N	N	Y	Y	Y	Y	Y	Y	Y	Y	Y	Y	Y	Z	Y	Y	Y	N	N	Y	N
Mitchell, 31	N	Y	N	N	N	N	N	N	Y	Y	Y	Y	Y	N	N	N	Y	Y	Y	Z	Y	Y	Y	N	N	Y	N
Murphy, 17	Y	Y	Y	N	N	N	Y	N	Y	Y	Y	Y	Y	Y	Y	Y	Y	Y	Y	N	Y	N	Y	N	N	Y	N
Nowak, 37	N	Y	Y	N	N	N	N	N	Y	Y	N	Y		Y	Y	Y	Y	Y	Z	N	Y	Y	Y	N	N	Y	N
Ottinger, 24	Y	Y	Y	N	N	Y	N	Y	Y	Y	Y	Y	Y	N	N	Y	Y	Y	N	N	Y	Z	N	Y	Y	Y	N
Pattison, 29	Y	Y	Y	N	N	N	Y	Y	Y	Y	Y	Y	Y	N	N	Y	Y	Y	N		Y	Z	Y	Y	Y	Y	N
Peyser, 23	Y	Y	Y	N	N	N	Y	Y	Y	Y	Y	Y		N	Y	N	Y	Y	N	N	Y	N	N	Y	N	Y	N
Pike, 1	Y	Y	Y	N	N	N	Y		Y	Y	Y	Y	Y	Y	Y	Y	Y	Y	N	N	Y	N	Y	Y	N	Y	N
Rangel, 18	Y		Y	Y	N	N	Y	Y	Y	Y	Y			Y	N	Y	Y	Y			Y			Y	N	Y	N
Richmond, 14	N	Y	Y	Y	N	Y	Y	Y	N	N	N		Y	N	Y	Y	Y	Y	Y	Z	Y	Y	Y	Y	N	Y	N
Rosenthal, 8	N	Y	Y	Y	N	Y	Y	Y	Y	N	N			N	Y	N	Y	Y	Y	Z	Y	Y	Y	Y	N	Y	N
Scheuer, 11	Y	Y	Y	Y	N	N	Y	N	N	N	Y	N		Y	N	Y	Y	Y	Y	Z	Y	Z	Y	Y	N	Y	N
Solarz, 13	Y	Y	Y	Y	N	Y	Y	Y	N	N	Y	N	Y	Y	N	N	Y	Y	Y	Z	N	Z	Y	N	N	Y	N
Stratton, 28	Y	Y	Y	Y	N	Y	Y	Y	N	Y	N	N		Y	N	N	Y	Y	Z		Z	N	Y	N	Y	Y	N
Walsh, 33	N	Y	Y		N	Y	Y	Y	N	Y	N	N	Y	N	N	Y	Y	Y	Z	Y	Z	N	Y	N	N	Y	N
Wolff, 6	Y	Y	Y	N	N	Y	Y	N	N	Y	N	N	N	Y	N	N	Y	Y	N		N	Z	N	N	N	Y	N
Wydler, 5	Y	Y	Y	N	N	N	Y	N	N	Y	N	N		N	Z	Z	Y	Y	N		N	N	Y	N	N	N	N
Zeferetti, 15	N	Y	Y	N	N	N	Y		N	N	N	N		N	Z	N	Y	Y	N		N	Z	Y	N	N	N	N

	1	2	3	4	5	6	7	8	9	10	11	12	13	14	15	16	17	18	19	20	21	22	23	24	25	26	27
Andrews, 4	N	Y	Y	Y	N	Y	Y	N	Y	N	N	Y	N	N	Y	N	Y	Y	Y	N	Y	Y	Y	N	N	N	N
Broyhill, 10	N	N	Y	N	N	N	Y	Y	Y	Y	Y	Y	Y	Y	N	N	Y	Y	Y	N	Y	Y	Y	N	N	Y	N
Fountain, 2	N	Y	Y	N	N	N	Y	N	Y	Y	Y	Y	N	N	N	N	Y	Y	N	Z	N		Y	N	N	Y	N
Hefner, 8	N	Z	Y	N	N	N	Y		Y	Y	Y	Y	Z	N	N	Z	Y	Y	Y	N	Y	N	N	N	N	Y	N
Henderson, 3	N	Y	Y	N	N	N	Y	Y	Y	N	Y	Y	Y	N	Z	N	Y	Y	N	N	Y	Z	N	N	N	Y	N
Jones, 1	N	Y	Y	N	N	N	Y	N	Y	Y	Y	Z	N	N	N	N	Y	Y	N		Y	Y	N	N	N	Y	N
Martin, 9	N	N	Y	N	N	N	Y		N	Y	Y	Y	N	N	N	N	Y	Y	Z	N	N	N	N	N	N	Y	N
Neal, 5	N	Y	Y	Y	N	N	Y	Y	Y	Y	Y	Y	N	N	Y	N	Y	Y	Y	Z	Y	Y	Y	N	N	Y	N
Preyer, 6	N	Y	Y	N	N	N	Y		N	Y	Y	Y		N	Y	N	Y	Y	Y		N	N	Y	N	N	N	N

	1	2	3	4	5	6	7	8	9	10	11	12	13	14	15	16	17	18	19	20	21	22	23	24	25	26	27
NORTH CAROLINA (Continued)																											
Rose, 7	N	N	N	Y	N	N	N	N	N	N	N	Y	N	N	N	N	N	N	N	Y	Y	N	N	N	Y	N	N
Taylor, 11	Y	N	N																	N							
NORTH DAKOTA																											
Andrews	N	N	N	N	Y	N	Y	Y	N	N	N	Y	Y	Y	Y	Y	Y	Y	Y	N	Y	Y	Y	N	N	N	N
OHIO																											
Ashbrook, 17	N	N	N	Y	Y	Y	N	N	Y	N	Y	N	Y	Y	Y	Y	N	Y	Y	N	N	N	N	N	Y	N	N
Ashley, 9	Y	Y	Y		Y	Y	Y	Y	Y	Y	Y	Y	Y	N	Y	Y	N	Y	Y		Y	Y	Y	Y	Y	Y	Y
Brown, 7	N	Y	Y		Y	Y	Y	Y	N	Y	Y	Y	Y	Y	Y	Y	N	Y	Y		N	N	Y	Y	Y	Y	Y
Carney, 19	Y	Y	N	Y	N	N	N	N	N	Y	Y	N	N	N	N	N	N	N	N	Y	Y	Y	N	Y	Y	N	N
Clancy, 2	Y	N	Y	N	Y	Y	Y	N	N	Y	Y	Y	N	Y	N	N	N	N	Y		N	N	N	Y	Y	N	N
Devine, 12	N	Y	N	Y	Y	Y	N	N	Y	Y	N	N	Y	Y	Y	Y	Y	N	N		Y	N	N	Y	Y	Y	N
Gradison, 1	N	N	N	N	Y	Y	N	N	Y	Y	N	Y	Y	Y	Y	Y	Y	Y	Y		N	N	Y	N	N	Y	Y
Guyer, 4	N	Y	N	Y	N	N	N	N	N	Y	N	N	N	N	N	N	N	N	Y		N	N	N	Y	Y	N	N
Harsha, 6	N	N	N	N	N	N	N	N	Y	N	Y	N	Y	Y	Y	Y	Y	Y	Y		Y	Y	Y	N	Y	Y	Y
Hays, 18	Y	N	N	N	Y	Y	N	N	N	N	N	N	N	N	N	N	N	N	Y		Y	Y	Y	N	Y	N	N
Kindness, 8	N	Y	N	Y	N	N	N	N	N	Y	N	N	N	N	N	N	N	N	Y		Y	Y	Y	N	Y	N	N
Latta, 5	N	N	N	N	N	N	N	N	Y	N	N	N	Y	N	N	N	N	N	Y		N	N	N	Y	N	N	N
Miller, 10	N	Y	N	Y	Y	N	N	N	N	Y	N	N	Y	Y	Y	Y	N	Y	Y		Y	Y	Y	Y	Y	N	N
Mosher, 13	N	Y	N	N	Y	Y	N	N	N	N	N	N	Y	Y	Y	Y	Y	Y	Y		Y	Y	Y	Y	Y	N	N
Mottl, 23	N	Y	N	N	Y	N	N	N	N	N	N	N	Y	Y	N	N	N	Y	Y		Y	N	Y	N	Y	N	N
Regula, 16	N	Y	N	N	Y	Y	N	N	Y	Y	N	N	N	N	N	N	N	N	Y		Y	Y	Y	N	Y	N	N
Seiberling, 14	Y	Y	Y	Y	Y	N	N	N	Y	Y	Y	Y	Y	Y	Y	Y	Y	Y	Y		Y	Y	Y	N	N	Y	Y
Stanton, J. V., 20	Y	Y	Y	N	Y	Y	N	N	Y	Y	Y	Y	Y	Y	Y	Y	N	Y	Y		Y	Y	Y	N	Y	Y	Y
Stanton, J. W., 11	Y	Y	N	Y	Y	Y	N	N	Y	Y	Y	Y	Y	Y	Y	Y	Y	Y	Y		Y	Y	Y	N	N	Y	Y
Stokes, 21	Y	Y	Y	Y	Y	N	N	N	Y	Y	Y	N	Y	N	Y	Y	Y	Y	Y		Y	Y	Y	Y	N	Y	Y
Vanik, 22	Y	Y	Y	Y	Y	Y	N	N	N	Y	Y	Y	Y	N	Y	Y	Y	Y	Y		Y	Y	Y	N	Y	Y	Y
Whalen, 3	N	N	N	N	Y	N	N	N	Y	N	Y	Y	N	Y	N	Y	Y	Y	Y		Y	Y	Y	N	N	Y	Y
Wylie, 15	N	N	N	Y	N	N	Y	N	Y	N	N	Y	N	N	N	N	N	Y	Y		Y	Y	Y	N	N	Y	Y
OKLAHOMA																											
Albert, 3	N	N	N	N	N	Y	Y	Y	Y	N	N	Y	N	Y	N	Y	Y	Y	Y	N	Y	N	Y	N	Y	N	N
English, 6	Y	Y	Y	Y	N	Y	Y	N	Y	Y	N	Y	N	N	N	N	Y	N	N	N	N	N	N	N	N	N	N
Jarman, 5	N	N	N	N	Y	Y	N	N	Y	N	Y	N	N	N	N	N	N	N	Y	Y	Y	Y	Y	N	N	N	N
Jones, 1	N	N	N	N	N	N	Y	N	Y	N	N	Y	Y	N	N	N	N	N	Y	N	N	N	N	N	N	N	N

	1	2	3	4	5	6	7	8	9	10	11	12	13	14	15	16	17	18	19	20	21	22	23	24	25	26	27
OKLAHOMA (Continued)																											
Risenhoover, 2	—	N	Y	N	N	N	Y	Y	Y	Y	Y	Y	N	N	Y	Y	N	N	N	Y	Y	Y	Y	—	N	N	Y
Steed, 4	Y	Y	N	N	N	N	Y	Y	N	Y	N	Y	N	N	Y	N	—	Y	Y	Y	Y	N	—	N	N	N	N
OREGON																											
AuCoin, 1	N	Y	Y	N	N	N	Y	Y	N	Y	Y	N	Y	N	—	N	Y	N	—	Y	N	N	—	Y	Y	Y	N
Duncan, 3	Y	N	Y	Y	N	N	Y	Y	N	Y	N	—	Y	—	N	N	Y	N	N	Y	N	N	N	Y	N	Y	N
Ullman, 2	Y	N	Y	Y	N	Y	Y	—	N	Y	N	Y	—	N	N	N	Y	Y	N	Y	N	N	Y	Y	N	Y	N
Weaver, 4	N	Y	Y	Y	N	Y	Y	—	N	Y	N	Y	Y	N	N	N	Y	Y	N	Y	N	N	N	Y	Y	Y	Y
PENNSYLVANIA																											
Barrett, 1	Y	N	Y	Y	N	Y	Y	Y	N	Y	N	Y	N	N	N	N	Y	—	Y	Y	N	Y	N	—	—	—	—
Biester, 8	N	Y	Y	Y	N	Y	Y	N	N	N	N	Y	Y	N	N	N	Y	Y	N	—	N	N	Y	Y	Y	Y	N
Coughlin, 13	Y	Y	N	N	Y	—	N	N	N	N	N	Y	Y	Y	Y	N	Y	Y	N	—	Y	N	Y	N	Y	Y	Y
Dent, 21	Y	Y	Y	Y	N	Y	—	Y	N	Y	N	Y	Y	—	Y	N	Y	Y	Y	—	—	Y	—	N	N	N	N
Edgar, 7	N	Y	Y	Y	N	Y	Y	Y	N	Y	N	Y	Y	N	N	N	Y	Y	N	Y	Y	N	—	Y	Y	Y	Y
Eilberg, 4	Y	Y	Y	Y	N	Y	Y	Y	N	Y	N	Y	N	N	N	N	Y	Y	N	N	Y	Y	Y	Y	—	—	—
Eshleman, 16	N	N	N	N	Y	N	—	—	—	N	Y	N	—	—	Y	Y	N	Y	Y	—	—	N	Y	—	N	N	N
Flood, 11	Y	Y	Y	Y	N	Y	Y	Y	N	Y	N	Y	N	N	N	N	Y	Y	N	Y	N	Y	Y	N	N	N	N
Gaydos, 20	N	Y	—	—	—	—	N	—	N	—	N	Y	N	—	Y	N	Y	Y	Y	—	—	Y	Y	Y	Y	Y	Y
Goodling, W., 19	N	N	N	N	Y	N	N	N	N	N	Y	N	Y	Y	Y	Y	Y	—	Y	—	Y	Y	Y	N	—	N	N
Green, 3	Y	Y	—	Y	N	—	Y	Y	N	Y	N	Y	N	N	N	N	Y	—	N	Y	N	Y	Y	Y	Y	Y	Y
Heinz, 18	N	Y	—	Y	Y	Y	N	—	N	Y	N	Y	Y	—	Y	N	Y	Y	N	—	Y	Y	Y	N	N	N	N
Johnson, 23	Y	N	N	Y	N	N	Y	N	Y	N	Y	N	Y	Y	Y	Y	N	—	Y	—	Y	Y	Y	N	—	—	—
McDade, 10	N	N	Y	N	Y	Y	Y	N	N	Y	N	Y	Y	N	N	N	Y	Y	N	—	Y	Y	Y	Y	N	N	N
Moorhead, 14	Y	Y	Y	Y	N	Y	Y	Y	N	Y	N	—	N	N	N	N	Y	Y	N	Y	N	N	—	Y	Y	Y	N
Morgan, 22	N	Y	Y	Y	N	Y	Y	Y	N	Y	N	Y	Y	N	N	N	Y	Y	N	Y	N	N	Y	Y	—	—	—
Murtha, 12	N	N	Y	Y	N	Y	N	Y	N	Y	N	Y	Y	N	N	N	Y	—	Y	—	Y	Y	Y	N	N	—	—
Myers, 25	Y	Y	N	N	Y	N	N	N	N	Y	N	N	Y	N	Y	N	Y	Y	Y	—	Y	N	Y	N	N	N	N
Nix, 2	Y	Y	Y	Y	N	Y	Y	Y	N	Y	N	Y	—	N	N	N	Y	Y	N	N	N	N	N	Y	—	—	—
Rooney, 15	Y	Y	Y	Y	N	Y	Y	Y	N	Y	N	Y	N	N	N	N	Y	Y	N	Y	Y	N	Y	N	N	N	N
Schneebeli, 17	N	N	N	N	Y	N	N	N	Y	N	Y	N	Y	Y	Y	Y	N	N	Y	—	Y	N	Y	N	N	N	N
Schulze, 5	N	N	N	N	Y	N	N	N	Y	N	Y	—	Y	Y	Y	Y	Y	N	Y	—	Y	Y	Y	N	N	N	N
Shuster, 9	N	N	N	N	Y	N	N	N	Y	N	Y	N	Y	Y	Y	Y	N	N	Y	—	Y	Y	Y	N	Y	N	N
Vigorito, 24	Y	Y	Y	Y	N	Y	Y	Y	N	Y	N	Y	Y	N	Y	N	Y	Y	N	Y	Y	Y	Y	N	N	N	—
Yatron, 6	N	Y	Y	N	Y	Y	N	Y	N	Y	N	Y	N	Y	Y	N	Y	Y	Y	Y	Y	Y	Y	N	—	—	—

	1	2	3	4	5	6	7	8	9	10	11	12	13	14	15	16	17	18	19	20	21	22	23	24	25	26	27
RHODE ISLAND																											
Beard, 2	N	N	N	N	Y	Y	Y	Y	N	N	Y	Y	N	N	Y	N	Y	Y	N		Y	Y	Y	N	N	Y	N
St. Germain, 1	Y	Y	Y	Y	N	Y	Y	Y	Y	Y	N	N	Y	N	Y	N	Y	Y	N		Y	Y	Y	N	Y	Y	N
SOUTH CAROLINA																											
Davis, 1	Y	N	N	N		N	N	N	Y	Y	Y	N	N	Y	Y	Y	Y	Y	Y	—	Y	Y	Y	N	N	N	N
Derrick, 3	Y	Y	Y	Y	N	Y	N	N	N	Y	Y	N	N	Y	Y	Y	Y	Y	Y	—	Y	Y	Y	N	N	N	N
Holland, 5	N	N	N	N	N	N	N	N	Y	N	Y	Y	N	Y	Y	N	N	Y	Y	—	Y	N	N	N	N	N	N
Jenrette, 6	N	N	N	N	N	Y	N	N	Y	Y	Y	Y	Y	Y	Y	N	N	Y	Y	—	Y	Y	Y	N	N	N	N
Mann, 4	N	N	Y	N	Y	Y	N	N	N	Y	N	N	N	N	Y	Y	N	N	Y	—	N	N	N	N	Y	N	Y
Spence, 2	Y	Y	Y	N		Y	N	N	N	Y	Y	Y	Y	Y	Y	Y	N	N	N	—	Y	Y	Y	N	N	N	N
SOUTH DAKOTA																											
Abdnor, 2	N	N	N	N	N	N	N	N	Y	N	Y	N	Y	N	Y	Y	Y	Y	Y	—	Y	Y	Y	N	N	N	N
Pressler, 1	N	Y	N	N	Y	Y	Y	Y	Y	Y	Y	N	Y	N	Y	Y	Y	Y	Y	—	Y	Y	Y	Y	Y	Y	Y
TENNESSEE																											
***Allen, 5	N	N	N	N	—	N	N	N	Y	Y	Y	N		Y	Y	Y	Y	Y	Y	—	Y	Y	Y	N	N	N	N
Beard, 6	N	N	N	N		N	N	N	N	N	N	N	—	Y	Y	N	Y	Y	N	—	Y	Y	Y	N	N	N	N
Duncan, 2	N	N	N	N	Y	N	N	Y	N	N	N	N	N	N	N	N	N	N	N	—	N	N	Y	Y	Y	Y	Y
Evins, 4	N	N	N	N	Y	Y	Y	Y	N	Y	N	Y	Y	N	Y	Y	N	Y	Y	—	Y	Y	Y	N	N	Y	N
Ford, 8	N	Y	Y	N	N	Y	N	Y	N	Y	Y	N	—	Y	N	Y	Y	Y	N	—	Y	Y	Y	N	N	N	N
Jones, 7	N	N	N	N	Y	Y	N	Y	Y	Y	N	N	Y	N	Y	N	N	Y	Y	—	Y	N	N	Y	Y	Y	N
Lloyd, 3	N	N	N	N	Y	Y	N	N	N	Y	Y	Y	—	N	Y	N	Y	N	N	—	Y	N	N	N	N	N	N
Quillen, 1	N	N	N	N	Y	Y	N	Y	Y	Y	Y	Y	—	Y	N	Y	N	N	Y	—	Y	Y	N	N	N	N	N
TEXAS																											
Archer, 7	N	N	N	N	Y	Y	Y	Y	N	N	Y	Y	Y	Y	Y	N	Y	N	N	—	Y	Y	Y	N	N	N	N
Brooks, 9	N	N	N	N	N	N	Y	Y	N	Y	N	N	Y	Y	Y	N	N	Y	Y	N	N	N	N	N	N	N	N
Burleson, 17	N	N	N	N	N	Y	Y	N	N	Y	Y	Y	Y	N	Y	Y	N	Y	Y	Y	N	N	N	N	N	Y	N
Casey, 22	N	N	N	N	Y	Y	Y	N	Y	N	Y	Y	Y	Y	Y	N	N	N	Y	N	Y	Y	Y	Y	Y	N	N
Collins, 3	N	N	N	N	Y	Y	N	Y	N	N	Y	Y	—	Y	Y	Y	N	Y	Y	—	Y	Y	Y	N	N	Y	N
de la Garza, 15	N	N	N	N	Y	N	Y	Y	N	Y	Y	Y	Y	N	Y	N	N	Y	Y	—	Y	Y	Y	Y	N	N	N
Eckhardt, 8	Y	Y	N	N	N	Y	N	N	N	Y	N	N	—	N	Y	N	N	N	N	—	Y	N	N	N	N	N	N
Gonzalez, 20	N	N	N	N	N	N	N	N	Y	Y	N	N	N	N	Y	N	N	Y	N	Y	Y	Y	N	N	N	Y	N
Hightower, 13	N	N	Y	N	Y	Y	Y	Y	N	N	N	N	—	N	Y	N	N	Y	Y	Y	N	N	Y	N	N	N	N
Jordan, 18	N	Y	Y	Y	N	Y	Y	Y	N	Y	Y	Y	—	Y	Y	Y	Y	Y	Y	—	Y	N	N	N	N	Y	N
Kazen, 23	N	N	N	N	Y	Y	Y	N	N	Y	Y	Y	N	N	Y	Y	N	Y	N	—	N	Y	N	N	N	N	N
Krueger, 21	N	N	N	N	Y	Y	N	Y	Y	Y	Y	Y	—	N	Y	Y	Y	Y	Y	—	N	N	N	N	N	N	N

	1	2	3	4	5	6	7	8	9	10	11	12	13	14	15	16	17	18	19	20	21	22	23	24	25	26	27
TEXAS (Continued)																											
Mahon, 19	Y	N	Y	N	N	N	Y	—	N	N	N	N	N	N	N	N	Y	Y	Y	N	N	Y	Y	Y	N	Y	Y
Milford, 24	Y	N	Y	N	Y	N	Y	Y	N	Y	N	Y	Y	N	Y	Y	Y	N	Y	N	N	N	Y	N	N	N	N
Patman, 1	Y	N	N	N	Y	N	Y	—	N	N	N	N	Y	N	Y	N	N	N	Y	N	N	N	Y	N	N	N	N
Pickle, 10	Y	N	Y	N	Y	N	N	Y	N	N	Y	N	Y	N	N	N	N	N	Y	N	N	Y	Y	N	N	N	N
Poage, 11	Y	N	N	Y	Y	N	N	—	N	N	N	Y	Y	Y	N	N	N	N	Y	N	N	N	Y	N	N	N	N
Roberts, 4	N	N	Y	N	Y	N	Y	N	Y	Y	N	N	Y	N	Y	N	Y	Y	Y	N	Y	Y	Y	Y	Y	Y	N
Steelman, 5	N	N	N	N	Y	N	Y	N	N	Y	N	Y	Y	Y	Y	Y	Y	Y	Y	N	Y	Y	Y	Y	N	N	N
Teague, 6	N	Y	Y	N	Y	N	N	Y	N	N	Y	N	Y	Y	N	Y	N	Y	N	N	Y	N	Y	N	N	N	N
White, 16	N	N	N	N	Y	N	Y	Y	N	Y	Y	N	Y	Y	Y	Y	Y	Y	Y	N	Y	Y	Y	Y	N	N	N
Wilson, 2	N	N	N	Y	Y	N	N	Y	Y	N	Y	N	Y	Y	Y	Y	N	Y	Y	N	Y	Y	Y	Y	N	N	N
Wright, 12	Y	Y	Y	Y	Y	Y	Y	Y	Y	Y	Y	Y	Y	Y	Y	Y	Y	Y	N	N	Y	Y	Y	Y	N	N	N
Young, 14	Y	N	Y	N	N	Y	Y	Y	Y	Y	N	N	—	Y	Y	Y	Y	Y	N	N	Y	Y	Y	N	N	N	Y
UTAH																											
Howe, 2	N	Y	Y	Y	N	N	N	Y	Y	Y	N	N	Y	Y	Y	N	N	Y	Y	N	Y	N	Y	Y	N	Y	Y
McKay, 1	N	N	N	N	N	N	N	Y	N	N	N	N	Y	N	Y	N	N	Y	Y	N	N	N	Y	Y	N	N	N
VERMONT																											
Jeffords	N	Y	Y	Y	N	N	N	N	N	Y	N	N	Y	Y	Y	N	N	Y	Y	Y	N	N	Y	Y	N	Y	N
VIRGINIA																											
Butler, 6	Y	N	Y	Y	N	Y	Y	Y	Y	Y	N	N	Y	Y	Y	N	Y	Y	Y	N	Y	Y	Y	N	N	N	N
Daniel, D., 5	Y	N	N	N	Y	Y	Y	N	Y	Y	Y	Y	Y	Y	Y	Y	Y	Y	Y	N	Y	Y	Y	Y	N	N	N
Daniel, R., 4	Y	Y	Y	N	Y	Y	Y	N	Y	Y	N	Y	Y	N	Y	N	Y	Y	Y	N	Y	Y	Y	N	N	N	N
Downing, 1	Y	N	N	N	Y	Y	Y	N	Y	Y	Y	Y	Y	N	Y	N	Y	Y	Y	N	Y	Y	Y	N	N	N	N
Fisher, 10	Y	Y	Y	N	Y	Y	Y	N	Y	Y	N	Y	Y	Y	Y	N	Y	Y	Y	N	Y	Y	Y	Y	N	N	N
Harris, 8	N	Y	Y	N	Y	Y	N	Y	Y	Y	N	N	Y	Y	Y	Y	Y	N	Y	N	Y	Y	Y	Y	N	N	N
Robinson, 7	N	Y	Y	N	Y	N	Y	N	Y	Y	N	Y	Y	Y	Y	N	Y	Y	Y	N	Y	Y	Y	Y	N	N	N
Satterfield, 3	Y	Y	Y	Y	Y	Y	Y	N	Y	N	Y	N	Y	Y	Y	N	Y	Y	Y	N	Y	Y	Y	N	Y	N	N
Wampler, 9	N	Y	Y	Y	Y	Y	Y	N	Y	Y	Y	N	Y	Y	Y	Y	Y	Y	Y	—	Y	Y	Y	Y	N	N	N
Whitehurst, 2	Y	N	Y	N	Y	N	Y	N	Y	N	N	Y	Y	Y	N	Y	Y	N	Y	—	Y	Y	Y	N	N	N	N
WASHINGTON																											
Adams, 7	N	N	Y	Y	N	N	N	N	N	Y	N	N	Y	N	Y	N	N	Y	Y	—	N	Y	Y	Y	N	Y	N
Bonker, 3	N	N	Y	N	N	N	N	N	N	Y	Y	N	Y	N	Y	N	N	Y	Y	Y	N	N	Y	N	N	N	N
Foley, 5	Y	N	Y	Y	N	N	N	N	N	Y	Y	N	Y	Y	Y	N	N	Y	N	Y	N	N	Y	Y	N	N	N
Hicks, 6	N	N	Y	N	N	N	N	N	N	Y	N	N	Y	Y	N	N	N	Y	N	N	N	N	Y	N	Y	N	N
McCormack, 4	Y	Y	Y	N	N	N	Y	Y	N	Y	N	Y	Y	N	Y	N	N	Y	Y	Y	N	Y	Y	N	N	N	Y

	1	2	3	4	5	6	7	8	9	10	11	12	13	14	15	16	17	18	19	20	21	22	23	24	25	26	27
WASHINGTON (Continued)																											
Meeds, 2	Y	Y	—	Y	Y	N	Y	N	Y	N	Y	Y	N	N	Y	N	Y	Y	N	—	N	Y	Y	Y	Y	Y	N
Pritchard, 1	Y	—	Y	Y	N	Y	Y	Y	N	Y	N	Y	Y	N	N	Y	Y	Y	N	N	N	Y	Y	N	N	N	N
WEST VIRGINIA																											
Hechler, 4	N	N	Y	N	Y	Y	Y	N	N	Y	N	Y	N	N	N	N	N	N	N	Y	N	N	N	Y	Y	Y	Y
Mollohan, 1	Y	Y	Y	N	N	Y	Y	N	N	N	Y	N	N	N	N	N	N	N	N	Y	N	N	N	N	N	N	N
Slack, 3	Y	Y	Y	N	Y	Y	Y	N	N	Y	N	Y	N	N	N	N	N	N	N	—	Y	N	N	Y	Y	Y	Y
Staggers, 2	Y	Y	—	N	N	Y	Y	N	N	N	N	Y	N	N	N	—	N	N	N	—	N	N	N	N	Y	Y	N
WISCONSIN																											
Aspin, 1	N	Y	Y	N	N	Y	Y	N	N	Y	N	Y	Y	N	N	N	Y	N	N	Y	N	N	Y	Y	Y	Y	Y
Baldus, 3	N	Y	Y	N	N	Y	Y	N	N	Y	N	Y	N	N	N	N	Y	N	N	Y	N	N	N	Y	Y	N	Y
Cornell, 8	N	N	Y	N	N	Y	N	N	N	Y	N	Y	N	N	N	N	Y	N	N	Y	N	N	N	Y	Y	N	Y
Kasten, 9	Y	Y	N	Y	Y	Y	Y	Y	N	N	Y	Y	Y	Y	Y	Y	Y	Y	Y	Y	Y	N	Y	N	Y	N	N
Kastenmeier, 2	N	Y	Y	N	N	Y	N	N	N	Y	N	N	N	N	N	N	Y	N	N	Y	N	N	N	Y	Y	N	Y
Obey, 7	N	Y	Y	N	Y	Y	Y	N	N	Y	N	Y	N	N	N	N	Y	N	N			N	N	N	Y	Y	Y	Y
Reuss, 5	N	Y	Y	N	N	Y	Y	N	N	Y	N	Y	N	N	N	N	Y	N	N			N	N	N	Y	N	N	N
Steiger, 6	Y	Y	—	Y	N	Y	Y	Y	N	Y	N	Y	Y	Y	N	N	Y	N	Y	—	N	N	N	Y	Y	N	N
Zablocki, 4	Y	Y	N	N	N	Y	Y	N	N	Y	N	Y	N	N	N	N	N	N	N			N	N	—	N	N	N	N
WYOMING																											
Roncalio	N	Y	Y	N	Y	Y	Y	N	N	Y	N	Y	N	N	N	N	N	N	N			N	Y	N	N	Y	N	N

* Pettis entered Congress May 6, 1975
** Fary entered Congress July 15, 1975
*** Allen entered Congress December 2, 1975

TABLE II—POSITIVE PROPOSALS

A. *Natural Gas Deregulation*
   PROBLEM: The Federal Power Commission has regulated the price of natural gas at artificially low levels. Consequently, natural gas producers have had little incentive to increase supply, and consumers have had excessive demand. This has resulted in serious shortages of this precious fuel.
   SOLUTION: Deregulate the price of natural gas; allow market forces, not the FPC, to determine the price of natural gas.
   BILLS: HR 5550, HR 10616, HR 10480, HR 11265.
   See Chapter 1, p. 16.

B. *Truth-in-Government Accounting*
   PROBLEM: The government's accounting practices are inaccurate, primarily because they fail to report certain major financial obligations.
   SOLUTION: Require the federal government to use "accrual accounting" methods—which businesses are legally required to use—so that the government's financial situation is more accurately stated.
   BILLS: HR 10855, HR 10856, HR 10857, HR 10880, HR 11202.
   See Chapter 2, p. 32.

C. *Balancing the Federal Budget*
   PROBLEM: Budget deficits tend to reduce private investment and stimulate inflation; generally, the goals sought by deficit spending can be better attained through other approaches.
   SOLUTION: Require that each year's budget be balanced, and repay the national debt.
   BILLS: House Joint Resolutions 5, 9, 19, 36, 63, 153, 183, 196, 251, 271, 318, 319, 357, 471, 531, 616, 646, 716; House Concurrent Resolutions 254, 257, 260, 261, 478; HR 1252, HR 2448, HR 4175, HR 5293, HR 5294, HR 5353, HR 7007, HR 8582. (Note: All of these bills require a balanced budget. Most do not require systematic

repayment of the national debt. Some introduce fiscal controls and budget specifications in addition to the budget-balancing requirement.)
See Chapter 2, p. 34.

D. *Tax Indexing*
PROBLEM: As inflation occurs, incomes tend to rise to avoid losing purchasing power, despite the increase in prices. However, even though real incomes may remain the same or decline (if they do not "keep up"), taxpayers move into higher tax brackets. Thus, inflation increases income taxes without legislation.
SOLUTION: Automatically adjust the tax tables (or computation method) so that the effects of inflation are neutralized and one moves into a higher tax bracket only if real income increases.
BILLS: HR 231, HR 424, HR 1816, HR 1817, HR 5430, HR 5867, HR 8829.
See Chapter 3, p. 40.

E. *Jobs Creation Act*
PROBLEM: Not only does the United States face problems of inadequate capital formation, but most tax policy actually tends to decrease investment and reduce employment and income.
SOLUTION: Revise the tax code in such a way that investment will be stimulated, thus increasing employment, income, and ultimately tax revenues.
BILLS: HR 7240, HR 7543, HR 7610, HR 7911, HR 8053, HR 8054, HR 8226, HR 10015, HR 10538, HR 10583.
See Chapter 3, p. 43.

F. *Fiscal Integrity Act*
PROBLEM: The federal budget and bureaucracy continue to grow constantly, along with the national debt. Fiscal integrity is absent because of the lack of control over the budgeting process.
SOLUTION: Alter the budget process to require disclosure of the impact of proposed legislation, and limit the growth of the budget through, among other things, balancing the budget each year. Other fiscal controls are also proposed in the Act.

235

BILLS: HR 1252, HR 2448, HR 4175, HR 5293, HR 5294, HR 5353, HR 7007, HR 8582.
See Chapter 3, p. 43.

G. *Regulatory Agencies*

PROBLEM: Federal agencies enact rules and regulations which are frequently unnecessary, creating needless compliance expense. Further, these agencies are so large and entrenched that Congress has little opportunity to regulate and scrutinize their activities.

SOLUTION: Require the agencies to provide a cost-benefit analysis of their proposals, and give Congress a veto power over them.

BILLS: HR 8231, HR 9312, HR 9313, HR 9314, HR 9390, HR 9801, HR 10164, HR 10399, HR 10400.
See Chapters 4, 7, pp. 58, 85.

H. *OSHA*

PROBLEM: OSHA currently embodies a punitive approach toward business; for example, standards sometimes impose more costs than benefits; employers cannot use alternative means of correcting health and safety problems; employers are forced to abandon equipment that is still useful in order to meet standards that may effect few benefits. This approach inhibits achieving the best results in the effort to maximize on-the-job health and safety.

SOLUTION: Amend (i.e., adopt a cost-benefit approach, allow use of alternative solutions, allow useful equipment to be used when it does not impose serious risks, exempt small businesses, etc.) or repeal OSHA to remove its negative effects.

BILLS: HR 7836, HR 7837, HR 11094 (reform); HR 131, HR 1086, HR 1964, HR 2699, HR 3792, HR 4553, HR 8520, HR 9136 (repeal).
See Chapter 5, p. 65.

I. *Gun Control*

PROBLEM: The number of crimes committed with guns is increasing at an alarming rate. Although everyone agrees that this must be corrected, some people are suggesting as a solution that the ownership of guns be restricted.

SOLUTION: Increase the penalties for using a gun in the commission of a crime. Also minimize the efforts of those who are attempting to restrict the ownership of guns. BILLS: HR 524, HR 6056, HR 8294, HR 8697 (penalties); HR 1087, HR 2217, HR 2590, HR 2897, HR 3110, HR 3637, HR 4200, HR 5106, HR 5384, HR 5712, HR 5779, HR 5781, HR 7775, HR 10774 (minimizing restrictions).
See Chapters 6, 15, pp. 75, 172.

J. *Welfare Reform*
PROBLEM: The welfare caseload has risen dramatically in recent years. A system of special exemptions, and loopholes combined with loose definitions of such terms as "continued absence," and "work related expenses" add up to a tremendous cost to the taxpayer.
SOLUTION: Tighten up exemptions, limit eligibility to the truly needy, redefine basic terms. The National Welfare Reform Act of 1975 does all this, with a resultant savings of $2.2 billion in taxpayers' money.
BILLS: HR 5133, HR 5134, HR 5135, HR 5006, HR 7146.
See Chapter 10, p. 110.

K. *Food Stamp Reform*
PROBLEM: Numerous loopholes exist in present eligibility standards which permit people capable of self-sufficiency to be carried at public expense. Lax income and asset tests worsen the problem. Insufficient cash and coupon accountability causes loose handling of federal funds and stamps. Opportunities for fraud and theft continue unabated.
SOLUTION: Reduce high income eligibility, close numerous loopholes, stiffen work requirements, streamline program administration, institute management improvements, and curtail opportunities for criminal activity.
BILLS: HR 8145, HR 8146, HR 8147, HR 8126, HR 8687, HR 9024, HR 9240, HR 9631, HR 10071, HR 10244, HR 10354, HR 10408, HR 10735.
See Chapter 11, p. 125.

L. *Social Security*
PROBLEM: Persons between the ages of 65 and 72 are severely penalized by the Social Security system. For

every dollar that is earned in outside income above a limit of $2,760, one dollar is deducted from benefits. Not only is this unfair, but it discourages these people from engaging in productive activity. Also, a married woman with a career may receive fewer benefits than she would if she were single or without a career.

SOLUTION: Remove the earnings limitation and the discriminatory clauses.

BILLS: HR 364, HR 2196, HR 2197, HR 2264, HR 2592, HR 2883, HR 3175, HR 3360, HR 3760, HR 5874, HR 6028 (earnings limitations); HR 6305, HR 7595, HR 8599, HR 9651 (earnings limitation and discriminatory clauses).

See Chapter 12, p. 134.

M. *China*

This resolution states the intent of Congress to assure the Republic of China that our close ties will continue and that they will not be compromised by our thawed relations with the Peoples' Republic of China.

BILLS: House Concurrent Resolutions 20, 360, 378, 279, 380, 381, 398, 419, 420, 421, 426, 451, 474, 488, 491.

See Chapter 17, p. 197.

	A	B	C	D	E	F	G	H	I	J	K	L	M
ALABAMA													
Bevill, 4							+						
Buchanan, 6												+	+
Dickinson, 2	+	+	+	+	+	+	+	+		+	+		+
Edwards, 1				+			+	+					+
Flowers, 7	+	+		+									+
Jones, 5													
Nichols, 3													+
ALASKA													
Young		+	+	+	+			+					
ARIZONA													
Conlan, 4		+	+		+	+		+	+	+	+	+	+
Rhodes, 1								+	+		+		
Steiger, 3				+			+	+		+	+		+
Udall, 2													
ARKANSAS													
Alexander, 1													+
Hammerschmidt, 3							+			+	+	+	+
Mills, 2													+
Thornton, 4													
CALIFORNIA													
Anderson, 32													
Bell, 27					+						+		+
Brown, 36	+										+	+	
Burgener, 43		+	+		+	+	+			+	+	+	+
Burke, 28													
Burton J., 5													
Burton P., 6													
Clausen, 2		+			+		+	+					
Clawson, 33		+	+		+					+	+		+
Corman, 21													
Danielson, 30											+		
Dellums, 8													
Edwards, 10													
Goldwater, 20		+	+		+	+	+			+	+	+	+
Hannaford, 34						+							
Hawkins, 29						+							
Hinshaw, 40			+	+		+	+			+	+	+	+
Johnson, 1													
Ketchum, 18	+	+	+		+	+	+	+		+	+	+	+
Krebs, 17													
Lagomarsino, 19			+			+	+	+		+	+		+
Leggett, 4													+
Lloyd, 35													+
McCloskey, 12	+	+										+	
McFall, 14													
Mineta, 13													
Miller, 7													
Moorhead, 22	+	+	+	+	+	+	+			+	+	+	+
Moss, 3													
Patterson, 38													
*Pettis, 37	+	+		+						+	+		
Rees, 23													
Rousselot, 26	+	+		+	+	+	+	+	+	+	+	+	+
Roybal, 25													+
Ryan, 11													+
Sisk, 15						+							
Stark, 9						+							
Talcott, 16		+	+		+	+	+			+	+		+
Van Deerlin, 42													
Waxman, 24												+	

Name	A	B	C	D	E	F	G	H	I	J	K	L	M
Wiggins, 39													+
Wilson, 31													
Wilson, Bob, 41			+			+	+	+			+		+
COLORADO													
Armstrong, 5	+	+	+		+	+		+		+	+	+	+
Evans, 3													
Johnson, 4								+			+	+	
Schroeder, 1													
Wirth, 2													
CONNECTICUT													
Cotter, 1													+
Dodd, 2													
Giaimo, 3													
McKinney, 4	+												
Moffett, 6													
Sarasin, 5			+		+	+						+	+
DELAWARE													
du Pont,							+						
FLORIDA													
Bafalis, 10			+	+	+			+	+	+			+
Bennett, 3			+										
Burke, 12													+
Chappell, 4	+		+					+	+	+	+		+
Fascell, 15				+									
Frey, 9								+	+	+			
Fuqua, 2						+		+					+
Gibbons, 7													
Haley, 8			+	+	+	+	+						
Kelly, 5			+		+	+			+	+	+		
Lehman, 13													
Pepper, 14				+		+							
Rogers, 11													
Sikes, 1					+		+						+
Young, 6					+	+		+	+		+		+
GEORGIA													
Brinkley, 3				+	+		+						+
Flynt, 6		+							+				+
Ginn, 1													+
Landrum, 9													+
Levitas, 4													+
Mathis, 2			+	+			+					+	+
McDonald, 7			+	+		+	+						+
Stephens, 10			+										+
Stuckey, 8	+			+								+	+
Young, 5				+									+
HAWAII													
Matsunaga, 1							+						
Mink, 2													
IDAHO													
Hansen, 2													
Symms, 1	+	+	+		+			+	+	+	+		+
ILLINOIS													
Anderson, 16	+						+						
Annunzio, 11													
Collins, 7													+
Crane, 12			+	+	+		+	+	+	+	+		+
Derwinski, 4		+	+		+	+	+	+	+	+	+		+
Erlenborn, 14	+		+			+					+		
**Fary, 5													
Findley, 20			+		+	+					+	+	
Hall, 15													

	A	B	C	D	E	F	G	H	I	J	K	L	M
Hyde, 6	+	+			+		+				+	+	+
Madigan, 21				+							+	+	+
McClory, 13	+	+		+							+	+	+
Metcalfe, 1													
Michel, 18					+			+	+	+			+
Mikva, 10													+
Murphy, 2													
O'Brien, 17			+	+	+								+
Price, 23													
Railsback, 19		+			+								+
Rostenkowski, 8													+
Russo, 3													+
Shipley, 22												+	
Simon, 24			+									+	
Yates, 9													
INDIANA													
Brademas, 3													
Evans, 6													
Fithian, 2													
Hamilton, 9													
Hayes, 8													
Hillis, 5					+			+					+
Jacobs, 11		+											
Madden, 1													
Myers, 7					+		+			+	+	+	+
Roush, 4													
Sharp, 10													
IOWA													
Bedell, 6													
Blouin, 2													
Grassley, 3	+	+		+			+	+	+	+	+		+
Harkin, 5													
Mezvinsky, 1													
Smith, 4													
KANSAS													
Keys, 2													
Sebelius, 1		+	+		+	+		+	+	+	+		+
Shriver, 4	+						+				+		
Skubitz, 5											+		
Winn, 3	+	+	+	+		+	+				+	+	+
KENTUCKY													
Breckinridge, 6													+
Carter, 5			+	+	+	+				+		+	+
Hubbard, 1							+	+					+
Mazzoli, 3													+
Natcher, 2													
Perkins, 7													
Snyder, 4			+				+	+	+	+	+		+
LOUISIANA													
Boggs, 7													
Breaux, 2												+	+
Hebert, 1													
Long, 8													+
Moore, 6			+	+	+			+		+		+	+
Passman, 5													+
Treen, 3	+	+	+	+	+	+	+	+	+	+	+	+	+
Waggonner, 4		+			+		+	+	+	+	+		+
MAINE													
Cohen, 2					+								+
Emery, 1			+		+		+	+			+		

241

	A	B	C	D	E	F	G	H	I	J	K	L	M
MARYLAND													
Bauman, 1	+	+			+		+	+	+	+			+
Byron, 6		+	+			+							+
Gude, 8				+									
Holt, 4		+	+	+	+	+	+	+	+	+	+	+	+
Long, 2		+										+	
Mitchell, 7													
Sarbanes, 3													
Spellman, 5						+							
MASSACHUSETTS													
Boland, 2				+							+		
Burke, 11													
Conte, 1													+
Drinan, 4											+		
Early, 3													
Harrington, 6													
Heckler, 10					+								
Macdonald, 7													
Moakley, 9				+							+		
O'Neill, 8													
Studds, 12													
Tsongas, 5													
MICHIGAN													
Blanchard, 18													
Brodhead, 17													
Broomfield, 19				+		+	+						
Brown, 3		+						+					+
Carr, 6													
Cederberg, 10				+							+		+
Conyers, 1													
Diggs, 13													
Dingell, 16													
Esch, 2		+		+	+								
Ford, 15													
Hutchinson, 4		+		+		+					+		+
Nedzi, 14			+			+							
O'Hara, 12						+							
Riegle, 7													
Ruppe, 11						+							
Traxler, 8													
Vander Jagt, 9		+			+			+	+	+			
Vander Veen, 5													
MINNESOTA													
Bergland, 7													+
Fraser, 5													
Frenzel, 3			+		+								+
Hagedorn, 2		+	+	+			+		+	+	+		+
Karth, 4													
Nolan, 6													+
Oberstar, 8													+
Quie, 1					+						+		+
MISSISSIPPI													
Bowen, 2			+			+							+
Cochran, 4	+	+	+			+	+				+	+	+
Lott, 5	+	+	+	+	+	+	+	+	+	+	+	+	+
Montgomery, 3	+	+	+		+	+		+	+	+		+	+
Whitten, 1													
MISSOURI													
Bolling, 5													
Burlison, 10				+				+					
Clay, 1													+
Hungate, 9													

	A	B	C	D	E	F	G	H	I	J	K	L	M
Ichord, 8		+	+			+			+	+	+		+
Litton, 6									+				+
Randall, 4													+
Sullivan, 3													
Symington, 2													
Taylor, 7				+	+		+			+	+		+
MONTANA													
Baucus, 1													
Melcher, 2													
NEBRASKA													
McCollister, 2	+	+		+	+	+		+		+	+		+
Smith, 3		+		+	+	+							+
Thone, 1		+	+		+	+	+			+	+		+
NEVADA													
Santini,													
NEW HAMPSHIRE													
Cleveland, 2					+		+				+	+	
D'Amours, 1						+						+	+
NEW JERSEY													
Daniels, 14													+
Fenwick, 5													
Florio, 1													
Forsythe, 6	+	+											+
Helstoski, 9				+									
Howard, 3												+	+
Hughes, 2													
Maguire, 7													
Meyner, 13													
Minish, 11													+
Patten, 15													
Rinaldo, 12			+										
Rodino, 10												+	
Roe, 8			+		+								+
Thompson, 4													+
NEW MEXICO													
Lujan, 1													
Runnells, 2	+	+	+		+	+	+		+	+	+		+
NEW YORK													
Abzug, 20				+									
Addabbo, 7													+
Ambro, 3													
Badillo, 21													
Biaggi, 10													+
Bingham, 22													
Chisholm, 12												+	
Conable, 35											+		+
Delaney, 9													
Downey, 2													+
Fish, 25				+				+					+
Gilman, 26				+		+				+			+
Hanley, 32						+							+
Hastings, 39				+		+			+		+	+	+
Holtzman, 16												+	
Horton, 34	+												
Kemp, 38	+	+	+	+	+	+	+	+	+	+	+	+	+
Koch, 18													
LaFalce, 36				+									
Lent, 4					+								+
McEwen, 30							+	+					+
McHugh, 27													
Mitchell, 31													+

243

	A	B	C	D	E	F	G	H	I	J	K	L	M
Murphy, 17												+	+
Nowak, 37													
Ottinger, 24		+										+	
Pattison, 29							+						
Peyser, 23													+
Pike, 1													
Rangel, 18													+
Richmond, 14												+	
Rosenthal, 8												+	+
Scheuer, 11													
Solarz, 13												+	
Stratton, 28													+
Walsh, 33		+	+		+		+		+			+	+
Wolff, 6												+	+
Wydler, 5												+	+
Zeferetti, 15												+	+
NORTH CAROLINA													
Andrews, 4		+		+									+
Broyhill, 10		+					+	+	+	+			+
Fountain, 2			+					+					+
Hefner, 8							+	+					+
Henderson, 3							+	+					+
Jones, 1									+				+
Martin, 9		+	+	+		+	+	+		+	+		+
Neal, 5													
Preyer, 6		+											
Rose, 7													
Taylor, 11													+
NORTH DAKOTA													
Andrews		+				+	+						
OHIO													
Ashbrook, 17					+			+	+				+
Ashley, 9													
Brown, 7		+			+		+				+		+
Carney, 19					+		+						
Clancy, 2			+		+				+	+			+
Devine, 12			+	+	+	+	+	+		+	+		+
Gradison, 1		+	+								+		
Guyer, 4		+		+		+	+		+				+
Harsha, 6			+				+						+
Hays, 18													+
Kindness, 8			+		+	+	+	+	+	+	+		+
Latta, 5			+		+		+		+	+	+		+
Miller, 10			+		+		+		+	+	+		+
Mosher, 13		+										+	
Mottl, 23			+										
Regula, 16			+			+				+	+	+	+
Seiberling, 14													
Stanton, J. V., 20													
Stanton, J. W., 11		+											
Stokes, 21												+	+
Vanik, 22													
Whalen, 3													
Wylie, 15											+		
OKLAHOMA													
Albert, 3													
English, 6													
Jarman, 5				+									+
Jones, 1		+	+										+
Risenhoover, 2			+				+		+				+
Steed, 4							+						

244

	A	B	C	D	E	F	G	H	I	J	K	L	M
OREGON													
AuCoin, 1							+						
Duncan, 3			+										+
Ullman, 2													
Weaver, 4							+						
PENNSYLVANIA													
Barrett, 1													
Biester, 8													+
Coughlin, 13	+			+							+	+	
Dent, 21													+
Edgar, 7													+
Eilberg, 4					+								+
Eshleman, 16			+		+		+	+	+	+	+		+
Flood, 11			+				+						+
Gaydos, 20				+									+
Goodling, W., 19					+	+	+				+		+
Green, 3				+	+	+					+		+
Heinz, 18													
Johnson, 23			+		+		+				+		+
McDade, 10				+									
Moorhead, 14					+								
Morgan, 22													
Murtha, 12			+	+		+			+				+
Myers, 25			+				+						
Nix, 2			+								+	+	+
Rooney, 15		+											
Schneebeli, 17	+												
Schulze, 5			+				+				+	+	+
Shuster, 9				+						+	+	+	+
Vigorito, 24		+					+						+
Yatron, 6						+							+
RHODE ISLAND													
Beard, 2													
St. Germain, 1												+	
SOUTH CAROLINA													+
Davis, 1		+	+	+	+								
Derrick, 3	+		+										+
Holland, 5			+				+						
Jenrette, 6			+				+						+
Mann, 4			+								+		+
Spence, 2		+	+		+	+	+			+	+		+
SOUTH DAKOTA													
Abdnor, 2	+	+	+	+	+	+	+	+					+
Pressler, 1					+				+				
TENNESSEE													
***Allen, 5													
Beard, 6		+	+		+	+		+		+	+		+
Duncan, 2	+		+		+	+		+		+	+		+
Evins, 4							+						
Ford, 8								+					
Jones, 7													
Lloyd, 3													+
Quillen, 1				+			+		+			+	+
TEXAS													
Archer, 7		+	+		+	+		+		+	+		
Brooks, 9													
Burleson, 17							+						+
Casey, 22	+	+											+
Collins, 3		+											+
de la Garza, 15		+	+	+	+	+	+	+	+	+	+		+
Eckhardt, 8													
Gonzalez, 20													+

	A	B	C	D	E	F	G	H	I	J	K	L	M
Hightower, 13	+							+				+	+
Jordan, 18													+
Kazen, 23													
Krueger, 21	+	+					+						
Mahon, 19													
Milford, 24			+	+		+		+	+	+			+
Patman, 1							+						+
Pickle, 10	+	+											+
Poage, 11							+						+
Roberts, 4	+	+								+	+		+
Steelman, 5					+		+						
Teague, 6			+										
White, 16									+				
Wilson, 2	+	+						+			+		
Wright, 12							+						+
Young, 14													+
UTAH													
Howe, 2													
McKay, 1													+
VERMONT													
Jeffords													+
VIRGINIA													
Butler, 6	+	+			+						+		+
Daniel, D., 5			+	+		+	+			+	+		+
Daniel, R., 4			+	+		+		+	+		+	+	+
Downing, 1			+										+
Fisher, 10													
Harris, 8													
Robinson, 7	+	+	+	+	+	+	+	+	+		+		+
Satterfield, 3	+	+								+	+	+	+
Wampler, 9			+	+		+				+	+		+
Whitehurst, 2	+	+			+			+	+	+			+
WASHINGTON													
Adams, 7													
Bonker, 3													
Foley, 5													
Hicks, 6													+
McCormack, 4													
Meeds, 2													+
Pritchard, 1	+	+										+	
WEST VIRGINIA													
Hechler, 4				+								+	
Mollohan, 1	+						+						+
Slack, 3													+
Staggers, 2													
WISCONSIN													
Aspin, 1													
Baldus, 3													
Cornell, 8													
Kasten, 9			+			+		+		+	+	+	+
Kastenmeier, 2													
Obey, 7													
Reuss, 5													
Steiger, 6			+			+							
Zablocki, 4													+
WYOMING													
Roncalio												+	

* Pettis entered Congress May 6, 1975
** Fary entered Congress July 15, 1975
*** Allen entered Congress December 2, 1975

246

REPUBLICAN STUDY COMMITTEE

Statement of Purpose

The Republican Study Committee is a group of conservative Republican Congressmen who favor progressive measures within the framework of constitutional government and who have pooled their resources to provide themselves with more effective research and legislative support.

Our purpose is to persuade rather than to divide; we will continue, as we have in the past, to cooperate closely with the Republican Leadership in the House of Representatives. At the same time we want to ensure that conservative alternatives are given a full and fair hearing both on the floor of the House and in the councils of the Administration.

—We believe that the preservation of individual liberties is the purpose of our constitutional system of government.

—We believe that our liberties are dependent upon a strong national defense second to none and upon a foreign policy that always places the just interests of the American people first.

—We believe that both spiritual and material prosperity are enhanced when government intrusion in the social, political, and economic lives of our citizens is strictly limited.

—We believe that the power of a strong central government, when increased at the expense of state and local government, is a threat to individual liberties.

—We believe that the American system of free, competitive, private enterprise best energizes the creative talents of our people and best serves the interests of consumers, workers, farmers and businessmen.

—We believe that unlimited government spending is the main cause of inflation which erodes the savings of our citizens and levies on them a heavy tax without their consent; accordingly, we believe in a balanced budget and frugal, efficient public services.

—We believe that most of the federal government's social policies have not significantly contributed to the general welfare of the people they were intended to help, and accordingly, we believe that reforms are needed in our domestic programs.

—We believe that the councils of "pragmatism" or "expediency" would set us adrift on the political seas without a compass; we believe finally that principle makes good politics.

To implement these principles in practice, we have combined our resources to establish a research and information center with a shared staff of specialists who will provide us with the facts we need to serve our constituents as informed legislators, and who will aid us in coordinating support for the bills and amendments introduced by our Members.

THE REPUBLICAN STUDY COMMITTEE
UNITED STATES HOUSE OF REPRESENTATIVES
134 HOUSE OFFICE BUILDING
WASHINGTON, D.C. 20515
202/225-0587

A Free Book ... if you order four others

1. **How to Start Your Own School**, Robert Love. Everything a parent or principal needs to know, by someone who did it himself. "An important and readable book that tells you how to do it"— *Human Events*. **$1.95**

2. **The Regulated Consumer**, Mary B. Peterson. The *Wall Street Journal* contributor shows how seven Federal regulatory agencies have been captured by the businesses they were supposed to regulate! How this hurts consumers everywhere, and what can be done about it. "This thoughtful, challenging book can perform a great service"— *Fortune*. **$2.95**

3. **The Defenseless Society**, Frank Carrington. A scathing look at how the Courts and Congress have tilted the battle against crime in favor of the criminal and against society, with proposals for restoring the balance. By the author of *The Victims*, executive director of Americans for Effective Law Enforcement. (April). **$1.25**

4. **The Case Against the Reckless Congress**, Hon. Marjorie Holt, ed. Nineteen Republican congressmen contribute chapters on the major issues before Congress. What is happening? Why? And *is your Congressman responsible?* Read and find out: all 435 Representatives' votes are recorded on these issues. (April). **$1.95**

5. **The Making of the New Majority Party**, William Rusher. "If anyone can invigorate the ideological comradeship of economic and social conservatives, it is William Rusher. This is a well-written and thoughtful book."—*The Wall Street Journal*. **$1.95**

6. **The Sum of Good Government**, Hon. Philip M. Crane. Often mentioned as a 1976 vice-presidential candidate, the brilliant conservative Illinois congressman offers a positive program for solving the problems of American government in our country's 200th year. (May). **$1.95**

7. **The Gun Owner's Political Action Manual**, Alan Gottlieb. Everything a gun owner needs to know to be politically effective in the firearms freedom fight. Includes voting records of all Congressmen on every pro-/anti-gun vote, how to use the media, and a large reference section on publications and organizations. (May). **$1.95**

8. **Sincerely, Ronald Reagan**, Helene von Damm. The personal correspondence of Ronald Reagan as Governor of California. Covers his views on almost every national issue. "Reading these letters restored my faith."—*James Cagney*. **$1.25**

9. **The Hundred Million Dollar Payoff: How Big Labor Buys Its Democrats**, Douglas Caddy. This classic available for the first time in paperback! (May). **$2.95**

10. **The Libertarian Challenge: A New Dawn for America**, Roger MacBride. The Libertarian Party presidential candidate calls for a return to first principles. (May). **$ .95**

Green Hill Publishers
Box 738
Ottawa, Illinois 61350
Please send me postpaid the following books:
(Circle numbers)   1   2   3   4   5   6   7   8   9   10
I understand that if I order four books, I get No._____ FREE.
I enclose $_____.*

_____

_____

_____ Zip code_____

*Illinois residents please add 5% sales tax
NOTE: Free book offer applies only when all books are shipped together. If not-yet-published books are ordered, entire order will be held until all books are available.

**How Parents Can Rescue their
Children from the Perils of
Public Education**

How to Start
Your Own School

by Robert Love

This is the story of how one group of parents formed their own successful independent school. Wichita Collegiate began in 1960, in an abandoned school building with four teachers, 28 students, grades one through six, and one retired principal. Today, the school has over 400 students in preschool through 12th grade, who average almost 90 points above the national average on College Entrance Exams and whose graduates attend such schools as Princeton, Baylor, Oxford, and Sewanee.

This "how to" book answers the many questions about certification, faculty, equipment, accreditation, and how everything was paid for. It is a complete working model and guide for those who want the best possible education for their children.

"An important and readable book that tells you how to do it."
—HUMAN EVENTS.

"A fascinating 'do it yourself' book."—THE FREEMAN.

QUANTITY PRICES*

1 copy $1.95	10 copies $12.50	100 copies $ 60.00
3 copies $5.00	25 copies $25.00	500 copies $275.00
5 copies $7.50	50 copies $35.00	1000 copies $500.00

*Illinois residents please add 5% sales tax

Everyone should know

The Case Against the Reckless Congress

This remarkable book can make the difference in the 1976 congressional elections. *Will you help turn things around in Washington?* Give copies of this book to your business associates, your friends and neighbors, your union or fraternal club, your political organization, your local newspaper editor. *Are you backing a conservative candidate this year?* You can help him by donating copies of this book to his campaign, or by making certain—on your own —that influential people in your District have this book. For the first time, the important votes of *every* Congressman are shown and explained. *No more can a Member who votes liberal hide behind conservative rhetoric . . . if you do your part and distribute copies of this book.*

QUANTITY PRICES

1 copy $1.95	10 copies $12.50	100 copies $ 60.00
3 copies $5.00	25 copies $25.00	500 copies $275.00
5 copies $7.50	50 copies $35.00	1000 copies $500.00

Everyone should know

The
Case
Against the
Reckless
Congress

This remarkable book can make the difference in the 1976
congressional elections. *Will you help turn things around
in Washington?* Give copies of this book to your business
associates, your friends and neighbors, your union or fraternal club, your political organization, your local newspaper editor. *Are you backing a conservative candidate
this year?* You can help him by donating copies of this
book to his campaign, or by making certain—on your own
—that influential people in your District have this book.
For the first time, the important votes of *every* Congressman are shown and explained. *No more can a Member who
votes liberal hide behind conservative rhetoric . . . if you do
your part and distribute copies of this book.*

QUANTITY PRICES

1 copy $1.95	10 copies $12.50	100 copies $ 60.00
3 copies $5.00	25 copies $25.00	500 copies $275.00
5 copies $7.50	50 copies $35.00	1000 copies $500.00

GREEN HILL PUBLISHERS, INC.
P. O. Box 738
Ottawa, Illinois 61350

Please send me postpaid_____copies of THE CASE AGAINST
THE RECKLESS CONGRESS, edited by Marjorie Holt. I enclose

_____

_____

_____

_____

_____ Zip Code_____